Knowledge Acquisition and Machine Learning: Theory, Methods, and Applications

Knowledge Acquisition and Machine Learning: Theory, Methods, and Applications

Katharina Morik
Universitat Dortmund, D-4600 Dortmund 50, GERMANY

Stefan Wrobel, Jörg-Uwe Kietz *and* Werner Emde
GMD, D-5205 Sankt Augustin 1, GERMANY

ACADEMIC PRESS
Harcourt Brace & Company, Publishers
London San Diego New York
Boston Sydney Tokyo Toronto

ACADEMIC PRESS LIMITED
24—28 Oval Road
London NW1 7DX

United States Edition published by
ACADEMIC PRESS INC.
San Diego, CA 92101

This book is printed on acid-free paper

A catalogue record for this book is available from the British Library
ISBN 0-12-506230-3

Printed and bound in Great Britain by Hartnolls Ltd, Bodmin, Cornwall

Contents

List of Figures

Preface

Knowledge-based systems offer more flexible ways of using a computer than former, standard approaches of programming could do. However, without a means to build up the knowledge base efficiently, the better performance of a knowledge-based system is outweighed by the efforts of constructing and maintaining the knowledge base. Therefore, knowledge acquisition and machine learning have become key issues in artificial intelligence. Frameworks for knowledge acquisition have been elaborated, and it became clear that building a knowledge base is equivalent to modeling an application domain. This process of modeling underlies all kinds of formalizing applications, whether they be in software or knowledge engineering. A better understanding of this process allows the development of tools that support users in their modeling tasks. Moreover, parts of the modeling activity can be performed by a learning system. Several learning algorithms have been developed and used for building up (parts of) a knowledge base. Theoretical investigations of learning in a restricted first-order logic further enhanced the scope of machine learning.

Incorporating learning algorithms into a knowledge acquisition environment provides for a new level of work-sharing between system and users. Users may delegate more routine procedures to the system and can concentrate on the relevant aspects of their applications. The computer assists its users in modeling a domain. The system MOBAL, like its predecessor BLIP, is such an assisting system, being a fully operational system which integrates knowledge acquisition and machine learning in restricted predicate logic.

About This Book

This book reports work on a series of systems over ten years. The systems METAXA, BLIP, and MOBAL are all based on a representation within a restricted higher-order predicate logic. Whereas learning algorithms based on attribute-value representations have a long tradition of successful applications and their formal properties are already about to be understood, learning in predicate logic is a rather new development. Moreover, learning algorithms which are able to use background knowledge and even the knowledge they acquired themselves are a central topic today. This book contributes experience with knowledge-intensive, logic-based learning to the current debate on inductive logic programming. It describes the knowledge representation as it is presented to the user (chapter 2) and as it is made effective by the inference engine IM-2 (chapter 3). Then, the tools are described which assist the user in modeling an application domain: the tool for structuring terms into sorts, STT (chapter 4), the tool for structuring predicates, PST (chapter 5), the tool for discovering rules, RDT (chapter 6), the tool for knowledge revision, KRT (chapter 7), and the tool for concept learning, CLT (chapter 8). Each chapter relates the reported work to current research and can be read independently of the book.

The systems BLIP and MOBAL illustrate a particular way of unifying knowledge acquisition and machine learning. The knowledge acquisition framework is introduced and discussed in chapter 1. Its effects on presenting the system's knowledge to the user are dealt with in chapter 2. The main underlying goal of this framework, namely to balance the modeling activity between system and user, naturally guides the design of the knowledge representation and of each tool. Each knowledge item (e.g., facts, sorts, predicate groups, rules, and rule schemata) can be added or revised either by the system or by the user. Hence, the knowledge representation must support the automatic as well as the manual acquisition of knowledge items. Another effect is that each tool must output items that can be used by other tools or by the user directly.

Experience with the systems is implicitly reported within the descriptions of the tools. Justification for design choices is often experience gained before with other choices. Experience with running the systems on applications is presented in chapter 9. Here, a warning to readers who are used to learning curves and evaluations in terms of percentage of correct predictions is appropriate. The reader will not find any of those tables. The reason is that the learning tasks of BLIP or MOBAL are not of the type to learn one concept and then classify previously unseen examples. Instead, all the tools contribute to building up a knowledge base together with the user. Diverse concepts and parts of concepts are learned and represented as rules by CLT and RDT. Potential concepts are learned and represented as classes of sorts by STT. Sets of predicates are determined and represented as groups of predicates by PST which the user might interpret as tasks and subtasks in the application. The criteria for evaluating the tools are theoretical estimates of efficiency, completeness, and correctness. The ultimate criterion for evaluating the systems is a practical one, namely the users being content.

The History

Starting 1981 at the Technical University Berlin from an idea to acquire inference rules for a natural-language question-answering system by model-based learning ([Habel and Rollinger, 1981] and [Habel and Rollinger, 1982]), Werner Emde developed the learning system METAXA. This system moved beyond the attribute-value representation employing a restricted higher-order logic. METAXA was the input of the Technical University Berlin into the project LERNER[1] which lasted from 1985 to 1989. LERNER aimed to integrate knowledge acquisition and machine learning. A new framework for knowledge acquisition, called sloppy modeling or balanced cooperative modeling, was developed by Katharina Morik and formed the basis for constructing a new type of a system: a system that assists a user by several means, among them different learning algorithms. An instance of such a system was BLIP, developed at the Technical University Berlin with an effort of seventeen man-years. In addition to the scientists Werner Emde, Katharina Morik (head of the Berlin LERNER-group), Sabine Thieme, and Stefan Wrobel, the students Oliver Bittkau, Christian Haider, Thomas Hoppe, Ingo Keller, and Jörg-Uwe Kietz significantly supported the system development. The industrial partners Nixdorf Computer AG and Stollmann ltd, provided practical demands and a medical application.

At the end of this German project, the Nixdorf Computer AG started a European initiative to make machine learning available within standard computer environments. The European project Machine Learning Toolbox MLT[2] started in 1989 and ends in 1993. Within this project, Jörg-Uwe Kietz, Katharina Morik and Stefan Wrobel - having moved from Berlin to the German National Research Center for Computer Science (GMD) at St.

[1]The project LERNER was funded by the German Ministry for Research and Technology under grant ITW8501B1. Industrial partners of the technical university Berlin were the Nixdorf Computer AG at Paderborn and Stollmann ltd at Hamburg.

[2]The project MLT is funded by the ESPRIT programme of the European Community under P2154. The consortium consists of ten partners, from universities, research institutes, and industry.

Augustin - enhanced the BLIP system to become MOBAL, a system which is available to the public and in use at the sites of MLT-partners. In addition, Edgar Sommer, Volker Klingspor, and Roman Englert contribute to the work on machine learning at GMD. Sixteen man-years have already been invested in the development of MOBAL and its integration into the overall MLT environment.

The main difference between BLIP and MOBAL is the new architecture of the latter. Whereas BLIP had a given flow of control with all algorithms integrated, MOBAL is organized as a toolbox. The algorithms are still integrated, but can also be used as tools in their own right. This allows the user to call an algorithm or to let the system choose when to apply which tool. Some parts of BLIP became parts of MOBAL with only a few changes. For instance, the inference engine IM-2 of Werner Emde was only ported from Symbolics Prolog to Quintus Prolog and some inference services have been optimized. Also the concept formation algorithm, CLT, of Stefan Wrobel remained more or less the one already implemented within the BLIP system. The sort taxonomy tool, STT, of Jörg-Uwe Kietz was enhanced in that it can now be used for more tasks within MOBAL than within BLIP. The knowledge revision tool, KRT, of Stefan Wrobel was enhanced in that it now allows to modify several rules at once. More important, it now performs a minimal base revision that preserves the structure of the original theory. Some ideas already prototyped within BLIP became regular tools within MOBAL. For instance, the idea of Katharina Morik to group together predicates as an analogy to sorting terms was fully elaborated and implemented by Volker Klingspor becoming the predicate structuring tool, PST. The chapter on PST is based on a text of Volker Klingspor. Some parts, however, have been completely renewed based on our experience with the corresponding BLIP algorithms. Due to theoretical insights in the logic of induction, the model-based rule learning algorithm, RDT, replaced the former rule learning of BLIP. Also the human-computer interface was reimplemented and constantly enhanced.

Cooperation with industrial partners has led to an orientation towards practical issues. Theoretical results have been used and tested with respect to their practical impact from the very beginning. For applications, good algorithms are not sufficient. They have to be embedded into a user-friendly human-computer interface, must be robust and well-documented. If scientific work relies on Ph D students, this work cannot be carried out. In contrast, the joined projects LERNER and MLT enabled us continuously to enhance the system with respect to its usability. The cooperation also provided us with real-world applications. In particular, the medical domain of newborn children with jaundice was investigated by Stollmann ltd in cooperation with the expert Dr. Müller-Wickop. Another medical domain has been provided by the Foundation of Research and Technology, Hellas, in cooperation with the expert Professor Charissis. Currently, GMD and Alcatel Alsthom Recherche are working on an application called SPEED. The security policy of access to distributed computers is to be modeled.

MOBAL is available via anonymous ftp from ftp.gmd.de and several people outside the consortium of MLT already use the system[3]. As we are interested in feedback from MOBAL users electronic mail concerning the experience of using the system, critical remarks, and proposals for further enhancements are welcome. MOBAL is running on SUN computers under SunOS4.1 and is written in Quintus-Prolog. Its human-computer interface is written in the HyperNeWS environment, developed by the Turing Institute at Glasgow on the basis of OpenWindows2. A licence for HyperNeWS can be obtained there free of charge for non-commercial use.

Acknowledgements

Over the years, colleagues have supported us in several ways. We wholeheartedly thank those who are mentioned in the history above. In addition, all members of the Berlin AI group KIT contributed to the exciting working atmosphere, as did the members of the GMD's AI group FIT.KI.[4] This includes Professors Hans-Jochen Schneider of the Technical University Berlin, the GMD institute directors Professor Thomas Christaller and Dr. Peter Hoschka, as well as the secretaries Cordula Lippke, Monika Wendel, and Ulrike Teuber and, last but not least, colleagues who are specialized in all kinds of trouble-shooting: Siegfried Dickhoven, Eva Hüttenhain, and Helmut Jungblut.

The European scientific community of machine learning, as brought together by Professor Yves Kodratoff in 1985, with its lively discussions on predicate logic and learning relations encouraged us to go beyond attribute-value representations. Also Professor Ryszard Michalski shared our view that our approach is feasible - even before the first system was fully operational. The knowledge acquisition community, particularly Professors Brian

[3]The reader who wants to exploit the results of our research by using the system or our theoretical results must do this on his or her own risk.

[4]Note that in German AI is abbreviated KI.

Gaines and Bob Wielinga, inspired us by helpful comments and questions.

We thank the German Ministry for Research and Technology and the Commission EC for the funding and the project reviewers for their advice. All users of our systems pushed us to keep on working on the user- friendliness of Blip and Mobal.

A rough translation of the final technical report of the Lerner project from German into English was the starting point of this book. We thank Stefanie Kühnel for this translation and Uwe Schnepf for its formatting. The copy-editor of Academic Press helped us to improve our English.

Finally, our moving from one city to another, as well as our long working hours, were sometimes hard for our private lives. Thanks to all our friends, who backed us up, anyway.

Chapter 1

The Knowledge Acquisition Framework

1.1 The Knowledge Acquisition Problem

Having abstracted the structure of the first expert system MYCIN, thus creating EMYCIN as an expert system shell [van Melle, 1981], the problem of how to acquire knowledge for knowledge-based systems was realized. At the beginning, expert systems were developed to fit a particular domain and a certain task, but later on researchers aimed at eliciting and representing the domain-related knowledge for a given interpreter with a fixed control structure. Filling the expert system shell has been found to be the major problem when applying expert systems[1]. Then the acquisition of task structures, i.e. inference strategies applied to particular rule sets, became a knowledge acquisition problem, too. The solution of the two problems, acquiring domain knowledge and acquiring problem solving methods, relies on the separation of different types of knowledge.

The experience gained when working with R1, the DEC computer configuration system, emphasized another aspect: the maintenance and testing of knowledge bases [Bachant and McDermott, 1984]. On the one hand this aims at modifying the represented knowledge as a result of changes in the domain, and on the other hand aims at detecting and rectifying errors in the knowledge that is represented.

Of all the different approaches to easing knowledge acquisition and main-

[1] A more detailed description of projects in the field of knowledge acquisition in artificial intelligence (AI) can be found in section 1.2.

tenance, machine learning methods are those which come closest to realizing the idea of automation. Parts of knowledge bases can be automatically created on the basis of a few examples. In order to automate an on-going activity of knowledge acquisition and knowledge enhancement, a learning system has to recognize by itself the need when and where to improve the knowledge base and at least to provide a few suggestions on how to achieve a better knowledge base. However, the creation of a knowledge base merely on the basis of machine learning procedures is not desirable, as the users (the so-called knowledge engineers) like to add or modify facts and rules themselves. Therefore, instead of exclusively concentrating on the development of learning techniques, it is much more important to integrate manual knowledge acquisition techniques (knowledge editor, knowledge elicitation system, knowledge maintenance system) and automated knowledge acquisition methods (machine learning).

1.2 Domain Modeling for Expert Systems

First-generation expert systems such as MYCIN provide users with exactly one data structure which enables them to represent knowledge. Production rules are used to represent knowledge of the task as well as knowledge of the consultation strategy and knowledge of the domain. Filling such an expert system shell means having to program knowledge with the help of production rules. To facilitate the user's programming task, knowledge acquisition tools such as editors, inspectors, explanation components and user interfaces have been developed. These tools supply the expert system shell with additional functionality:

- inspectability of the knowledge base,
- explicability of the system's behavior,
- modifiability of the knowledge base.

As we will see later on, this increased functionality, however, cannot go beyond the limitations inherent in the uniform representation of knowledge. Tools depend on the knowledge representation formalism they use. Hence, knowledge acquisition issues led to recent advances in the field of knowledge representation for expert systems, which, in turn, resulted in an improvement of the knowledge acquisition procedure for the user. Consequently, the attitude towards the knowledge acquisition process has changed completely:

from the programming-like coding of existing knowledge to interactive domain modeling, which creates knowledge.

Interarctive domain modeling will be described later. First, we will outline some well-known shortcomings of the uniform representation technique used for early expert systems so as to show that even the best tools cannot overcome functional shortcomings of an expert system (section 1.2.1). Afterwards, we will deal with recent developments in the field of knowledge representation for expert systems and knowledge acquisition systems (section 1.2.2). A few assumptions, which were put forward regarding the knowledge acquisition problem, and which turned out to be false, will be discussed in section 1.2.3. Finally, we will focus on the attitude towards knowledge acquisition as a modeling process (section 1.2.4).

1.2.1 Shortcomings of Early Expert Systems

This section describes the shortcomings of the uniform knowledge representation style in previous MYCIN-like expert systems, as far as they affect the problem of knowledge acquisition. Three well-known examples will be presented: the integration of multiple derivations, object-level representation, and the combining of different types of knowledge. These examples have already been discussed in connection with the explicability of expert systems [Swartout, 1983], [Neches *et al.*, 1985], [Wahlster, 1981], [Clancey, 1986]. Now, we will concentrate on their significance in the context of knowledge acquisition.

Shortliffe [1976] and then many other authors who work in this field have solved the problem of integrating multiple derivations of the same conclusion by reinforcing the evidence of this conclusion. This procedure, however, requires that the premises of all rules that derive the same conclusion be independent of each other. This means that entering a new rule into the knowledge base entails checking whether its premises are independent of all other premises with the same conclusion. The identity of premises is, of course, easy to find out, but it is particularly important to rule out that one premise is the specialization of another one. As the representation does not explicitly refer to specialization relations and these cannot be easily calculated by the system, the user is the only one to check the independence of premises. A tool can only represent all the rules with the same conclusion, but it cannot monitor their compliance with the rule of the independence. Only if the representation formalism would express specialization or generalization relations between premises, a tool can check the independence of premises and the reinforcement because of multiple derivation can be safely applied. This demonstrates the dependence of a tool's performance on the representation formalism used.

A famous example shows how object-level representation makes it difficult to modify the knowledge base. It is cited by Clancey [Clancey, 1986] and others and points at heuristics hidden in MYCIN rules. MYCIN behaves as if it obeys the following heuristic rule:

> If the genus of a micro-organism can be determined
> but not its species
> Then take the most probable species for that genus.

The heuristic principle is not coherently represented but manifests itself in all the rules that govern the determination of the species. If the user intends to change the heuristics, he or she will have to modify all these rules. In this case, a tool cannot even be used to discover and present to the user all the rules involved, as they do not reveal that they are responsible for the system's behavior. Moreover, the modification of a rule about the species can lead to a change in the system's behavior which was not intended by the user. No tool can support the user when modifying the heuristics nor give advice on the consequences of a modification. To avoid this problem some researchers [Neches *et al.*, 1985] recommend the explicit representation of methodological knowledge.

The combining of different types of knowledge also proves that a lack of functionality cannot be remedied by imposed tools. In particular, the combining of consultation and domain-related knowledge has been criticized. The following two MYCIN rules are uniformly represented:

> When the age of a patient is over 17, and the patient is an alcoholic,
> then diplococcus might cause an infection.

and

> When the age of the patient is under 7,
> then remove tetracycline from the list of drugs under consideration.

In fact, the first rule constitutes indirect dialog handling (never ask a minor whether he or she is an alcoholic). The second one is a domain-related rule (tetracycline impedes the formation of the bone structure in adolescents). But how can we modify the knowledge base, when the number of alcoholic children is increasing? How can a tool search for the rules that will have to be modified in order to achieve a change in the system's dialog behavior? When the user deletes the first premise of the first rule, which is not logical in the context of this domain, no tool is able to inform her that the dialog behavior of the system will be changing. It is not evident that the premise encodes knowledge of dialog handling. This is why Puppe [Puppe, 1986] provides his expert system shell MED2 with particular representation items for dialog handling. Clancey [Clancey, 1986] recommends a representation of knowledge which is categorized according to different types of knowledge, and uses a consultation structure for the heuristic classification. Swartout and Smoliar [Swartout and Smoliar, 1989] point to the art of accurately modeling the different knowledge types of an expert system, which enables knowledge maintenance in the first place. They also recommend adhering to the explicability feature as a guideline for this purpose. We underline the necessity of categorizing the types of knowledge in order to ensure the learnability of rules [Emde and Morik, 1989]. This illustrates how the intention to provide a better support for the knowledge acquisition and maintenance processes has led to new developments in the field of expert systems. For instance, one of the major reasons for the expert system shell TWAICE[2] to undergo a change towards the categorization of knowledge types was the research done on the subject of knowledge acquisition.

1.2.2 Facilitating Knowledge Acquisition

As we have just seen, a major prerequisite for the support of knowledge acquisition is to define an adequate representation system. Gruber and Cohen consequently describe the problem of knowledge acquisition as being caused by the incongruity of representation formalisms and the expert's manner of formulating the problem [Gruber and Cohen, 1987]. The KL-ONE school of knowledge representation deals with the problem in a similar way providing a sound formalism to define the terminology which is used to describe knowledge [Brachman and Levesque, 1985]. The knowledge representation used for the BLIP system, which was developed to facilitate the acquisition and the modification of knowledge, is described in [Emde, 1989], [Wrobel, 1987] and in the chapters 2 and 3 of this book. This is why we will not discuss representation formalisms, here. Instead we would like to present a brief outline of knowledge acquisition systems in order to be able to assess the formalism designed for MOBAL.

[2]TWAICE is an expert system shell and a product of Nixdorf Computer AG, now SNI.

Knowledge acquisition systems can be classified using many different criteria. We will use the range of knowledge which has to be available, before the knowledge acquisition system can help the user to enter or modify knowledge. At the same time, this specifies system limitations with particular applications. To explain this we can present two contrasting examples. On the one hand, there are systems such as KRIMB [Cox and Blumenthal, 1987] which already contains a complete domain model and which only requires adding instances of existing expressions. Supposing it is known that animals feed on food, that cats are animals, that fish is food, that cats eat fish, then the system can support the user entering the information that a particular cat eats a certain kind of fish. The usefulness of such a system becomes obvious, when we look at another system, OPAL [Musen *et al.*, 1987]. It is a knowledge acquisition system that is part of an expert system designed for cancer therapy (ONCOCIN). It provides users, usually physicists, with the forms they usually had to fill in anyway. The system is able to add new patient data to the existing knowledge base. Because of the already given domain model, the system can check integrity of new data. It is a human-computer interface which is especially tailored to achieving a particular purpose in a domain.

On the other extreme, we have the example of a conventional text editor. It does not prescribe any particular structure, is independent not only of the purpose of data and of the domain that yields the data but also of any representation formalism. Character identity can be used by the text editor to compile data of the same kind. Additionally, it is independent of the target system, which is supposed to interpret the knowledge, once it has been entered. But, of course, it is not able to conduct integrity or consistency checks, and it cannot use semantic criteria to search for particular facts or rules[3].

We classify in table 1.1 some knowledge acquisition systems with respect to the knowledge which needs to be given in advance. The knowledge requirements listed in the lower line comprise those of the lines above.

Between the extremes of a text editor and an intelligent interface, there are several mediate positions.

Less knowledge than the one required for OPAL is needed for systems such as MOLE [Eshelman *et al.*, 1987]. There it is assumed that:

[3] I take this example of a "free" system seriously, as it has turned out that computer scientists being the users like to work with a text editor, when they enter or modify knowledge.

Prerequisite Knowledge	Sample System
none	text editor
a particular knowledge representation formalism such as, e.g. KL-ONE	AQUINAS, BLIP, KRITON, KREME, KLUSTER, MOBAL
problem solving methods	PROTEGE-II, OMOS
a particular inference engine with a problem-solving strategy	MOLE, SALT, TEIRESIAS
a particular domain	OPAL, KRIMB

Table 1.1: Knowledge Acquisition Systems

- the task of the expert system is of the heuristic classification type,
- there are hypotheses to explain symptoms,
- there are symptoms that distinguish between hypotheses,
- there is knowledge of how to combine hypotheses.

These assumptions are true of applications that are as diverse as the diagnosis of car engine problems, the recommendation of an appropriate meal for a party, or a medical diagnosis. The given structure enables the system to set up default values and to check whether two hypotheses can be distinguished and to detect intermediate concepts between symptoms and hypotheses[4] . Systems of this type benefit from of the fact that they are directly linked to an inference engine. SALT [Marcus, 1988] follows the propose-and-revise strategy. This strategy is general enough to allow for a number of applications. At the same time it is constraining enough to help the acquisition of knowledge.

TEIRESIAS [Davis, 1982], one of the first knowledge acquisition systems, also belongs to this type, as it uses the syntactic shape of the rules and the strategy of the inference engine's interpreter for which it acquires knowledge.

[4]Considering the issue of multiple derivations, we can determine whether a hypothesis is more general than another one or independent of this one, when we look at the subset relations between symptom sets in these systems. This is possible, as it is explicitly stated which hypothesis covers which symptoms.

The approach of such systems is similar to the one of programming environments for a particular programmming language. The user is regarded as an AI programmer whose task is to encode knowledge with the help of the system.

A generalization of this approach is the current investigation in appropriate building blocks for building up the problem-solving strategy of the target system. The approach covers a variety of systems and ideas[5]. The reasoning chain leading from OPAL to PROTEGE-II is a good illustration of this approach. OPAL being a convenient interface for a particular system was generalized to be specifiable by the knowledge acquisition system PROTEGE. This system helps to build up the domain model and to specify OPAL to become a corresponding knowledge editor. From there, the knowledge is loaded into the empty expert shell E-ONCOCYN. Of course, the link between OPAL and PROTEGE made knowledge acquisition more flexible than with OPAL alone. However, the problem-solving method remained fixed. The next step was to build the overall problem-solving method using building blocks. Luc Steels proposed particular components of expertise [Steels, 1990]. Others claimed building blocks of combined abstracted domain knowledge and problem-solving steps [Chandrasekaran, 1989]. PROTEGE was generalized to put mechanisms and methods to good use in knowledge acquisition [Puerta *et al.*, 1991]. PROTEGE-II indexes a library of mechanisms by generic tasks. The user configures methods to become an application's problem-solving strategy. The user may also change the offered methods and become an AI programmer again. The resulting knowledge base is loaded into the performance system, E-ONCOCYN. A similar approach has been put forward by the OMOS system [Linster, 1992]. Domain knowledge and problem-solving methods are at first acquired seperately before a mapping yields an operational model. MODEL-K, a system on the basis of the KADS framework, also explicitly expresses links between the domain level and the inference level [Karbach and Voß, 1992]. The models built using MODEL-K or OMOS are translated into the EMYCIN-like expert system shell BABYLON [Christaller *et al.*, 1989]. Models of MODEL-K at first are not operational. They need to be run partially by calling the interpreter for a particular (sub-)task or be made operational by a programming effort called operational refinement. The result is then compiled into BABYLON.

Independence of a particular performance system is proved by systems like KREME [Abrett and Burstein, 1987], which are based on a knowledge

[5] An overview of the diverse systems is given in [Karbach *et al.*, 1991].

representation system whose knowledge base still has to be compiled into an expert system. This independence enables the system to provide the user with the choice of how to model a domain. It takes into account that the requirements of the consultation system differ from those prescribed by the knowledge acquisition system[6]. AQUINAS [Boose and Bradshaw, 1987], KRITON [Diederich *et al.*, 1987] and BLIP [Morik, 1987] fall into the same category of systems. BLIP and MOBAL only acquire and express domain knowledge. This is operational so that the user may inspect and revise it. The task structure of MOBAL does not determine particular problem-solving methods or mechanisms. It is used to structure the domain knowledge according to the application. It expresses the insight that knowledge acquisition should focus on those parts of the infinite domain which will be used for problem-solving further on. Only in this respect are domain and task knowledge related within the MOBAL system. The domain knowledge, however, is not compiled into a performance element, because that would disturb its continuous update. Instead, BLIP and MOBAL are linked with an expert system shell which provides the query sets and the overall problem-solving strategy for consultations with the end-user. Both systems have been successfully coupled with the expert system shell TWAICE [Emde *et al.*, 1989]. In this scenario, the expert system asks for facts which are derived by BLIP or MOBAL and reacts by whatever is specified if a fact cannot be derived (e.g. asking the user for more data). As all domain knowledge which is used during consultations of the expert system is maintained by BLIP or MOBAL, the disadvantages of decoupling the knowledge acquisition system from the performance element are prohibited. The advantages of keeping the domain knowledge separate from the dialog and problem-solving strategy are guaranteed. The same domain knowledge can be used for different application problems.

Most systems which acquire knowledge automatically, i.e. by using machine learning methods, only rely on their own representation formalism, and are thus independent of a target system. When considering KL-ONE-like system's[7] representation formalisms, the learning system KLUSTER [Kietz and Morik, 1991a] which forms a KL-ONE terminology on the basis of facts also belongs to the systems that only rely on a representation formalism for domain knowledge.

---

[6] Refer to [Swartout, 1983] who explicitly describes the compilation of the acquired knowledge base.

[7] These systems are also called term-subsumption systems or terminological logics.

With respect to the place within the modeling cycle where the system supports the knowledge engineer, the first three groups of systems are involved in a much earlier stage of modeling than the last two groups. It is already a challenge to elicit the domain model, which will then have to be transformed or encoded. When we classify the knowledge acquisition systems following the notion of the knowledge acquisition process they have been developed for, we will obtain a new categorization, where the last two groups and some of the building blocks group transfer a model into a formalized structure. In contrast, systems such as PROTEGE-II, AQUINAS, BLIP, KLUSTER, and MOBAL also comprise the elicitation or the structuring of this model. The following section will deal with the problem of knowledge elicitation and the suggestions put forward to solve it.

1.2.3 The Problem of Knowledge Elicitation

When we regard knowledge acquisition as being the transfer of one representation into another, then we tacitly assume that there is an initial representation. This assumption, however, is questionable in two respects. On the one hand - and this is the opinion of a number of scientists who are involved in knowledge elicitation - it is not easy to obtain this (existing) knowledge. On the other hand - and this is how we argue - this initial representation does not necessarily exist. There is an art to questioning experts about their expertise. The techniques used for this purpose include questionnaires, protocol analysis, and interview techniques. By questionnaire techniques we understand surveys of experts who have a choice of different possible answers. One technique, in particular, is known as the personal construct theory [Kelly, 1955], which is based on the repertory grid method. Repertory grids are scales which range between extreme properties and which are used to indicate the extent to which a particular property applies to a certain object. Objects and properties can be requested. Then scales are set up so that the expert only has to mark whatever is applicable. This procedure can easily be automated. Actually, the systems AQUINAS and ETS [Boose, 1985], for example, are based on this technique. Protocol analysis is the information theory based analysis of statements made about the problem-solving behavior of an expert. The procedure can be automated. KRITON, for example, statistically analyses a text using key words and relations between them, thus producing objects and rules which still have to be confirmed by the user, but which for a start provide a guideline.

There are a number of interview techniques. To meet the knowlege acquisition requirements for expert systems LaFrance has developed a structured interview strategy based on particular question types [LaFrance, 1987]. The results of such an interview can be formalized in a mediating representation and will then be transformed into the final or another mediating representation (see [Johnson, 1987]. The KADS technique can also be viewed as a method to structure interviews. KADS [Wielinga and Breuker, 1986] divides the knowledge (domain and problem-solving knowledge) which is to be elicited into four levels:

- the domain level with concepts and relations between them
- the inference level with meta classes and knowledge bases, which structure the domain knowledge as required by the task,
- the task level with the problem-solving strategy, which is developed with the help of the metaclasses and knowledge bases.
- the strategic level which describes how to use the strategies.

The result of the method is a classification of the knowledge. However, it is not formalized. The informal model can be used - in an analogy to specifications in software engineering - in the process of implementing the the knowledge-based system. Newer developments allow the knowledge engineer to formalize the specification and to edit it within a system, e.g. SHELLEY [Anjewierden *et al.*, 1990]. However, this system does not reason with the knowledge. An approach to close the gap between specification and an operational model is the language MODEL-K [Karbach and Voß, 1992]. Of course, MOBAL can be used to represent a conceptual model of KADS in an operational and maintainable way.

Machine support of interview techniques is difficult to achieve for two reasons. On the one hand, the support provided by a system requires a formal knowledge representation. This formalism limits the expressiveness of the experts' statements. However, this is the very advantage of the interview technique: it allows experts to be free in formulating. On the other hand, interviewing itself is not easy to automate, because the interview is influenced by a number of social factors:

- the experts' self-confidence,
- the experts assessment of the consequences the interview will have on their working environment and that of their colleagues,

- the role in which the experts view themselves during the interview,
- the experts' social status within the group, just to mention a few.

These factors often have a decisive influence on whether experts are motivated enough to be as thorough and accurate as possible in defining their expertise. Experienced interviewers will take these factors into account. They not only interpret the experts' statements with regard to the application domain, but also with regard to social factors. Thus, they are in a better position to assess and - using certain dialog techniques - even increase the reliability and completeness of the experts' statements. They can also be flexible in asking follow-up questions. As it only makes sense to discuss the usefulness and compatibility of an expert system in a particular domain with a human being and not with a system, such a discussion is part of an interview. Consequently, interviews are conducted as a conversation between humans, with the result then being transferred into a mediating representation.

1.2.4 Knowledge Acquisition as a Modeling Process

The above knowledge acquisition techniques (section 1.2.3) all center on the problem of how to extract knowledge from an expert. They all require that the knowledge be requestable, i.e. conscious and explicable. But this need not be the case. A human being's expertise need not be based on knowledge, even though a knowledge-based system may represent it as knowledge. It can also be available in the form of skills. Skills are unconscious, the result of routine and not immediately accessible by way of introspection. Speaking and understanding, for example, are skills which cannot be explained by members of the language community. Depending on the state of the art, linguists are able to explain linguistic phenomena[8]. Consequently, we have to distinguish between practicians and theorists.

The knowledge elicitation techniques mentioned in the last section require that the experts who are interviewed know how to describe their expertise. These techniques do not take into account that the explicit knowledge can markedly differ from the skills that constitute the expertise. This means that the experts may convey standard knowledge, although they act

[8] And this is even true independently of their command of the language. This is similar in the case of musicians and music critics, poets and literary scientists: a good musician can make a poor music critic and vice versa, and it can happen that a good poet interprets his/her own works worse than a literary scientist, who, in turn, creates mediocre prose.

differently. The reason is that they do not have other knowledge consciously. They may even think that they act accordingly[9]. Perhaps, there does not even exist any knowledge of a domain, instead the domain is made up of a series of activities which help humans to acquire the necessary skills. Interview questions, the request to tell one's thoughts (think-aloud protocol) and the demand to mark the properties of objects in a scale prompt the experts to come up with an ad-hoc explanation [Garfinkel, 1973]. This explanation is a naive theory that was not examined and modified by the usual scientific procedure[10]. In our opinion, this shows the main problem that knowledge acquisition is beset with: it is not always possible to extract existing knowledge, frequently it has to be created first [Morik, 1989]. The process of knowledge acquisition is hence not the transfer of existing knowledge into a given formalism but the modeling of a domain.

By *modeling* we mean the explicit description of competence. In this respect, competence is a cognitive process with cognitive entities, which we have to assume in order to describe a certain behavior and to show what the observed behavior produces. This concept of competence comprises knowledge and skills. It is - unlike that used by [Chomsky, 1965, pages 14ff] - largely geared to the behavior that is based on knowledge or skills. This definition of *modeling* takes into account that the description of competence, in turn, influences the notion of competence. Thus, the notion is reflexive. In this respect, we do not assume the existence of real, objective competence, which only has to be elicited. Instead, the description of competence is regarded as being an intersubjective constructive process. The competence description itself is referred to as a model. For knowledge-based systems we demand that the model be operational. Consequently, a model is an explicit, explicable and operational domain theory. Hence, it constitutes precisely what is to be developed in the knowledge acquisition process. The modeling process becomes comparable to the process of constructing a scientific theory about particular skills.

This new notion of knowledge acquisition has also been termed *sloppy modeling* [Morik, 1989]. It accounts for a number of observations:

---

[9]Herkner reports a series of experiments, which suggest that a human will develop a model of own behavior in the same way as modeling another human's behavior[Herkner, 1980, pages 46 ff]. Self-observation does not rely on information or techniques that are different from those used for the observation of others. As a result, it is subject to the same errors.

[10]For common sense theories and scientific theories refer to [Schütz, 1962], [Garfinkel, 1967].

- Experts supply incomplete and inconsistent knowledge, because they instantly develop a naive theory about their competence, when they are being interviewed.

- The experts' descriptions of their actions differ from their observed behavior since they tend to verbalize their knowledge but not the competence which underlies their actions.

- Experts modify their knowledge during the knowledge acquisition process; they adapt it to the model which has been interactively created with a knowledge engineer, because the modeling process will perhaps be the first occasion for them to develop a distinct model of their competence.

The word *sloppy* is used to stress that a model never reaches a finite state which will remain appropriate forever. It indicates that there is never even a part of the evolving model that can be taken for granted. It therefore points at the need for revisions concerning all parts of a model. The basic set of assumptions summarized by the term *sloppy modeling* are:

- A model is always incomplete, on the one hand, because the domain changes, and on the other hand, because our knowledge of the domain changes, too. Modeling is an infinite process.

- A model is more or less adequate, on the one hand for the uses of the knowledge, and on the other hand for the tasks the model is to perform. Modeling is an approximative process, which is expected to provide increased adequacy.

- A model is to be consistent in itself and reflect the present state of the art. This cannot be achieved at once. Modeling is a deficient process.

We do not want to discuss here the useful results brought about in philosophy (epistemology, theory of science), psychology and sociology. We have already dealt with the intersubjectivity, reflexivity and interactivity of models or the modeling process. Instead, we only want to present some additional justification for our assumptions made about the modeling process (cf. also [Morik, 1991]). They can be interpreted in such a way that modeling is an infinite, approximative and deficient process. Hence, the model is not the result of the transformation of one structure into a given, different structure, and will not terminate when an initial structure has been processed. The knowledge acquisition problem can then no longer be dismissed as being caused by the incongruence of the representation formalism and the expert's description (see section 1.2.2). But rather, the process of modeling only comes to a temporary end, just as scientific findings only have a temporary character. It goes without saying that this process requires a lot of effort.

Scientists working in the field of software engineering have only recently started to pursue these ideas, with the slogan being *reality construction* [Floyd *et al.*, 1988]. They also place the emphasis on the interactivity of software engineering, its integration into social reality, the intersubjectivity and reflexivity of the concepts as well as on the notorious difficulties caused by the different representation techniques applied by developers and users[11].

Findings can become invalid by new events. In any case, new findings make the existing domain model incomplete, until the new findings have been modeled and incorporated into the domain model. The modeling of a domain cannot reach a final state, since the domain itself is subject to change, and since our knowledge of the domain changes. But nevertheless, the modeling process is evaluated at any time.

In principle, there are infinitely many possibilities to model a domain. The model determines the aspects of the domain that are represented or omitted. It also defines how phenomena are regarded: what is an object, a property, a relation? These definitions are evaluated according to their adequacy for particular uses of the knowledge and particular tasks that are to be carried out with the model. The adequacy of particular models in the field of knowledge representation has often been discussed [Freksa *et al.*, 1984]. It is not an absolute criterion, but can only be fulfilled to a varying degree. Of course, an adequate model should be consistent and reflect the present state of the art, i.e. be accurate. While it is possibile to evaluate the consistency within a model, accuracy refers to the model interpretation of the real world or at least the expert's view of the real world. A problem lies in the method of verification (how do we verify consistency?) and validation (how do we know that the model accurately reflects the expert's view of the world?) [O'Keefe *et al.*, 1987].

The new view of the knowledge acquisition process has some implications

---

[11] A quotation which also applies to knowledge acquisition: "Since formalization is central to all development of computer programs, how can we understand it without losing touch with the richness of the world we started from? By formalization we not only describe reality in a concise way. We also construct reality in selecting features to incorporate in our model and in making up its description. And we shape reality as well, since we act and see according to our description."[Floyd *et al.*, 1988, chapter B7]

for a system that is designed to support the process. How can the assumptions of sloppy modeling help us to gather the requirements that a system for knowledge acquisition has to fulfill? Such a system should not be used only once. Systems such as ID3 [Quinlan, 1983] which transform and augment information at the same time can only be part of a knowledge acquisition system. Also, systems such as PROTEGE-II or MODEL-K which build up a model and then compile it into a performance system are inappropriate with respect to the requirement of infinite modeling. On the whole, the system:

- has to accommodate the continuous increase in knowledge, and
- must be operational for use even if the model is incomplete.

We have drawn these requirements from the assumption that knowledge acquisition is infinite.

Revisions not only involve overcoming inconsistencies but also approaching an adequate model. Hence, any decision taken in the modeling process must be revisable, with the system supporting this revision. It is not sufficient to change particular facts or rules of the model: the lay out of the model, the items used for describing it, must be revisible. For instance, the decision that a particular entity of the world is to be represented as a property with particular possible values may turn out to be inadequate. A representation of this entity as an object may lead to a better model. Also this type of revision must be supported by the system. This requirement rules out stepwise refinement techniques, as they depend on the accuracy of the previous decision concerning the modeling process.

A knowledge acquisition system needs to be interactive and should immediately show the user the consequences of his/her decisions (see section 2.3). It is another view of the well-known advantages of rapid prototyping and the requirement of the system being operational from the very beginning. This can be concluded from the interactivity of knowledge acquisition. But, the system need not be the main interaction partner of the knowledge engineer or expert. The communication between experts and knowledge engineers remains most important and cannot be replaced by any human-computer interaction. The system, however, should support this interaction by enabling them to test various possibilities how to carry out the modeling.

The systems BLIP and MOBAL have been developed to fulfill the requirements of revisability and incrementality. The description of any part of MOBAL shows techniques that can be used to fulfill the requirements: the inference engine (chapter 3), for example, handles inconsistencies; the knowledge revision tool (chapter 7) helps to overcome the inconsistencies; the forming of concepts (chapter 8) is governed by exceptions to rules; the sort taxonomy tool (chapter 4) can be used incrementally and the learning of rules (chapter 6) is an incremental learning method.

1.3 Machine Learning

This section will briefly introduce machine learning, and will explain the most important terms that are used in the other sections. One of the first questions a layman will ask when being introduced to machine learning is bound to be: what is machine learning? But this question is more difficult to answer than you may think. We would like to present two definitions. The first one has been suggested by Herbert Simon [Simon, 1983, pages 28]:

> Learning is any change in a system which enables it to perform the same task or a task of the same type better the next time.

Some have criticized this definition for including too much (not every performance-enhancing change is learning) and for ruling out learning without purpose. This definition requires that the purpose of learning be known. But at least at the very moment of learning this need not be true. Scott [Scott, 1983] contends that humans (and Simon subsumes humans under his concept of "system") can process information which enables them to perform a task without even knowing of that task. For instance, while walking in a city you may happen to realize that there is a library. You realize this without knowing of any purpose for this information. If later on somebody asks you whether there is a library in that city you are able to answer the question. You learned about the library. However, you didn't know that this could become useful. Most often, nobody comes to ask questions about what you experienced while walking. Michalski [Michalski, 1986] objects against this definition that purposes can be defined differently. The example he puts forward is forced labor: workers in a labor camp gradually learn to work less, while pretending to be busy. On the surface, they seem to get more and more stupid, whereas in fact, they manage to realize their own purposes better. Hence, Simon's definition can only be applied in retrospective, but cannot provide a constructive guideline.

Michalski proposes the following definition [Michalski, 1986, page 10]:

> Learning is the construction and modification of representations of what has been experienced.

This definition will not preclude representations from being modified to achieve a particular purpose. But it will not confine all learning processes to that. By including the two terms "experience" and "representation" in the definition, the emphasis is placed on the aspects which are also of particular importance for machine learning:

- What is experience, and how can we describe it in operational terms? When we say of experts that it is their very experience which makes them experts, what exactly do we mean by that? Does expertise involve a more concise and more effective representation of the domain-related knowledge? Are there any problem-solving strategies which have been deduced from many examples, and which have then been optimized to be applied to other problems? There are some comments on these issues in the above paragraphs (section 1.2).

- Concepts of which representation formalism can be learned? What are the necessary restrictions of the representation formalism to make learning efficient? In section 1.3.2 we point at some new learnability results for logic-based learning. Chapter 6 shows the particular restrictions of the hypothesis space chosen for MOBAL's rule discovery tool.

- Which representation lnaguage is adequate for learning a certain concept? How does learning affect a representation language? The relation between knowledge representation and machine learning will be discussed later on in various sections (chapters 2 and 3, see also [Morik, 1989].)

1.3.1 Standard Techniques of Machine Learning

Machine learning most often induces a general concept from a number of examples by generalizing the common features of the examples. This approach is based on *induction*. Induction is a justified generalization. Standard techniques of machine learning induce one or several concept descriptions from examples, the description language for concept descriptions being an attribute-value representation. Famous learning techniques are the *top-down induction of decision trees* (TDIDT) with the implementations by Quinlan [Quinlan, 1983] and Bratko [Cestnik *et al.*, 1987] and the *conceptual clustering* technique by Michalski [Michalski, 1983]. Instances of one (TDIDT) or several (conceptual clustering) concepts are entered into the system. They are then used to induce the description of a concept in the form of a decision tree (TDIDT) or a declarative description (conceptual clustering). The induction is statistically justified, i.e., all or very many instances of a concept are covered by the description, and there are none or only a few non-instances covered by the description. This description of the concept is then used to recognize new instances ("recognition function"). Principally, there are several possibilities to describe a set of instances. Frequently, we look for the most specific generalization, or for the most general discrimination of examples and counter-examples.

The search for a *generalization* can be regarded as a search in space, with the most general discrimination forming the upper boundary and most specific generalizations of instances (examples) forming the lower boundary of this space. This versions space and the systematic search in it was introduced by Mitchell [Mitchell, 1982]. In contrast to the techniques of TDIDT or conceptual clustering, this method takes one example after the other and modifies the boundaries of the versions space accordingly. The learning procedure limits the current set of the most general discriminations when a negative example has been entered. The result is the creation of a new set of such most general discriminations, which no longer covers the new negative example. In the case of a positive example, the most specific generalizations will be generalized. A new set of most specific generalizations is created which also covers the new positive example. If the intersection of the boundaries contains only one hypothesis, this is the learned concept description. No further example will change this hypothesis. The versions space technique requires that the instance descriptions can be precisely ordered according to a "more-general-than" relation.

Particular difficulties in inductive learning are caused by noisy data, limitations of the description language (missing term problem), incremental learning and closed-loop learning. By *noisy data*we mean inaccurately classified objects (the objects described are not instances of the class as indicated or they are instances, although they were marked as non-instances), wrong descriptions of objects, or even faulty background knowledge. It is realistic to assume that there are errors in the learning data. Strategies for coping with such errors include, for example, allowing a very low percentage of negative examples to be covered by a most specific generalization. These counter-examples will then be regarded as noisy data. Another possibility would be to collect counter-examples until they provide an opportunity to revise the description of a concept [Emde, 1987]. Of course, it is still uncertain whether the results are accurate in view of the unreliable learning material, but when there are possibilities to revise the results, the system is at least in a position to rectify the errors once they have been detected.

The problem of limitations of the description language refers to the fact that the representation language determines the scope of possible concept descriptions. This limitation provides the advantage that insignificant description parts will not lead the learning procedure in the wrong direction. Implicitly, the fact that a feature is mentioned means that it is relevant for the concept or the rule to be acquired. Hence, we also speak of representational bias. But what will happen if the description of the concept or the rule to be acquired is outside the score of possible descriptions? How is it possible to realize that a significant feature is missing in the examples, because it could not be expressed with the means of the representation language? How can the representation language be automatically enlarged? This problem, which is closely connected with representational bias, can specifically be described as the *new term problem.* MOBAL contains a learning procedure which forms new predicates to overcome language limitations.

A learning procedure is *incremental* when not all the examples are supplied at once, but a subset of examples is used for each learning step. Thus, each learning result is only an intermediate result, which is modified by supplying new examples. This requires the representation to support such modifications, and the procedure not to abstract from any information that may be relevant for later examples. Heuristic approaches show sequencing effects: the learning result depends on the sequence in which the examples are presented. The versions space is a procedure which when being supplied with the same examples in a different order will still produce the same final result.

By *closed-loop learning* we are referring to an incremental learning procedure which includes intermediate results in the background knowledge and uses them for further learning. This learning procedure provides the big advantage that it is not the user who has to supply all the background knowledge, and that the learning procedure can be more efficient owing to an increasingly large background knowledge. It is often the case that only an increased background knowledge will enable the system to learn a particular rule or develop a particular concept. Thus, learning results improve further learning. The disadvantage is that sometimes the background knowledge is unnecessarily comprehensive, with the result that the learning process will become increasingly inefficient.

1.3.2 Logic-based Learning

Whereas the representational power of standard learning techniques is only the one of propositional logic, Gordon Plotkin showed early on how the inductive process of generalization can be formalized within predicate or first-order logic [Plotkin, 1970], and [Plotkin, 1971]. Plotkin's results concerning the complexity of learning in predicate logic were at first disappointing, and, for a long time probably prevented many researchers from looking for efficient algorithms using predicate logic. About ten years later, induction in predicate logic was again investigated by some researchers [Vere, 1977], [Shapiro, 1981], [Emde *et al.*, 1983], [Kodratoff, 1986], [Kodratoff and Ganascia, 1986]. Today, learning in predicate logic or *logic-based learning* has become a hot research topic. Logic-based learning produces learning results in a (restricted) predicate logic. Predicate logic allows to formulate relations in an elegant way which users (human experts from other faculties than computer science) can easily understand. Moreover, the learning result can be interpreted by the system. It is an operational or executable description. In contrast, the decision trees produced by TDIDT algorithms cannot be interpreted by these systems. Logic-based learning goes beyond neural networks or standard machine learning approaches in that it is capable of using background knowledge. It goes beyond explanation-based learning in that it does not require the background theory to be complete. It goes beyond statistics in that the hypothesis generation and the interpretation of results is done automatically. Logic-based learning is reliable in applications in that it induces only those hypotheses that are consistent with the set of examples. Therefore, the user can interpret the learning result with respect to the learning data.

In the framework of logic-based learning, the task of *inductive learning* can be presented using the following items:

- a background theory B,
- a set of positive examples E^+ and a set of negative examples E^-,
- a hypothesis space,
- a (partial) ordering relation $\leq$ for hypotheses, and
- B $\not\models E^+$.

Inductive learning finds a hypothesis H such that:

1) B, H, E $\not\models \bot$

2) B, H $\models E^+$

3) B, H $\not\models E^-$

As the logical inference is applied, its undecidability is inherited by the process which tests whether a hypothesis fulfills the above conditions. The partial ordering can be used to select either the *most specific generalization* or least general generalization as Plotkin puts it, or the *most general discrimination* between positive and negative examples. If the most special generalization is to be found, an additional requirement for the hypothesis is:

4) $\forall$ H' (H' $\leq$ H $\Rightarrow$ H $\leq$ H'),
where H' fulfills the conditions 1) - 3).

We may base the partial ordering on logical inference. The most specific generalization H of E with respect to B is implied by all other consistent hypotheses:

if H $\leq$ H' then H' $\models$ H

An alternative ordering is to use *subsumption* in order to select an appropriate hypothesis as Gordon Plotkin did.

Wray Buntine introduced an improvement of Plotkin's learning in the context of background knowledge, the generalized θ-subsumption [Buntine, 1988]. He restricts the representation formalism to Horn clause logic without functions as terms[12] and describes a decidable generalization of clauses as follows. σ and θ being substitutions, C_{body} being the body of a clause, and C_{head} its head, we can say:

Clause C1 is more general with respect to a theory B than C2 iff
$\exists\ \sigma$ such that $C1_{head}\ \sigma = C2_{head}$ and
B, $C2_{body}\ \theta \models \exists\ (C1_{body}\ \sigma\ \theta)$

This can be operationalized by

- turning constants of C2 into variables of C1,
- dropping atoms of C2 so that the set of literals of C1 is a real subset of the set of literals of C2,
- ensuring that resolving C1 with B leads to C2'.

[12]If we view constants as unary functions, these are of course included, but all others are excluded.

An alternative approach to this view of induction is to regard induction as the inverse of resolution[13]. At first sight, it seems possible to base an algorithm for induction on the inversion of the algorithm for deduction, namely resolution. Hence, several scientists worked on this approach [Muggleton and Buntine, 1988], [Wirth, 1989], [Rouveirol and Puget, 1989]. However, the control of the inverse substitution is difficult and the complexity of such an algorithm is exponential in the number of literals involved (see [Jung, 1993] for an overview).

The framework of *identification in the limit* [Gold, 1967], [Angluin and Smith, 1983] allows us to assess inductive inference. The criterion is that if it happens that a correct theory was built, then no further input will change it. We never know when a correct theory has been found. If an inductive algorithm is proved to identify a theory in the limit, then we only know that the algorithm will not change the theory after the limit. Ehud Shapiro [Shapiro, 1983] presented a system MIS which identifies a theory in the limit if the languages for the examples (LE) and for the theory (LH) are admissible. The system applies two operators, the contradiction backtracing operator and the refinement operator. The contradiction backtracing operator identifies by a minimal number of questions to the user which rule of the theory has to be retracted so that the theory no longer covers negative examples. This operator has become a method for debugging logic programs. The proof for MIS identifying a theory in the limit depends on the admissability of LE and LH, on the monotonicity of logic, on a depth-bound of inference, and on the completeness of its refinement operator. This operator incrementally produces more and more complex formulae. It is evoked whenever the theory does not yet cover all valid facts (positive examples). The operator is complete in that it can produce all well-formed formulae. As this is not tractable, RDT of MOBAL only produces a subset of all well-formed formulae, namely those corresponding to user-given rule schemata. This makes RDT's learning efficient but incomplete. The property of identification in the limit does not hold for RDT. If a correct theory entails formulae which do not correspond to given rule schemata, MOBAL will not identify the theory. If, however, the theory is expressible using rules corresponding to given rule schemata, RDT will identify it effectively.

A theoretical approach that determines the learnability of representation classes is that of *probably approximately correct learning* - PAC for short

[13] Another alternative - which unfortunately has not been studied further - is the view of induction as non-monotonic reasoning [Helft, 1989].

- [Valiant, 1984][14]. The learning task within this framework is to identify a concept. The correctness of the learning result is weakened by allowing a small failure (at most ε) and ensuring the identification of the concept only with the probability 1-δ. Neither the learning task of PAC-learning nor its basic assumptions formalize the learning scenario of MOBAL. Nevertheless, the learnability theory could be used to prove some important results for logic-based learning. Existentially quantified conjunctive formulae cannot be learned polynomially [Haussler, 1989]. The main focus of current work on logic-based learning is to find restrictions of the hypothesis language that still offer the advantages of learning in predicate logic but are tractable. Non-recursive ij-determinate clauses can be learned polynomially [Džeroski *et al.*, 1992], but no proper superset of this formalism is efficiently learnable [Kietz, 1993]. Concepts in an alternative representation formalism, namely the termsubsumption formalism (KL-ONE), could also be shown to be efficiently learnable [Kietz and Morik, 1993]. The representation formalism of MOBALwhich is also used by its learning tool RDT is presented in 2. The hypothesis space of RDT is not only determined by this formalism, but users can specify application specific restrictions which restrict the hypothesis space further.

1.4 A Characterization of MOBAL

MOBAL has been developed to reflect the assumptions about the modeling process (see section 1.2.4), namely that modeling is an infinite process. Design goals for the system as a support to the manual knowledge acquisition process were to maintain incomplete and revisable knowledge, to check its consistency, and to enable the user to inspect the knowledge base. In particular, the inspection is eased by an immediate display of the consequences which the user's activities have. For the automatic knowledge acquisition process a model-based, incremental and even closed-loop learning procedure was developed. From the beginning, we worked in the framework of predicate logic. Users are allowed to restrict learning to those rules that are instantiations of given rule schemata. This restriction reduces the hypothesis space of learning (see chapter 6, in particular, section 6.4 and section 6.5). The goal was to cope with noisy data, to not apply the closed-world assumption (which is the opposite of the assumptions underlying sloppy modeling) and to provide an approach which overcomes limitations of a description lan-

[14] A current introduction into PAC-learning is [Kearns, 1990].

guage whenever necessary. RDT learns most general discriminating rules. This results in a high predictiveness. It requires, however, that learned rules can be refined if needed. This requirement is fulfilled by KRT and CLT (see chapters 7 and 8).

It was a design goal in its own right to integrate completely manual and automated knowledge acquisition. By complete integration we mean that the coordination of knowledge uses (learning, checking consistency, communicating) is also performed by the system, and that the representation of a system component is also "understood" by other system components. This rules out approaches which require the user to determine when to call which system component. It does not rule out, however, allowing the user to guide the system. So-called edit-and-compile cycles, e.g., for revisions and updates, are also excluded. Actually, these systems do not guarantee that dependencies between activities or their results are managed by the system, since the operations are opaque for the system.

Both the user and the learning components of the system build up the emerging domain model, which is managed by the inference engine. Operations of the user on the domain model as well as operations of the system are supported by the same environment. The work-share between system and user is flexible. All items which can be input or deleted by the user can also be added or deleted by the system.

- Users are free to enter rules or to let rules be learned by RDT.
- Users are free to input concept descriptions or to let them be learned by CLT.
- Users may revise the set of rules or let KRT select the rules to be retracted or refined.
- Users are free to define sorts and declare predicates with respect to the sorts of their arguments. If they don't want to do it, STT does it for them.
- Users are free to enter the task structure of the application as a predicate structure. They may also call PST to structure a set of rules.
- Users must at least enter some facts. Further facts can be deduced from (learned) rules.
- Users must choose or enter a set of rule schemata.

- Users are free to change the default values of all parameters, including the criteria for accepting or rejecting hypotheses.

Consequently, we describe this approach towards the integration of manual and automatic knowledge acquisition as *balanced cooperative modeling*.

Chapter 2

The Knowledge Representation Environment

The knowledge representation of MOBAL can be viewed from three different angles:

- the knowledge engineer works with the knowledge structures as they are presented by the human-computer interface,
- the software developer who wants to couple MOBAL with a performance system or integrate a module of MOBAL into another system uses the access routines provided by the programmer's interface,
- the reader of this book - whether a user of the system or not - might be interested in the meaning of the knowledge structures.

This chapter describes MOBAL's knowledge representation environment from all three of the above perspectives. In the next section (section 2.1), we introduce MOBAL's knowledge representation informally by verbally describing meaning and purpose of the different knowledge sources and giving examples of their use (section 2.1). After this, we give a formal syntax and semantics definition of the core elements of our representation and discuss the properties and complexity of possible inference procedures (section 2.2). In the second half of the chapter, we give an overview of the design goals, general structure, and use of MOBAL's knowledge acquisition environment and user interface (section 2.3). Then, the programmer's interface is presented (section 2.4). We do not document the details of the access routines in this book but refer the reader to MOBAL's user guide [Sommer *et al.*, 1993b]. The exact data structures and inference procedures used in MOBAL's inference to operationalize the representation are described in chapter 3.

2.1 MOBAL's knowledge representation

The MOBAL system is an environment for building up, inspecting, and changing a knowledge base. We describe the knowledge sources which constitute a domain model in MOBAL from the point of view of the knowledge engineer. The different knowledge sources are:

- **facts**, expressing relations, properties, and concept membership of objects
- **predicate declarations**, defining the arity of the predicate and symbolic sort names for its arguments
- **sorts**, expressing the hierarchical structure of the objects (constant terms) used in the domain model
- **rules**, expressing inferential relations between predicates, necessary and sufficient conditions of concepts and hierarchies of properties
- **integrity constraints**, expressing constraints on the knowledge base that are to be monitored by the system
- the **topology**, expressing general semantic relationships by grouping predicates into sets and showing their possible inferential relationships
- **metapredicates**, which are rule schemata specifying the translation of *metafacts* into rules
- **metafacts**, a declarative representation of inferential knowledge that is translated into rules via metapredicates
- **metarules, metametafacts, and metametapredicates** are rarely used constructs that relate to metafacts in the same way that rules, metafacts, and metapredicates relate to facts.

As indicated by the use of the term "meta", the representation incorporates restricted higher-order logic elements. Fortunately, as we will see in section 2.2.5, inferences in this representation are still tractable. Also, it should be noted that users need not be familiar with the metalevel constructs to use MOBAL, since they are created automatically whenever needed. This means that in most cases, a user can formulate a domain model using only facts and rules. Metapredicates are also used in MOBAL's inductive rule learning component RDT to restrict the hypothesis space (see chapter 6). In the following, we describe the different representational constructs and knowledge sources in more detail.

2.1.1 Facts

Facts are used to state relations, properties of objects and concept membership. Facts are function-free literals that must not contain variables. The form of a positive fact is $p(t_1, ..., t_n)$ where p is a n-ary predicate and t_j is a constant or a number. The form of a negated fact is not($p(t_1, ..., t_n)$). Examples of facts are

large(cadillac)
not(small(cadillac))

Each fact has an associated *evidence point* specifying the fact's truth value. A positive fact is interpreted as having the evidence point true and a negated fact has the evidence point false. In addition, the evidence points both and unknown are possible in MOBAL. The former is assigned to contradictory facts about which both positive and negated evidence is available, e.g. because the user has input a positive statement and the system has derived its negation via rules. Contradictory facts can also be directly input as both($p(t_1, ..., t_n)$), as in

both(medium(ford))

The evidence point unknown is the evidence point for facts that are not currently inferrable from the knowledge base.

Note that every fact which is to be interpreted as false must be explicitly negated. This explicit negation has some advantages compared with the closed world assumption. It enables the user to input incomplete examples and to build up the model incrementally. The closed world assumption requires the user to know in advance which statements are necessary to complete the description of an example, but, as was stated above, modeling does not start with such a precise idea. Therefore, leaving out some statements in one example does not mean the negation of these statements. Hence, MOBAL interprets missing information simply as unknown.

Also note that the mapping from a fact to a truth value can in principle obey a fuzzy logic because MOBAL's inference engine IM-2 handles continuous truth values in a two-dimensional evidence space (see section 3.2.4 and [Emde, 1991]). In this continously valued representation of evidence points, a pair of integers, each between 0 and 1000, independently represent positive and negative evidence. The symbolic truth values above are the cornerpoints of this space. True corresponds to [1000,0], false to [0,1000], both to [1000,1000], and unknown to [0,0]. Such evidence points can in principle be specified by the user, e.g. as

owner(luc,diane) – [700,200]

which says there is a moderate amount of positive evidence and a little amount of negative evidence for this fact. In general, however, it is difficult for users to work with such continous-valued evidence points, so normally only the four above-mentioned cornerpoints of the evidence space are used.

2.1.2 Predicate declarations

The arguments of a predicate are of a particular *sort*. While MOBAL's sort taxonomy tool STT automatically and dynamically builds up a sort structure of its own (see chapter 4), the user can also declare symbolic sort names for the arguments of a predicate. Given the declaration

p/2: <sort1 >, <sort2 >

STT will automatically add all objects that are used in the first argument position of predicate p to the sort sort1. Such named sorts are fully integrated into the automatically constructed sort lattice, but it is also possible to declare relationships between them (see below and chapter 4).

2.1.3 User sort declarations

In addition to the dynamic sort lattice that is automatically constructed by STT, it is also possible to declare certain relationships between named sorts (so-called *user sorts*) and thus permanently fix them in the sort lattice. For example, the user can specify required inclusions of named user sorts. This is done using the relation :< between sorts, for example

child :< person
woman :< person,female

where the second is equivalent to

woman :< person
woman :< female

Chapter 4 describes in detail how these declarations are processed and how they are incorporated into the dynamic sort lattice of STT.

2.1.4 Rules

In MOBAL, rules are clauses with at least two literals and a marked head. The head of a rule is referred to as its *conclusion*, and all other literals are referred to as *premises*. There is no restriction on the number of positive or negated literals in a rule. In MOBAL, rules are not written in clausal form, but in implication form as

$$L_1\& \ldots \& L_n \rightarrow L_{n+1}$$

When writing down rules, we will usually not specify the list of variables explicitly, but simply use the Prolog convention and write variables with a capital first letter. A simple example of a rule is

small(X) → not(large(X))

Rules may also make use of a number of *built-in predicates* of the inference engine in their premises. There are two groups of such predicates. The first performs arithmetic functions (eq, ge, gt, le, lt, add, sub, mult, div), and the second computes *autoepistemic operations*, i.e., operations the result of which depends on the current state of the knowledge base (unknown, count, max_of, min_of). These predicates thus result in non-monotonic effects. Section 3.2.2 describes the built-in predicates and their use in more detail. As an example of the use of numeric comparisons, consider the following threshold rule for fever (using a centigrade scale):

temperature(Person,T) & gt(T,37) → fever(Person)

As an example of an autoepistemic operator, the following rule expresses a default:

person(X) & unknown(marital_status(X,Y)) → single(X)

Each rule has an attached special data structure called a *support set* which determines the rule's domain of applicability. For a rule with n variables, the support set is an expression that specifies an n-dimensional set, and it is required that for every application of the rule, the tuple of variable values be a member of this set. The exact syntax of support set specifications is described in section 7.3.2, and their evaluation in section 3.2.3, so we give only a short example here. From our TRAFFIC-LAW domain (see section 9.1), consider the rule

involved_vehicle(X,Y) & owner(Z,X) → responsible(Z,X)

which states that the owner of a vehicle is responsible for all traffic violations in which the vehicle was involved. If we specify as support set for this rule

(X,Y,Z) ∈ (minor_violation × all × all) \ {(event1,car1,person1)}

this means that the rule may only be applied in cases where X is bound to a constant known to be a minor_violation, and where the tuple of variables is not equal to (event1,car1,person1). Support sets are mainly used by the knowledge revision component to achieve minimal knowledge base revisions (see chapter 7).

2.1.5 Integrity constraints

It is difficult to state disjunctive or negative information using rules. As an example, consider expressing the constraint that every employee of a company must either be a senior manager or an operator. This information cannot be expressed with rules. As an example of the difficulty of negative information, assume we wanted to state that an operator must not be a manager and *vice versa*. We could express this using the two rules

operator(X) → not(manager(X))
manager(X) → not(operator(X))

which is the right thing to do if we are really interested in all the negative facts about managers and operators. In many cases, however, we just want to make sure the constraint holds without wanting to see all the negative inferences explicitly. MOBAL's *integrity constraints* allow the statement of exactly this kind of information. An integrity constraint is a clause just like a rule, but it may have more than one head literal. In fact, its head can be empty or a disjunctive normal form expression. The first example above can be expressed by the integrity constraint employee(X) → (senior(X) & manager(X)) ; operator(X)

whereas the second example can be expressed as

manager(X) & operator(X) →

with an empty conclusion which is to be read as "fail" or "false". MOBAL checks integrity constraints either permanently or upon explicit user request. Violations are placed on the system's *agenda* and can be resolved by the user at a convenient time. MOBAL supports this by offering a menu of fact additions or deletions that if performed would restore integrity.

2.1.6 The topology

The predicate **topology**, also known as the *predicate structure*, expresses general semantic relationships between predicates by grouping predicates into sets called *topology nodes* and showing their possible inferential relationships by links between these nodes. As an example, consider the topology node

violation - [illegal_parking, responsible, unsafe_vehicle_violation]
<- [places,circumstances,laws]

This node contains the predicates illegal_parking, responsible and unsafe_vehicle_violation, all of which state information about the traffic violation that was committed. The node has three children, namely the nodes places, circumstances and laws, which means that inferential relationships between the predicates in these three nodes and all predicates in the node violation are considered as possible. More precisely, a rule is considered to match a topology if all premise predicates are taken from the same node as the conclusion predicate or from one of its immediate children. In this way, the topology shows which information can in principle have an influence on which other information. The topology graph can thus be viewed as a generalization of *determinations* [Davies and Russell, 1987]. A determination states a relation between particular predicates, whereas the topology generalizes this to *sets* of predicates.

The system does not prevent the user from entering rules that do not correspond to the current topology. In fact, the predicate structuring tool PST can be used to automatically *generate* a topology that corresponds to the current set of rules in the knowledge base (see chapter 5). The topology is also used by the inductive rule learning component RDT to restrict its hypothesis space. RDT considers only rule hypotheses that match the current topology (see chapter 6).

2.1.7 Metapredicates and metafacts

Metapredicates are part of MOBAL's higher order knowledge structures. They define a translation between a *metafact* and a domain level rule by specifying a *rule schema* that when instantiated becomes a regular rule. Consider for example the metapredicate

opposite(P,Q): P(X) → not(Q(X))

which defines the "opposite" relationship between two predicates. In this metapredicate definition, P and Q are predicate variables, the part before the colon is called the *metapredicate header*, and the rest is the rule schema. In a knowledge base that contains the metafact

opposite(large,small)

the inference engine will automatically apply the metapredicate and enter the rule

large(X) → not(small(X))

into the knowledge base. If the rule schema is to include constants as arguments, these can also be included in the metapredicate header, as in the following metapredicate for treshold:

threshold(P,C,Q): P(X,Y) & gt(Y,C) → Q(X)

Using this metapredicate, the metafact

threshold(temperature,37,fever)

can be translated into the rule

temperature(X,Y) & gt(Y,37) → fever(X)

Since rules have associated supports set, metafacts also have support sets that carry over to the generated rule. Metapredicates have an important function in the rule learning module RDT, where they function as *rule models.* This means that when given a set of metapredicates as rule models, RDT will consider only those rule hypotheses that are instances of the given schemas, i.e., can be derived from them by instantiating predicate variables.

Since metapredicates can be arranged in a hierarchy, this allows an efficient search based on safe pruning (see chapter 6).

Users who do not want to get involved with the metalevel or need help in writing metapredicates can use MOBAL's *model acquisition tool* MAT which automatically creates metapredicate definitions from sample rules by abstracting variable and predicate names and, if necessary, reordering the premises to ensure proper evaluation. At present, work is under way to find methods of automatically generating metapredicates from the structure of facts in the knowledge base. As a first result, Edgar Sommer's [Sommer, 1993] INCY algorithm is capable of heuristically proposing new metapredicates that can then be used by RDT.

2.1.8 Metarules, metametapredicates and metametafacts

MOBAL's metalevel structures can in principle be extended to an unlimited number of metalevels. Since metafacts are just facts on the metalevel, *metarules* about these metafacts can be written which in turn can be produced from *metametafacts* with the help of *metametapredicates.* Even though the same process could be repeated to offer constructs on a third or higher metalevel, these are very hard to use and have not been included in MOBAL. As an example of a metametapredicate, consider

m_symmetrical(mp): mp(P,Q) → mp(Q,P)

which expresses the symmetry of a metapredicate mp[1]. Using this metapredicate, the metametafact

m_symmetrical(opposite)

can be translated into the metarule

opposite(P,Q) → opposite(Q,P)

Given the metafact

opposite(large,small)

the above metarule derives the metafact

[1]When entering this metametapredicate into MOBAL, each literal in the rule schema must be augmented by an additional argument representing the support set of the respective metafact. This is necessary in order to specify which premise support set is to be inherited by the conclusion.

opposite(small,large)

which can be translated into the domain level rule

small(X) → not(large(X))

as described in the preceding section. Metametafacts and metarules are thus a convenient way of declaratively representing inferential knowledge so that it can be reasoned about. In this example, we have used metametaknowledge to perform the inference

large(X) → not(small(X)) ⇒ small(X) → not(large(X))

One important use of this facility is the introduction of metarules that prevent inconsistencies in the rule set. As an example, consider the metapredicate

inclusive(P,Q): P(X) → Q(X)

Clearly, there can be only one of the inclusive or opposite relationships between two predicates. This can be ensured by adding to the knowledge base the metarules

inclusive(P,Q) → not(opposite(P,Q))
opposite(P,Q) → not(inclusive(P,Q))

In this fashion, some of the obvious inconsistencies in rule sets can be prevented. Note that metarules and metametafacts do not have associated support sets in the current implementation.

2.2 Formal Properties

In the preceding sections, we have looked at our knowledge representation language from a particular perspective, namely the static perspective of expressive power. In other words, we have informally defined a syntax for possible statements in our representation, and were then primarily interested in whether the information we found necessary for developing models of an application domain could be expressed with those statements. The complementary dynamic perspective on knowledge representation was assumed implicitly, but never made explicit: what does it mean to enter a certain statement into the knowledge base, i.e., which inferences will be supported by the knowledge base? Which mechanism uses the available facts and rules to answer a query about a goal predicate in the knowledge base?

These questions focus our attention on the fact that a knowledge representation is not simply a language, but is really part of a knowledge representation system that is to store statements of the language, perform inferences with those statements, and answer questions about what is in the knowledge base or implied by it. This perspective is also called the *functional* view of knowledge representation [Levesque and Brachman, 1985]. As a user of a knowledge representation system, we need to know:

- What do statements in the representation mean? What is their *semantics*?
- Which inferences does the knowledge representation system provide? Are these correct and complete with respect to the semantics of the representation?
- Are the inferences provided in reasonable time?

From a pragmatic point of view, these questions can be answered simply by referring to the implemented system. In our case, the representation is stored and manipulated by IM-2, MOBAL's inference engine, and a detailed technical description of IM-2's inference mechanism is available (see chapter 3). Using the description, or its operational incarnation as a program, it can be determined which inferences will be provided, and which ones not. Through empirical tests, we can estimate how long it takes to answer queries on average knowledge bases.

Such a system-oriented characterization of a representation has some disadvantages however, which indicate the need for a formal characterization. First, the operational description does not provide a succinct characterization of the inferences delivered by the representation system, and does not provide a definition of the meaning of a statement independent of the implementation. Second, if we want to guarantee certain properties of the representation, we need to prove them, which cannot be done without first having a precise formal definition of the representation. Third, by providing a description that is independent of the program, we have a much better basis for scientific communication about the system.

In the following, we will therefore develop a formal characterization of the core subset of the representation that was introduced in section 2.1. This subset, which we refer to as $\mathfrak{R}$, includes all the elements that are central to the inferential and computational properties of the representation, i.e., facts and rules on the object level, and metapredicates, metafacts, and metarules on arbitrary metalevels. We have omitted the formalization of support sets and of evidence points other than **true**, **false**, **unknown** and **both**. Facts that are **unknown** simply are not included in the knowledge base, and facts that are contradictory are represented by including both the fact and its negation in the knowledge base. Thus, in the formalization, it is sufficient to rely on positive and negated facts for representing all four evidence points.

The remainder of the section is organized as follows. We will first specify the syntax of the representation subset described above (section 2.2.1, and then define a classical two-valued semantics for this subset (section 2.2.2). After describing a proof theory for our representation (section 2.2.3), we use the semantics definition as a reference point against which we measure the completeness and correctness of the inferences that are provided by the system (section 2.2.4). After an examination of the computational complexity of inference in $\Re$ (section 2.2.5), we change our focus to the treatment of inconsistencies in our representation (section 2.2.6), and provide an alternative, multi-valued semantics for $\Re$ (section 2.2.7). We relate this semantics to the possibility of non-monotonic treatment of inconsistencies in IM-2 (section 2.2.8), and conclude with brief pointers to related work (section 2.2.9).

2.2.1 Syntax

Let $\Omega = \mathcal{M} \cup \mathcal{C} \cup \mathcal{V} \cup \mathcal{P}$ be the *alphabet* of $\Re$, where $\mathcal{M} :=$ {"(", ")", ",", ":", "& ", "$\rightarrow$ "} is a set of punctuation and connective symbols, $\mathcal{C}$ is a set of constant symbols (c_1, c_2, or other lowercase letters), $\mathcal{V}$ is a set of variable symbols (X, Y, or other uppercase letters), and $\mathcal{P}$ is a set of predicate symbols (p, q, r, or other lowercase letters), where $a : \mathcal{P} \rightarrow \mathbb{N}^+$ denotes the arity of a predicate symbol. Define the set of *terms*

$$\mathcal{T} := \mathcal{C} \cup \mathcal{V} \cup \mathcal{P}.$$

We let τ denote a type function

$$\tau : \mathcal{T} \rightarrow \mathbb{N}$$

that assigns a type to each term such that

$$\tau(t) \begin{cases} = 0 & \text{if t} \in \mathcal{C} \\ \geq 0 & \text{if t} \in \mathcal{V} \\ \geq 1 & \text{if t} \in \mathcal{P} \end{cases}$$

We write v^t to denote $v \in \mathcal{V}$ with $\tau(v) = t$, and $p^{t,a}$ to denote $p \in \mathcal{P}$ with $\tau(p) = t$ and $arity(p) = a$. Note that instead of type, we will often say *level*, and that type is not identical to order (variables of type t are instantiated to terms of type t, and not of type $t - 1$, see sections 2.2.2 and 2.2.3).

We can now define the atomic formulae of $\Re$. If $p^{t,a} \in \mathcal{P}$ is a predicate symbol of type t and arity a, and $T_1, \ldots, T_a \in \mathcal{T}$ are terms, then

$$L = p^{t,a}(T_1, \ldots, T_a)$$

is a *positive literal* iff (if and only if) for all $k \in \{1, \ldots, a\}$, $\tau(T_k) < t$[2]. We define functor(L) := $p^{t,a}$, and args(L) := $\{T_1, \ldots, T_a\}$. If L is a positive literal, $L^- = \mathsf{not}(L)$ is a *negative literal*, and functor(L^-) := functor(L), args(L^-) := args(L). For a literal L, we define vars(L) := args$(L) \cap \mathcal{V}$; if vars$(L) = \emptyset$, we say that L is *ground*, otherwise *nonground*; we further define $\tau(L) := \tau(\text{functor}(L))$. All ground positive and negative literals together make up the set $\mathcal{A}$ of atomic formulae of $\Re$. In MOBAL, these are called *facts* ($\tau = 1$), *metafacts* ($\tau = 2$), and *metametafacts* ($\tau = 3$).

If $L_1, \ldots, L_n, L_{n+1}$ are literals of type t, then

$$R = L_1 \& \ \ldots \& \ L_n \rightarrow L_{n+1}$$

is a *rule* iff vars$(L_{n+1}) \subseteq$ vars(R), where vars(R), the variables of a rule, are defined as vars$(R) := \bigcup_{i \in \{1,\ldots,n\}} \text{vars}(L_i)$. This restriction ensures that conclusion variables are always bound in the premises. We will assume that there is a canonical, fixed ordering on the variables of a rule, i.e., vars(R) is assumed to be an *ordered* set. We define $\tau(R) := t$. As stated above and defined below (section 2.2.2), the semantics for $\Re$ treats all variables as implicitly universally quantified. We use *clause* to denote a fact or a rule of $\Re$. A clause has the form of a rule as defined above; if $n > 0$, the clause is a rule, if $n = 0$ and the clause is ground, it is a fact.

We can now complete the syntax definition of $\Re$ with a definition of metapredicates as follows. If R is a rule of type t, and RS is obtained by replacing in at least one literal of R the functor predicate with a variable of type t, then RS is a *rule schema* or rule model, and $\tau(RS) := t$. If

[2]Note that we do not require the existence of a literal argument of type $t - 1$. This is done to allow, for example, a metafact of the form size_class(10,20,small) which, given the metapredicate

size_class(V1,V2,C): size(X,S) & S $\geq$ V1 & S $\leq$ V2 $\rightarrow$ class(X,C),

corresponds to the rule size(X,10) & S $\geq$ 10 & S $\leq$ 20 $\rightarrow$ class(X,small).

$\{v_1, \ldots, v_m\}$ are the variables introduced into R to produce RS, and L is a positive literal of type $t+1$, then

$$MP = L : RS$$

is a *metapredicate* definition iff $\{v_1, \ldots, v_m\} \subseteq \text{vars}(L)$, and $\text{vars}(L) \subseteq \text{vars}(R) \cup \{v_1, \ldots, v_m\}$, i.e., all predicate variables in RS must be bound in L, and L may not use variables that are not in RS. We define $\tau(MP) := t+1$.

The set of well-formed formulae of $\Re$ consists of the atomic formulae, rules, and metapredicates as defined above. In MOBAL, only formulae of types 1, 2, and 3 are used; formulae of type 1 are said to be on the object or domain level, formulae of type 2 are said to be on the metalevel, and formulae of type 3 are said to be on the metametalevel. Metametarules are not used. This completes the definition of $\Re$.

Note that if negated premises are disallowed, the subset of $\Re$ of type 1 (the base level) corresponds to the language of function-free Horn clauses (DATALOG programs [Ceri *et al.*, 1990]) which are generative.

2.2.2 Semantics

What is the meaning of a statement of $\Re$? When can we say a fact, rule, or metapredicate is true in a domain? What is the semantics of $\Re$?

The standard way of answering this question is by specifying an *interpretation*, i.e., a mapping from the constants and predicates of $\Re$ to the objects and relations of the domain that the knowledge base is supposed to describe. The meaning of a knowledge base is then given by defining under which circumstances its statements are true in the domain of interpretation, i.e., which worlds or domains are logical *models* of a given knowledge base. For $\Re$, such a Tarskian semantics [Mendelson, 1987] can be defined as follows[3].

We will first define what we mean by an interpretation for $\Re$. Let D be a non-empty set, the set of individual domain objects. Then define D^t and D^* recursively as follows:

$$D^0 := D,\ D^t := (\bigcup_{a \in \mathbb{N}^+} \text{pset}(\underbrace{D^{t-1} \times \ldots \times D^{t-1}}_{a \text{ times}})) \cup D^{t-1}, \text{ and } D^* := \bigcup_{t \in \mathbb{N}} D^t,$$

where $\text{pset}(S)$ denotes the powerset of a set S, i.e., D^t is the set of all relations (of any arity a) over D^{t-1}, and D^* is the union of all these sets.

[3] See section 2.2.7 for an alternative, multi-valued semantics for $\Re$.

An *interpretation* is a function

$$I : \mathcal{C} \cup \mathcal{P} \rightarrow D^*$$

from the constants and predicates of $\Re$ to D^* with the following properties:

$I(c) \in D$ for all $c \in \mathcal{C}$, $I(c_1) = I(c_2)$ only if $c_1 = c_2$ and
$I(p^{t,a}) \in \text{pset}((D^{t-1})^a) \subseteq D^t$ for all $p^{t,a} \in \mathcal{P}$.

In other words, each constant is mapped to a distinct element of the domain (the "unique names assumption"), and each predicate of type t and arity a is mapped to a relation of the same arity over D^{t-1}.

We can now define what it means for an $\Re$-statement to be true. A positive ground literal (fact) $L = p^{t,a}(T_1, \ldots, T_a)$ is true in an interpretation I if and only if

$$(I(T_1), \ldots, I(T_a)) \in I(p^{t,a}),$$

i.e., if the objects or relations that correspond to the fact's arguments are indeed in the relation that corresponds to the fact's predicate. Similarly, a negated ground literal (fact) $L = \mathsf{not}((p^{t,a}(T_1, \ldots, T_a))$, is true in I if and only if

$$(I(T_1), \ldots, I(T_a)) \notin I(p^{t,a}).$$

To define truth for rules, we need to define how domain values can be substituted for variables in a rule. A *domain substitution* δ (for an interpretation I) is a function $\delta : \mathcal{C} \cup \mathcal{P} \cup \mathcal{V} \rightarrow D^*$ with the following properties:

$\delta(v) \in D^t$ if $\tau(v) = t$ for all $v \in \mathcal{V}$, and $\delta(s) = I(s)$ for all $s \notin \mathcal{V}$.

In other words, δ substitutes for each variable a domain object of the fitting type, and is equal to I for all non-variables. Using domain substitutions, we can define truth in δ for (ground or nonground) literals in the obvious way: a positive literal $L = p^{t,a}(T_1, \ldots, T_a)$ is true in δ if and only if $(\delta(T_1), \ldots, \delta(T_a)) \in \delta(p^{t,a})$, and a negated literal $L = \mathsf{not}((p^{t,a}(T_1, \ldots, T_a))$, is true in δ if and only if $(\delta(T_1), \ldots, \delta(T_a)) \notin \delta(p^{t,a})$.

We can now define when a rule is true. A rule $R = L_1 \& \ \ldots \& \ L_n \rightarrow L_{n+1}$ is true in an interpretation I if and only if for all domain substitutions δ for I, either there exists $i \in \{1, \ldots, n\}$ such that L_i is not true in δ, or L_{n+1} is true in δ. This defines the meaning of & and $\rightarrow$ in the usual fashion: an implication is true if one of its antecedents is false, or its conclusion is true (or both).

Finally, we have to define truth for metapredicates. A metapredicate $MP = L : RS$ is true in an interpretation I if and only if for all domain substitutions δ for I, the following holds: whenever L is true in δ, RS is true in δ as well. In other words, a metapredicate is true if for any true fact using the metapredicate, the rule defined by the metapredicate is true as well.

Whenever a formula of $\Re$ is not true (in I) it is *false* (in I). An interpretation I is called a logical *model* of a set of $\Re$-formulae Γ if all formulae in Γ are true in I. A formula F is *logically implied* by Γ (written $\Gamma \models F$) if and only if F is true in all models of Γ. This definition of $\models$ specifies the set of inferences that we would like to get from an inference engine for $\Re$. In the next section, we will therefore describe the basic inference rules that are implemented in IM-2, and then discuss whether they are correct and complete with respect to $\models$.

2.2.3 Inference Rules for $\Re$

To define the inference rules we want to use for $\Re$, we need to define a notion of substitution that respects the types of variables, and thus differs a little from the usual definition of substitution in first-order logic. A *substitution* in our context is a (usually partial) function $\sigma : \mathcal{V} \rightarrow \mathcal{T}$ with the following property:

$$\tau(\sigma(v)) = \tau(v) \text{ for all } v \in \mathcal{V} \text{ on which } \sigma \text{ is defined.}$$

In other words, a substitution always replaces a variable by a term of the appropriate type, which in $\Re$ may be a variable or a predicate or constant. Following standard logical practice, we write the application of a substitution σ to a term t as $t\sigma$. We will often write $\{V_1/t_1, \ldots, V_n/t_n\}$ for a substitution that replaces V_i by t_i (for $1 \leq i \leq n$).

Following the description of IM-2 in [Emde, 1991], and matching its implementation in MOBAL, we can now define the inference rules for $\Re$ as follows. They define the *one-step derivation operator* $\vdash_1$.

(I) Let Γ be an $\Re$-theory, $R = L_1 \& \ldots \& L_n \rightarrow L_{n+1}$ is a rule in Γ, and $F_1, \ldots, F_n$ facts in Γ. If σ is a substitution such that

$$L_i\sigma = F_i \text{ for all } i \in \{1, \ldots, n\},$$

then

$$\Gamma \vdash_1 L_{n+1}\sigma.$$

(II) Let Γ be an $\Re$-theory, $MP = L : RS$ a metapredicate in Γ, and F a fact in Γ. If σ is a substitution defined only on vars(L) such that

$$L\sigma = F,$$

then

$$\Gamma \vdash_1 RS\sigma.$$

It should be noted that in inference rule (I), we have not made special provisions for computed predicates (see section 3.2.2), i.e., they are treated as if they were asserted in the knowledge base. In inference rule (II), σ must be restricted to variables of L to avoid inferring rules that are more instantiated than necessary.

We can now define syntactical derivability as follows. Let Γ^* be the closure of Γ under $\vdash_1$. Then define that $\Gamma \vdash F$ if and only if $F \in \Gamma^*$.

The first inference rule given here is not very remarkable if we regard only the base level of the representation (facts and rules of type 1), and represents a typical forward chaining inference mechanism. Other inference rules, such as resolution, could have been used as well[4]. These inference rules are special only in their treatment of the higher-order constructs of $\Re$, as it is expressed by the second inference rule, which ensures that for every metafact, a corresponding rule is inferred.

2.2.4 Fact-correctness of $\vdash$ for $\Re^+$

Ideally, the inference rules that are used in a representation should define $\vdash$ in such a way that it derives all statements that are logically implied as defined by $\models$ (completeness), and none that are not logically implied (soundness). If a set of inference rules fulfills both of these requirements, we will call it *correct* for a representation. A quick look at the inference rules realized in MOBAL shows that this ideal goal is not met. Clearly, the above inference rules do not produce any rules that are logically implied by a knowledge base. If our knowledge base contains the rules

large(X) $\rightarrow$ heavy(X) and heavy(X) $\rightarrow$ stationary(X)

then the third rule

large(X) $\rightarrow$ stationary(X)

[4]In section 2.2.6, we will discuss why resolution cannot be chosen if the representation system is to tolerate inconsistencies gracefully.

is logically implied, but not derived by $\vdash$. The second source of incompleteness is due to the use of explicit negation in $\Re$. Given the knowledge base

large(X) → heavy(X), not(heavy(a))

the additional fact

not(large(a))

is logically implied, but not derived.

Nonetheless, things are not quite as bad as they might seem. If we adopt a restriction often used in logic programming and deductive database theory, and limit ourselves to the subset $\Re^+ \subset \Re$ that admits only positive literals in facts and rules, we can show (and do so below), that inference rules (I) and (II) above guarantee that all true facts and no false facts are derived from a knowledge base containing statements of arbitrary types. Even though this still leaves out the inference of rules as in our first example above, it is an important property that proves how the higher-order statements of $\Re$ can be correctly handled in a knowledge representation system.

Fact-completeness also meets the requirements of a functional knowledge representation: it is easy for a user to see which queries will be answered correctly (all factual queries), and which ones will not (anything else). As we will see in section 2.2.6, fact completeness on the positive subset of $\Re$ also provides an important hint as to how negation should be interpreted in $\Re$ — our inference rules provide all factual inferences that are possible if a fact and its negation are treated as if they were independent, i.e., as if they were expressed with separate predicates, because under this view, any $\Re$ theory can be regarded as consisting of positive literals only. Moreover, as we will discuss in section 2.2.7, it is possible even to capture this intuition formally by providing an alternative (albeit non-standard, multi-valued) semantics for all of $\Re$ according to which our inference rules are complete. First, however, we will prove the fact correctness of $\vdash$ for $\Re^+$ by showing that it is sound and complete.

Theorem 2.1 *$\vdash$ is sound and fact complete for $\Re^+$, i.e. for any $\Re^+$-theory Γ, if $\Gamma \vdash S$ for any statement S, then $\Gamma \models S$, and if $\Gamma \models F$ for any fact F, then $\Gamma \vdash F$.*

Proof:

Soundness It is obvious that $\vdash$ will not derive any incorrect theorems when we compare inference rules (I) and (II) with the semantic definition of rules and metapredicates; we therefore omit the proof for this lemma.

Completeness To prove the completeness of $\vdash$ for $\Re^+$, we will show that every $\Re^+$ theory Γ has a model in which a fact F is true only if $\Gamma \vdash F$, i.e., the only true facts are the ones in Γ^*. Knowing that such a model exists, we know that for any fact not $\vdash$-derivable from Γ, there is a model in which that fact is false, so the fact cannot be implied logically ($\models$) either, which means that $\vdash$ indeed produces all true facts.

We now prove the existence of such a model by constructing, for a given theory Γ, an interpretation called I in which only the facts in Γ^* are true, and then showing that indeed I is a model of *Gamma*.

Let Γ^* be the transitive inferential closure of Γ as defined above. With a given vocabulary, only finitely many facts are expressible in $\Re^+$, so Γ^* must be finite also. Let $F_1, \ldots, F_f$ be a fixed enumeration of the facts in Γ^* such that

$$\text{for all } i, j: \text{ if } 1 \leq i < j \leq f \text{ then } \tau(F_i) \leq \tau(F_j),$$

i.e., the facts are enumerated beginning with the domain level (type 1), and then proceeding to higher levels.

Then let $D := \mathcal{C} \cup \mathcal{P}$ be the base domain for the interpretation we want to construct, where $C \cap P = \emptyset$. For every predicate $p \in \mathcal{P}$ of arity a, define $\hat{p}$ as:

$$\hat{p} := \{(\underbrace{p, \ldots, p}_{a})\}.$$

Now we define a sequence of interpretations $I_j, j \in \{0, \ldots, f\}$ as follows, for $F_j = p'(A_1, \ldots, A_a)$:

$$I_j(c) \quad := \quad c \text{ for all } c \in \mathcal{C}, j \in \{0, \ldots, f\}$$

$$I_0(p) \quad := \quad \hat{p} \text{ for all } p \in \mathcal{P}$$

$$I_j(p) \quad := \quad \begin{cases} I_{j-1}(p) & \text{if } p \neq p' \\ I_{j-1}(p) \cup \{(I_{j-1}(A_1), \ldots, I_{j-1}(A_a))\} & \text{if } p = p'. \end{cases}$$

We are thus extending the interpretation in parallel with our enumeration of Γ^*. Since the type of a fact's arguments is required to be less than the type of its functor, $\tau(A_i) < \tau(p')$ for all $i \in \{1, \dots, a\}$ for all facts F_j. This ensures that all A_i appear before p' in our enumeration, so their interpretation is fixed when it is used, and so the recursive part of the definition is well-defined. The inclusion of a special tuple $\hat{p}$ in I_0 for predicates is necessary to guarantee the uniqueness of interpretations for predicates (constants map to themselves anyway, but several predicates could share, say, the empty relation as their interpretation). Note that $\hat{p}$ is a legal interpretation for p according to the definition in section 2.2.2, and that for all terms T, $I(T) \neq p$, so the addition of $\hat{p}$ does not influence the truth of statements in $\Re^+$.

We define our target interpretation as the last element of the above sequence, i.e.,

$$I := I_f,$$

and note as an important property that I is invertible, i.e., if $I(s_1) = I(s_2)$, then $s_1 = s_2$.

This concludes the construction of I. We now show that a fact $F = p(T_1, \dots, T_a)$ is true in I only if it is in Γ^*. So assume F is true in I. By definition, this means that $(I(T_1), \dots, I(T_a)) \in I(p)$. Since for all terms T, $I(T) \neq p$, $(I(T_1), \dots, I(T_a))$ cannot be equal to $\hat{p}$. Thus for $(I(T_1), \dots, I(T_a))$ to be in $I(p)$, by the construction of I, there must be a fact $F' = p(T'_1, \dots, T'_a) \in \Gamma^*$ such that for all $i \in \{1, \dots, a\}$, $I(T'_i) = I(T_i)$. Since I is invertible, however, this means $T'_i = T_i$, and therefore $F = F' \in \Gamma^*$.

As required, I thus makes only the facts in Γ^* true. We now need to show that $I = I_f$ is indeed a model of Γ, i.e., we need to show that all statements in Γ are true in I. By the construction of I, all facts in $\Gamma \subseteq \Gamma^*$ must be true in I. So it remains to be shown that all rules in Γ are true as well.

So, let $R = L_1 \& \ \dots \& \ L_n \rightarrow L_{n+1}$ be a rule in Γ, where

$$L_i = p_i(T_{1,i}, \dots, T_{a_i,i}) \text{ for all } i \in \{1, \dots, n+1\}.$$

Let δ be a domain substitution. According to the definition of truth for rules (see section 2.2.2), R is true if any antecedent literal is not true in δ; so assume that all antecedent literals are true in δ, i.e.,

$$(\delta(T_{1,i}), \dots, \delta(T_{a_i,i})) \in I(p_i)^5 \text{ for all } i \in \{1, \dots, n\}.$$

[5] Remember that δ is equal to I on all non-variables, so since p_i is not a variable, we can write either δ or I here.

By the construction of the model I, this means that for all $i \in \{1, \ldots, n\}$, there must be a fact $F_i = p_i(A_{1,i}, \ldots, A_{a_i,i}) \in \Gamma^*$ such that

$$I(A_{k,i}) = \delta(T_{k,i}) \text{ for all } k \in \{1, \ldots, a_i\}$$

because otherwise, $(\delta(T_{1,i}), \ldots, \delta(T_{a_i,i}))$ could not have been in $I(p_i)$[6]. Since I is invertible, this is equivalent to

$$A_{k,i} = I^{-1}(\delta(T_{k,i})) \text{ for all } k \in \{1, \ldots, a_i\}.$$

Having thus assumed that all premises are true in δ, we have to show that the conclusion is also true in δ, i.e., that

$$(\delta(T_{1,n+1}), \ldots, \delta(T_{a_{n+1},n+1})) \in I(p_{n+1}).$$

For this to be true, there must be a fact

$$F_{n+1} = p_{n+1}(A_{1,n+1}, \ldots, A_{a_{n+1},n+1}) \in \Gamma^*$$

such that $I(A_{k,n+1}) = \delta(T_{k,n+1})$ for all $k \in \{1, \ldots, a_{n+1}\}$ by the same argument as above. We now show that such a fact must indeed have been inferred with inference rule (I).

To this end, define a substitution σ on the variables of R such that

$$\sigma(V) := I^{-1}(\delta(V)),$$

i.e., apply the inverse of I on the domain object substituted by δ. Since I is invertible (see above), I^{-1} is defined. With σ defined this way, the following holds for all $i \in \{1, \ldots, n\}$:

$$\begin{aligned} L_i\sigma &= p_i(T_{1,i}\sigma, \ldots, T_{a_i,i}\sigma) \\ &= p_i(I^{-1}(\delta(T_{1,i})), \ldots, I^{-1}(\delta(T_{a_i,i}))) \\ &= p_i(A_{1,i}, \ldots, A_{a_i,i}) \\ &= F_i \end{aligned}$$

This means that inference rule (I) is applicable, and will derive the fact

$$\begin{aligned} L_{n+1}\sigma &= p_{n+1}(T_{1,n+1}\sigma, \ldots, T_{a_{n+1},n+1}\sigma) \\ &= p_{n+1}(I^{-1}(\delta(T_{1,n+1})), \ldots, I^{-1}(\delta(T_{a_{n+1},n+1}))) \\ &= p_{n+1}(A_{1,n+1}, \ldots, A_{a_{n+1},n+1}) \\ &= F_{n+1} \end{aligned}$$

[6] $(\delta(T_{1,i}), \ldots, \delta(T_{a_i,i}))$ cannot be the dummy tuple that was added to $I(p)$ because no term of $\Re$ is mapped to its elements, see above.

if we define $A_{k,n+1} = I^{-1}(\delta(T_{k,n+1}))$ for all $k \in \{1, \ldots, a_{n+1}\}$. Now we must show that indeed $I(A_{k,n+1}) = \delta(T_{k,n+1})$ for all $k \in \{1, \ldots, a_{n+1}\}$, which is easy since for all $k \in \{1, \ldots, a_{n+1}\}$:

$$\begin{aligned} I(A_{k,n+1}) &= I(I^{-1}(\delta(T_{k,n+1}))) \\ &= \delta(T_{k,n+1}) \end{aligned}$$

as required. Thus, $\delta(L_{n+1})$ is in I, and so the conclusion of the rule is true in δ, as was to be shown.

The proof for a metapredicate $MP = L : RS$ works along the same lines, so we will only sketch it here. If L is false in δ, MP is true anyway, so assume L is true in δ. We then need to show that RS is also true. If one of the premises of RS is false in δ, RS is true anyway, so assume all premises of RS are true. We then need to show that the conclusion of RS is also true, and this can be done very similarly to the construction for rules above. By defining substitutions just as above, we can show that using inference rule (II), Γ^* will contain a rule that will derive, using inference rule (I), the required conclusion.

We have thus shown that indeed there is a model for any theory Γ which makes only the facts in Γ^* true, thus showing completeness and completing our proof. □

2.2.5 Computational Complexity

We now know that the two inference rules we have specified provide a natural and interesting set of inferences for $\Re^+$, namely all facts that logically follow from a given knowledge base. This meets the second requirement of the list we set up at the beginning of section 2.2, leaving only the third one open: in what time can $\vdash$ be computed? For a knowledge representation system to be functional, the minimal requirement is certainly that $\vdash$ be decidable, i.e., that any query be answered in finite time; in practice, however, we usually require a polynomial upper bound on the time it takes to answer a query.

Our goal in this section, then, is to show that such a bound exists for $\vdash$ in $\Re^+$. Since the subset of $\Re^+$ of type 1 corresponds to the well-known language of function-free Horn clauses, the most interesting aspect of $\Re$ is its inclusion of restricted higher-order statements. In order to see more clearly the effect of these statements on the complexity of answering a query, we will subdivide the complexity analysis into two parts. First, we will show that the use of statements of type higher than 1 does not add exponential effort to the cost of reasoning in the base representation. We will then show that reasoning in the base representation is possible in polynomial time, which together shows that Re^+ queries can be answered in polynomial time.

Lemma 2.1 *Using a given base level inference procedure, and assuming that the maximal arity of predicates is A, and that rules have an arbitrary fixed maximal branching factor, any query regarding the full range of $\Re^+$ including higher-level statements up to level t_{max} in a knowledge base of size (in symbols) N can be answered in time*

$$t_{max} \cdot O(N^{A+2}) + t_{max} \cdot C_b(O(N^{A+1})),$$

where $C_b(M)$ denotes the time it takes to execute the base level inference procedure on a knowledge base of size M.

Proof: Since our goal is not to analyze the actual time complexity of the implementation of $\vdash$ in IM-2 with its various optimizations, we will simply use $\vdash$ forwards as a proof procedure to show that a polynomial bound exists. So, assume our proof procedure for answering a query Q about an $\Re^+$ knowledge base Γ is:

> *Metalevel proof procedure:* In order to answer a query about a (ground or nonground) literal Q, compute Γ^* as described below, and then check for each $F \in \Gamma^*$ whether F unifies with Q; if so, the required substitution is a solution to the query. To compute Γ^*, the transitive closure of Γ under $\vdash_1$, do the following. Let $t_{max} = max_{s \in \Gamma} \tau(s)$ be the highest level used in Γ. (In MOBAL, $t_{max} \leq 3$.) Beginning on level t_{max}, and proceeding down to the level of the query $\tau(Q)$, do the following for each level. First, use the base level inference technique to infer all facts on the current level from the rules on the current level. Second, for every fact ultimately derived, try to match it with every metapredicate, and if successful, enter the resulting rule in the next lower level according to inference rule (II).

If the base level proof procedure is correct, the above proof procedure correctly implements $\vdash$. This can be seen through the following argument. Since no metapredicates are ever generated, only the existing metapredicates can generate new rules. Since every metapredicate generates rules only on the next lower level, and we begin with the highest level above which there are no metapredicates any more, we are always assured that all rules that

can be inferred have already been inferred when we start using them on a level.

To analyze the complexity of this proof procedure, observe that for every fact generated by the base level inference procedure on a particular level, we have to check for every metapredicate whether it can be applied to generate a rule on the next lower level. Let $|F_t|$ denote the number of facts before the base level inference procedure was executed, $|F_t^*|$ the number of facts after application of the base level inference procedure, $|R_t|$ the number of rules, and $|MP_t|$ the number of metapredicates on the current level t. Now observe that certainly on every level, we cannot derive more facts than we can express with the given vocabulary. If the maximal arity of predicates is A, we have at most $|\mathcal{P} \cup \mathcal{C}|$ choices for the predicate and each of the A argument positions. Since each symbol must occur in the knowledge base somewhere,

$$|\mathcal{P} \cup \mathcal{C}| \leq N,$$

so the maximal number of facts F_{max} is:

$$F_{max} \leq N^{A+1}.$$

We therefore know that

$$|F_t^*| \leq F_{max} \leq N^{A+1}.$$

The total cost on a level is thus the cost of base level inference, plus the cost of applying all metapredicates. To determine the cost of the base level inference, observe that in the worst case, the next higher level was inferring all possible facts, each of which was translated into a rule. The length of each fact is at most $A+1$ symbols. If B denotes the maximal branching factor of rules, the length of each rule is at most $(B+1)(A+1)$ symbols, so we know that the size of the knowledge base for base level inference at level t is at most

$$N_t \leq (B+1)(A+1)|R_t|+(A+1)|F_t| \leq (B+1)(A+1)N^{A+1}+N = O(N^{A+1}).$$

Consequently, if we let $C_b(M)$ denote the cost of executing the base level inference procedure on a knowledge base of size M, the total cost of inference on one level is

$$\begin{aligned} C_1 &\leq C_b(O(N^{A+1})) + |F_t^*| \cdot |MP_t| \\ &\leq C_b(O(N^{A+1})) + N^{A+1} \cdot N \ = \ C_b(O(N^{A+1})) + O(N^{A+2}). \end{aligned}$$

This cost is incurred for a constant number of levels t_{max}, and we finally need to examine every element of the so-generated closure to see if it matches the query, so the total cost of answering a query is at most:

$$\begin{aligned} C_{total} &= t_{max} \cdot C_1 + F_{max} \\ &\leq t_{max} \cdot C_b(O(N^{A+1})) + t_{max} \cdot O(N^{A+2}) + N^{A+1} \\ &= t_{max} \cdot C_b(O(N^{A+1})) + t_{max} \cdot O(N^{A+2}). \square \end{aligned}$$

Lemma 2.2 *There is a base level proof procedure that computes all inferences in a time that is polynomial in the size of the knowledge base in symbols when a fixed vocabulary is used, and the maximal branching factor of rules and maximal predicate arity are fixed.*

Proof: We essentially follow the proof procedure that we developed in [Wrobel, 1987]. It is equivalent to the forward inference method of [Ceri *et al.*, 1990] for DATALOG languages.

> *Base level proof procedure:* Use all rules for forward inferences by matching their first premise, then for each instantiation matching their second premise, etc. For every successful instantiation of all premises, add the instantiation of the conclusion according to inference rule (I). Once through with all rules, repeat with all of them unless no new fact was derived.

Since the inference operator (I) is monotonic, i.e., only adds new inference, the order in which rules are used for inference does not matter. Furthermore, since the set of statements is necessarily finite, termination of the process is guaranteed, so the above proof procedure correctly performs the base level inferences as required by $\vdash$.

We derive a generous bound on the time it takes to execute the above procedure, and show that it is polynomial in the size of the knowledge base. In the actual implementation of IM-2, various optimizations are made in forwards and in backwards mode that we do not take into account (this would be necessary only to analyze IM-2's actual time complexity which is not our goal here).

In this proof, let M denote the size of the knowledge base given to the base level inference procedure. Let $|R|$ denote the number of rules, and $|F_0|$ the number of facts when we start inferring. If the maximal branching factor (maximal number of premises) of a rule is B, then the cost of performing the first forward inference step is

$$C_1 \leq |R| \cdot |F_0|^B,$$

since for every rule, we must in the worst case match its first premise against all facts, and for each such instantiation, match the second premise against all facts, etc. for up to B premises[7]. Since the first step generated additional facts (but no additional rules), the number of facts that form the basis for the second step is $|F_1| > |F_0|$, so the cost of the second step is at most

$$C_2 := |R| \cdot |F_1|^B.$$

In any case, however, $|F_i|$ can never exceed the number of well-formed facts constructible from the available vocabulary, F_{max} that was developed in the previous proof. If we define $N \geq |\mathcal{C} \cup \mathcal{P}|$,

$$F_{max} \leq N^{A+1},$$

Therefore, the cost of any step is at most

$$C_i \leq |R|(N^{A+1})^B = |R|N^{(A+1)B}.$$

Now, how many rules can there be in a knowledge base of size M? Each rule has at least one symbol, so $|R| \leq M$, and thus the cost of any step is at most

$$C_i \leq MN^{(A+1)B}.$$

How often do we need to repeat this single step in the worst case? Since we terminate whenever a step does not generate a new fact, every step must generate at least one new fact, which means, since there can be at most F_{max} facts, that there can be no more than F_{max} steps, and so the total cost of forward chaining is at most

$$C := F_{max}C_i \leq N^{A+1}MN^{(A+1)B}.$$

Since $M > N$, this is polynomial in the size of the knowledge base M. (Please note that if this proof procedure is applied in the context of the metalevel proof procedure for $\Re$, N corresponds to the size of the original knowledge base.) □

We can now state the theorem we were looking for.

Theorem 2.2 *A fact-correct set of inferences for $\Re^+$, as defined by $\vdash$, can be provided in time polynomial in the size of the knowledge base if the maximal number of levels, maximal arity, and maximal branching factor are fixed.*

[7]Note that since the arity of predicates is at most A, and there are no function symbols, matching a premise against a fact can be regarded as a constant time operation.

Proof: From lemma 2.1, we know that answers can be provided in polynomial time if there is a polynomial proof procedure for the base level; this however was shown in lemma 2.2. □

The result shown above carries over to all of $\Re$, because our inference simply treat negated literals as is they belonged to a new predicate independent of the corresponding unnegated predicates (this notion is further explored below). To reason in all of $\Re$, we can thus simply transform the original knowledge base into one with twice as many predicates, which means that the above theorem continues to hold.

Corollary 2.1 *The set of inferences for $\Re$ as defined by $\vdash$ can be provided in time polynomial in the size of the knowledge base if the maximal number of levels, maximal arity, and maximal branching factor are fixed.*

2.2.6 Reasoning with Inconsistencies

In section 2.2.4, we were able to show that $\vdash$ correctly provides all factual inferences for $\Re$, albeit only if we restricted the representation to statements without negated literals. In this section, we briefly discuss the difficulties involved in properly handling negation in the inference rules for $\Re$. Since the problem of negation is independent of whether metalevel statements are used or not, we refer to the base level only.

At first sight, specifying a proof procedure that will provide a complete set of inferences for $\Re$, including negation, seems to present no problem. The semantics in section 2.2.2 clearly defines what it means for an $\Re$ fact or rule with negated literals to be true or false. Furthermore, there are known inference procedures such as resolution [Lloyd, 1987] that will work properly when negation is used, and derive all facts, positive or negated, that follow from a knowledge base. For example, resolution will correctly infer:

$$\{\mathsf{p(X)} \rightarrow \mathsf{not(q(X))},\ \mathsf{p(a)},\ \mathsf{q(b)}\} \vdash_{resolution} \{\mathsf{not(q(a))},\ \mathsf{not(p(b))}\}$$

whereas the inference rule (I) we have specified will only produce

$$\{\mathsf{p(X)} \rightarrow \mathsf{not(q(X))},\ \mathsf{p(a)},\ \mathsf{q(b)}\} \vdash_1 \{\mathsf{not(q(a))}\}$$

Resolution will even correctly infer from apparently useless rules such as:

$$\{\mathsf{p(X)} \rightarrow \mathsf{not(p(X))}\} \vdash_{resolution} \{\mathsf{not(p(a))},\ \mathsf{not(p(b))},\ \ldots\}$$

So why was resolution not used as a proof procedure in the inference engine of MOBAL, and why were the rules of section 2.2.3 used instead even though they are incomplete when negation is used? The reason for this choice is in the intended behavior of the inference system on *inconsistent* knowledge bases. According to the standard logical semantics defined in section 2.2.2, a knowledge base logically implies all statements that are true in all models. A knowledge base with a contradiction has no models, so this condition is vacuously true, and consequently, all statements are logically implied by an inconsistent theory. Indeed, resolution will also use contradictory information for inferences, and will be able to derive any query from a knowledge base containing contradictory information:

$$\{\mathsf{p(a)},\ \mathsf{not(p(a))}\} \vdash_{resolution} \{\mathsf{q(a)},\ \mathsf{q(b)},\ \mathsf{not(q(c))},\ \ldots\}$$

since the empty clause can be produced during the refutation proof simply by resolving the two literals in the original knowledge base. This can of course be prevented by requiring resolution only between the goal clause and clauses in the original theory, but then resolution is no longer complete according to our semantics.

In a learning system, it is very important to avoid this inference behavior on inconsistent knowledge bases, as during a learning process it is quite likely that the knowledge base will be in a transient inconsistent state, e.g. because a learned rule contradicts a new example input by the user. If we want to avoid producing *all* statements as inferences in such a situation, we *must* by definition give up completeness, which is exactly what has been done in MOBAL. The inference rules specified in section 2.2.3 allow us to work properly with inconsistent knowledge bases by treating a statement and its negation independently, i.e., using these inference rules, $p \vee \neg p$ is not a tautology.

There are two conceptually different approaches to characterizing the power of these inference rules formally. The first approach, which we have taken in the preceding sections, is to use a standard logical semantics for the representation, specify a set of incomplete inference rules for this representation which can handle inconsistencies gracefully, and characterize in which ways the inferences realized by the inference rules differ from the ones to be expected from the standard logical semantics. The advantage of this strategy is that a well-known semantics can be used, which should be easier to follow for most readers, and that only the differences need to be explained. This is precisely why we have chosen a standard two-valued semantics as our main reference point in the preceding sections.

The second approach, also chosen by many authors, is to use a non-standard semantics that is fitted exactly to the set of inferences we want to produce. The advantage of this strategy is that a nice completeness result can be obtained; the price to pay is that these semantics are usually more difficult to understand, e.g. because they rely on multiple truth values and fixpoint constructions. To allow the reader this alternative view of our representation as well, we will now provide such a multi-valued semantics for $\Re$.

2.2.7 A Multi-valued Semantics for $\Re$

As pointed out above, the basic intuition behind the multi-valued semantics for $\Re$ is to treat a statement and its negation independently, i.e., as if the negation of a fact were expressed by an independent predicate, i.e., reading not(p(a)) as not_p(a). Doing this means that the truth of a statement S is independent of the presence or absence of $\neg S$. To capture this intuition formally, we can use the semantics defined by Blair and Subrahmanian [Blair and Subrahmanian, 1989] in their work on paraconsistent logic programming with generally Horn programs (GHPs)[8].

Definition 2.1 (Generally Horn) *Let $\mathcal{T}_v$ be the set of truth values unknown, false, true, both. A* generally Horn clause *is a statement of the form, for $n \geq 0$,*

$$L_1 : T_1 \& \cdots \& L_n : T_n \rightarrow L_{n+1} : T_{n+1},$$

where the L_i are positive literals[9]*, and the $T_i \in \mathcal{T}_v$ for all i.*

Since $\mathcal{T}_v$ is exactly the set of MOBAL truth values (see section 2.1.1), this form of writing down statements with a truth value annotation is just a syntactical variant of the representation introduced in section 2.1.1. In fact, as described in chapter 3, MOBAL's inference engine IM-2uses a very similar annotated format internally. It is also quite easy to map our language $\Re$ to a particular subset of GHPs, since the main difference is that with generally Horn clauses, contradictory statements can be represented by a single annotated fact, so unlike in $\Re$, they do not need to be represented by a fact and its negation.

[8]We will use a slightly different syntax, however, and omit parts that we do not need for $\Re$.

[9]As shown in [Blair and Subrahmanian, 1989], negated literals are unnecessary as they can be represented by letting $T_i = false$.

Definition 2.2 ($\Re$-GHP) *The subset of generally Horn programs corresponding to statements from $\Re$ ($\Re$-GHP) is defined as follows. Let Γ be an $\Re$ theory. The corresponding* GHP *G is defined as follows:*

- *If $f \in \Gamma$ is a positive fact, and* not$(f) \in \Gamma$*, then $f : both \in G$.*
- *If $f \in \Gamma$ is a positive fact, and* not$(f) \notin \Gamma$*, then $f : true \in G$.*
- *If* not$(f) \in \Gamma$ *is a negated fact, and $f \notin \Gamma$ then $f : false \in G$.*
- *If $L_1\& \cdots L_n \rightarrow L_{n+1}$ is a rule in Γ, then $(\forall)P_1 : T_1\& \cdots P_n : T_n \rightarrow P_{n+1} : T_{n+1}$ is in G, where for all i, $P_i : T_i = L_i : true$ if L_i is a positive literal, and $P_i : T_i = L_i' : false$ if $L_i =$ not(L_i') is a negated literal.*

$\Re$-GHP *is the union of all G for any $\Re$-theory Γ.*

In the terminology of Blair and Subrahmanian, $\Re$ corresponds to GHPs where all unit clauses must be ground (facts), and all non-unit clauses are well-annotated, universally quantified implications[10].

The meaning of the truth values used as literal annotations must be defined such that it captures the above intuitions about the use of inconsistent information. Following Blair and Subrahmanian, we therefore define the following ordering on truth values:

$$both \geq_{\mathcal{T}_v} true \geq_{\mathcal{T}_v} unknown; both \geq_{\mathcal{T}_v} false \geq_{\mathcal{T}_v} unknown.$$

We can now define a multi-valued semantics for $\Re$ (in the syntactical form of GHPs)[11]. We follow standard practice for the definition of nonstandard semantics and regard an interpretation I as a function from the Herbrand base of the language, i.e., the facts of $\Re$, to truth values.

Definition 2.3 (Satisfaction according to multi-valued semantics) *An interpretation I* satisfies *an $\Re$-GHP formula F ($I \models F$) under the following conditions.*

1. *I satisfies the ground annotated atom $F : T$ iff $I(F) \geq_{\mathcal{T}_v} T$.*

[10] Well-annotated means that only *true* and *false* are used as annotations.

[11] We omit the semantics for GHP statements that do not correspond to statements in $\Re$; the complete semantics can be found in [Blair and Subrahmanian, 1989].

2. *I satisfies the rule* $R = (\forall)P_1 : T_1 \ \& \ \ldots \ P_n : T_n \rightarrow P_{n+1} : T_{n+1}$ *iff for every instance of R (where ground terms have been substituted for variables using a substitution* δ*), there is some* $1 \leq i \leq n$ *such that I does not satisfy* $P_i\delta : T_i$*, or* $I \models P_{n+1}\delta : T_{n+1}$.

The reader will notice that the crucial difference to our two-valued semantics is the requirement that $I(F) \geq_{\mathcal{T}_v} T$ to satisfy a fact; this immediately implies that the meaning of $\rightarrow$ is not material implication, but corresponds to the inferences made by our inference rules. In particular, contraposition inferences are no longer admitted under these semantics. The theory

$$\mathsf{p(x)} \rightarrow \mathsf{q(x)},\ \mathsf{not(q(a))}$$

no longer logically entails not(p(a)), since q(a) could simply have the truth value *both*. Thus, this semantics *a priori* excludes the inferences we had identified as "missing" above. We can formally prove that under these semantics, our inference rules are indeed complete and correct.

Theorem 2.3 *Under the multi-valued semantics defined above, the inference rules specified in section 2.2.3 are sound and complete.*

Proof: To prove this theorem, we use a result from [Blair and Subrahmanian, 1989] who show that the least model of a GHP G is the least fixpoint of the following operator T_G:

$$T_G(I)(A) = lub\ \{T \mid (\forall)P_1 : T_1 \ \& \ \ldots \ P_n : T_n \rightarrow A : T \text{ is a ground instance of a statement in } G, \text{ and } I \models P_i : T_i \text{ for all } 1 \leq i \leq n\},$$

where *lub* refers to the least upper bound in the lattice defined by $\geq_{\mathcal{T}_v}$. Comparing T_G with our inference rule (I), we see that using the correspondence of $\mathfrak{R}$ theories to GHPs put forth in definition 2.2, this inference rule does exactly the same as T_G: if some of the inference rules that match A in G have a positive conclusion, A will be inferred; if some have a negative conclusion, not(A) will be inferred. Given that our correspondence from definition 2.2 realizes a least upper bound operation on $\mathcal{T}_v$, we thus know that a single application of $\vdash_1$, i.e., all possible single step applications of inference rule (I), corresponds to a single application of T_G.

This is so because in the case where all rules concluding about a particular predicate have the same conclusion "sign" (all positive or all negated), the resulting fact will have the corresponding "sign" (truth value). If there are rules with both positive and negated conclusions for a particular predicate, both positive and negated instances will be derived and added to the closure of the theory. According to our translation, this corresponds to a truth value of both, which is exactly the least upper bound of the two values.

We thus only need to note that the semantics defined here are monotonic, i.e., the truth value of a statement can only increase, so that once a statement (in the $\Re$ formulation) has been inferred, it never needs to be taken back. Thus, the closure of our inference rules computes the smallest fixed point of T_G, and thus the least model of a theory under the four-valued semantics given here. □

We thus have two semantics available for our representation $\Re$, a standard two-valued one where our inferences are fact complete for the positive subset, and a four-valued one for which our inference rules are complete[12]. Depending on the preferences of the reader, each can be used to understand the properties of our representation.

2.2.8 Nonmonotonic Treatment of Inconsistencies

With the inference rules described above, we have ensured that MOBAL can gracefully tolerate contradictions in its knowledge base by treating a statement and its negation independently. This formalization of the problem allowed us to use a *monotonic* semantics for MOBAL's representation, i.e., the inferences made with a statement are not invalidated when the negation of that statement is added to the knowledge base. More formally, in a monotonic logic, we can assure that

$$\text{If } \Gamma_1 \models S \text{ then } \Gamma_1 \cup \{S'\} \models S.$$

In practice, however, this may not always desirable, since we may reasonably argue that from a contradictory statement, we should not infer anything, i.e., should not use this statement for inferences. This kind of treating inconsistencies is referred to as *blocking*, since any use of inconsistent statements for inferences is blocked. MOBAL's inference engine IM-2 allows the user to choose whether blocking is to be used or not (see section 3.2.4). If blocking is used, the behavior of the system becomes *nonmonotonic*, since whenever the negation of a statement is added to the knowledge base, all inferences drawn from this statement must be retracted.

[12] Even though we have not actually defined the four-valued semantics for higher-order statements and metapredicates, the definitions given here can be extended in analogy to the path taken for the two-valued semantics.

For the formal semantics and inference rules given above, this means that they correctly describe the behavior of MOBAL's inference engine only when blocking of inferences with inconsistent entries is not used. If blocking is used, which is the standard in MOBAL, the above inference rules and semantics correctly describe the system's behavior only on consistent knowledge bases. For inconsistent knowledge bases, when blocking is used, the inference engine actually provides *fewer* inferences than those defined by our inference rules. Since the set of inferences that are left out has been determined by pragmatical considerations that have not yet been captured formally, we refer the reader to chapter 3 which provides a procedural description of the inference process. At present, work is under way to develop a formal nonmonotonic semantics that also captures blocking.

2.2.9 Related Work

The language and proof theory described here are based on our original description published in [Wrobel, 1987]. In the deductive database community, the language $\Re^+$ defined here has acquired the name DATALOG, and its properties have been investigated. A very relevant book is the one by Ceri, Gottlob, and Tanca [Ceri *et al.*, 1990], where a proof theory that is almost identical to ours is developed, but based on a minimal Herbrand model semantics. They also use a forward inference procedure as proof procedure, and arrive at similar statements about the size of the proof tree as were given in section 2.2.5. The book also contains chapters on optimizing the query answering process for DATALOG.

Higher-order statements have been used relatively rarely in other knowledge representation or learning systems, but have recently been picked up by a number of researchers. Silverstein and Pazzani [1991] use *relational cliches*, which are almost identical to metapredicates, for learning, but do not introduce them into their representation. Similarly, DeRaedt and Bruynooghe [1992] have used rule schemata for learning by analogy, but again without introducing them into the representation. Muggleton and Feng [1992] try to integrate higher-order schemata fully into a representation for a learning system by using a restricted variant of *lambda-calculus*.

2.3 The Human-Computer Interface

2.3.1 Design Goals

The human-computer interface is the knowledge acquisition environment of the system. We have identified six requirements that should be met in order to ensure an effective support to an interactive modeling process. They can be summarized by the following key words [Wrobel, 1988b]:

- Flexibility
- Revisability
- Integrity and Consistency Maintenance
- Immediate Feedback
- Inspectability
- Transitionality

Flexibility One of the major assumptions of our knowledge acquisition paradigm is that at the beginning of the acquisition process we do not yet have an explicit, explainable and accessible model of the domain and of the expert's competence, but that such a model will only emerge during the acquisition process itself. Thus, we can say that the developer generally does not have the structures and concepts that would enable him/her simply to "transfer" the existing knowledge into the system in an organized and goal-directed manner. Rather, the modeling process is characterized by various ideas about the content and structure of the emerging model. Consequently, users are likely to divide their attention among various activities perhaps just to return to the first one after a while. To support such an interaction the system must be able to accept new information as soon as it is available, and must not compel its users to enter certain answers to make a specific input at times. Instead of lengthy dialogs, whose structure is predefined by the system, the users should be provided with small, continuously available operations.

Revisability The demand for the knowledge acquisition environment to be revisable, like the demand to be flexible, is a consequence of the basic assumption that the model will develop during the acquisition process, and that as a result, the necessity to modify a decision previously made about the content or the structure of the model can arise at any time. Thus, in addition to (monotonic) extensions of the model, the knowledge acquisition system must support revisions, modifications and, in particular, a global restructuring of the model. The implications of changes should automatically be propagated to dependent data (data dependency maintenance, see section 3.4). Similarly, the learning component must be able to deal with data revisions (knowledge revision, see chapter 7).

Integrity and Consistency Maintenance In a knowledge acquisition system based on several mutually dependent knowledge sources (facts, rules, metafacts, predicates, sorts, etc.) it is difficult to ensure that the entries in one knowledge source correspond to those in other knowledge sources, i.e. that the arity of a predicate does not, for example, differ in its definitions and facts. In accordance with database terminology, we will refer to such requirements as *integrity conditions*. In many acquisition systems, in particular those whose goal was to provide as large a variety of formalisms as possible, the maintenance of integrity conditions was left completely to the user. This task, however, is foreign to the model-building process — it is a system-oriented, not a knowledge-oriented task [Newell, 1982] and the user should be relieved of it. Integrity conflict resolution should take place automatically wherever possible, otherwise the user must have the option to postpone resolving the conflict and to carry it out at a convenient stage in the process. The same applies to the monitoring and maintenance of the logical *consistency* of a knowledge base (see chapter 7).

Immediate Feedback When developing a domain model using a representation formalism, it is difficult for users to keep in mind the consequences of their modeling decisions and their data input, since local changes (that, for example, result from inferences) may have global implications. Consequently, when a model is being developed, the traditional development cycle of a program, consisting of editing, input and error detection as commonly used in the past for knowledge acqusition systems, is no longer acceptable. The system must provide the user with an of the consequences of each input, i.e. each input must immediately be processed by all system parts (inferences, sorts, learning), and the modifications that result must immediately be displayed in the interface.

Inspectability The demand to provide adequate facilites that can be used to inspect the content of a knowledge base is traditionally a major concern of those working in the field of knowledge acquisition. The use of a browser and other graphical representation facilities has long since been common. But it is still necessary to develop them further, e.g., when it comes to dealing with rather large domain models. This requires the use of an adequate focus mechanism that fits the structure of the model in order to select the knowledge elements that are displayed.

Transitionality The demand for transitionality has long since been put forward in connection with interface research projects [Badre, 1984]. A user interface should be built in such a way as to enable a smooth transition from beginner-oriented to expert-oriented interaction formalisms, with the result that the user can automatically learn the latter ones by using the former ones. In the knowledge acquistion context this means that a user can start with a domain-oriented model and later on deal with the advanced facilities provided by the system level (such as the MOBAL metaknowledge). In the case of *balanced cooperative modeling* with a learning component such as MOBAL, transitionality can also mean that the transition from the purely manual acquisition to an acquisition that supports learning can be smooth, i.e. that both system parts use the same interface and the same knowledge sources.

2.3.2 Basic Structure of the Interface

The human-computer interface of MOBAL (see figure 2.1)[13] offers a main menu from which the different operations of MOBAL can be selected, such as loading or saving of knowledge bases, displaying knowledge base entries or calling one of the learning tools. The FILE menu lets the user load, save, delete, or print out domain models, or quit the system. The VIEW menu allows the user to bring up windows displaying the different knowledge sources, or a window providing access to MOBAL's parameters. All currently open display windows are dynamically included in the WINDOWS menu. The CALL menu, finally, allows the user to ask queries from the inference engine, enter Prolog expressions, or explictly invoke certain operations of MOBAL's tools RDT, CLT, STT, PST.

[13]The current human-computer interface was built using the HyperNeWS environment of the Turing Institute, Glasgow.

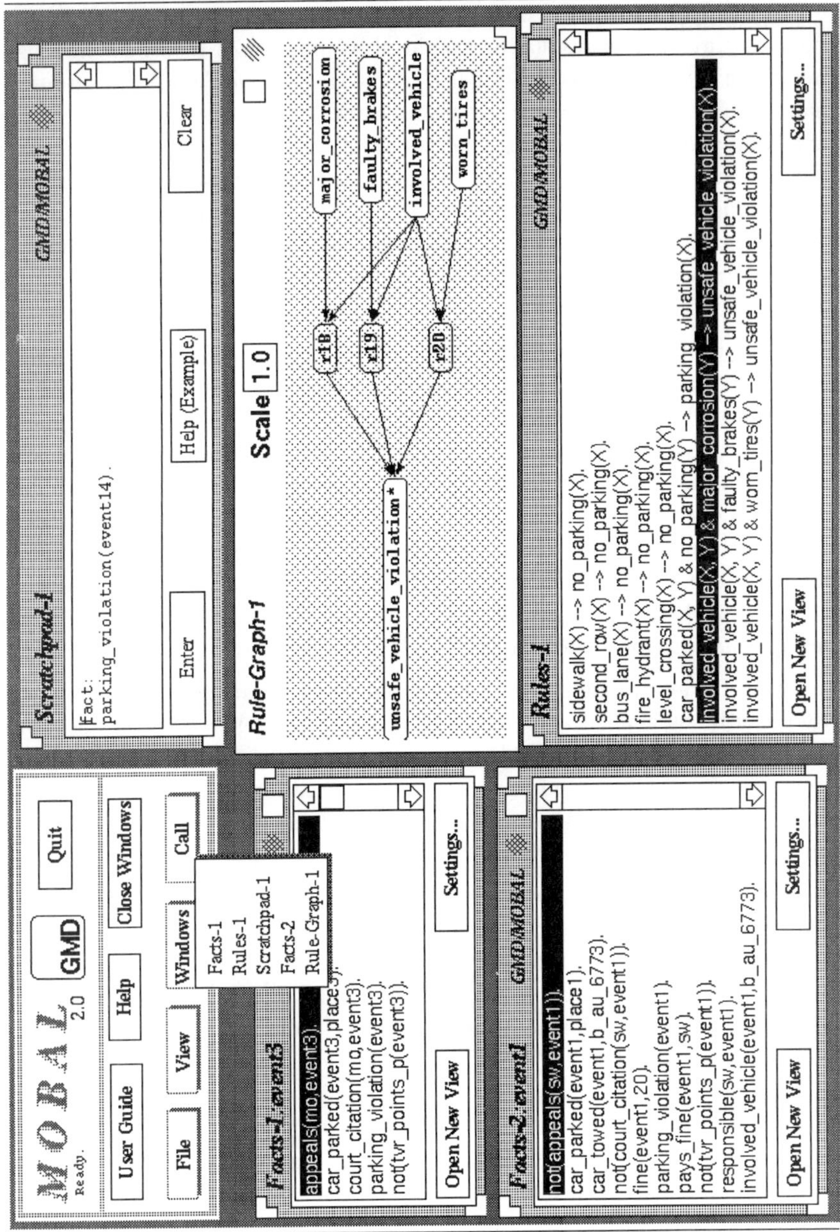

Figure 2.1: Screen Copy (Partial) of a MOBAL Interface Configuration

To display knowledge base entries, the user, via the VIEW menu, can open any number of textual or graphical windows each of which shows exactly one kind of representational element (facts, rules, etc.). In addition, each window can be focused so that it shows only a selected subset of the available entries. The textual windows are dynamic and immediately reflect changes in the knowledge base. Associated with each window is an item operations menu that pops up when an entry in the window is selected. These menus generally offer operations for deleting entries and for showing detailed information about an entry, augmented with specific operations for the particular representational element shown by the window.

The graphical display of knowledge sources distinguishes between knowledge that can be represented as a tree and knowledge that can only be represented by a general graph. For the former, which includes rules, sorts, and the topology, MOBAL offers automatic layout routines that place nodes on the canvas. For other knowledge sources, such as facts or predicates, the graphical display is based on the idea of incremental exploration. This means that the graphical display is started with one core node and all its neighbors. The user can then click on any of the neighbor nodes which causes the node to be expanded, i.e., all its neighbors are also shown in the graphic. Here, no automatic layout is attempted by the system.

New entries are added by typing them into a *scratchpad* window, where they can be assembled and then read in by the system whenever appropriate. A help window associated with the scratchpad shows the format of each item for input. The same format can also be used for saving and loading domains, which allows easy porting or merging of domains. The corresponding operations are found on the FILE menu.

Revisions of all knowledge items are supported by MOBAL and the consequences are immediately propagated. If a rule or fact is deleted, all its consequences are deleted, too. Consequences are the facts derived from this rule or fact. If the user detects a (derived) fact which he wants to reject, he can either delete it in the fact window, or if it is a derived fact, call the knowledge revision tool KRT to modify the knowledge base so that the rejected fact is not derived any more (see chapter 7. The user may also simply enter the negation of the incorrect fact, which causes the fact to become contradictory, thus generating and agenda entry and triggering knowledge revision. The sort taxonomy is also dynamically updated to reflect all changes to the knowledge base. The system does not, however, retract rules when the facts from which the rule was learned are deleted.

Balanced Cooperation between System and User

In this section, the balanced cooperation of system and user is described with respect to adding knowledge items. It is shown that for each type of knowledge there exists a tool which creates items of this type and there is an interface which supports the user in adding items of this type.

The user may input *predicate declarations* with named *sorts*. This is sometimes useful, when it is easy to forget what argument type was supposed to occur where in a predicate. The predicate declaration then serves as a reminder of, say, where to put the person name in the predicate owner. If, however, the user prefers to just type in facts, or just wants to read an existing file of facts, he or she need not input predicate declarations. STT will generate sorts and predicate declarations automatically based on the input facts that are seen.

The user may input a *topology of predicates* in order to structure the domain model beforehand, e.g., with respect to steps of problem solving which uses the (learned) rules[14]. For instance, the leaf nodes of the topology may consist of predicates which refer to the given data (observations) in an application. Intermediate nodes may refer to intermediate problem solving results. The root node may consist of predicates which refer to possible results of problem solving (possible solutions). In this way, the topology is a task structure for the performance element which uses the built-up knowledge base in an application. If, however, the user does not know the overall domain structure, PST can construct it on the basis of the rules.

The user may input *rules* and set the parameter such that the model acquisition tool MAT is called in order to obtain rule models from them. Or, the user may set the parameter to "direct rule input" so that MAT is not called for an inputed rule. The user may also input some rule models and call RDT for discovering rules. Thus, here again, there is a flexible work share of system and user.

The user must input some *facts*. Facts are necessary for learning, inferring, and building the sort taxonomy. On the other hand, facts can also be added by the system's inferences. By selecting inference depths (maximum inference path lengths) for forward and backward inferences (these are parameters of the inference engine), the user can control how far the space of possible inference is to be explored by the inference engine.

Hence, for each knowledge item there is a system tool adding it to the

[14]One should never forget that learning serves the acquisition of a rule base for a particular application where the rules are put to use.

knowledge base, and there is the option that the user enters it. Balanced modeling is the flexible use of the tools for supporting the user to add items or to have the system adding items to the knowledge base.

2.4 The Programmer's Interface

The programmer's interface (PI) offers Prolog predicates to be used directly by other Prolog programs or indirectly to define an interface for another programming language using the Quintus Prolog facilities (e.g., a C interface to MOBAL). Using the predicates of the programmer's interface gives access to the full range of MOBAL's knowledge representation, inference, and learning. The first set of predicates to be used are the ones for initializing or reinitializing MOBAL and for starting its human-computer interface. The predicate mobal does all this and is the convenient start of working with MOBAL. The remaining predicates of the PI can be logically organized in the following groups:

- predicates for reading in or storing knowledge bases in various formats,
- predicates for calling the tools,
- predicates for setting parameters, and
- predicates for adding or deleting any of the knowledge items, and for querying about existing or inferable items

Access to the knowledge structures is given abstract data types. The abstract types are declared by item structures. The predicates to access knowledge items follow a strict name convention. They start with the item type (e.g., fact) followed by an underscore followed by the name of the part of the structure to access. The predicate is of 2-place arity with the first place being the item structure and the second place being the part of the item to be accessed. For instance, if the proposition of a fact is to be accessed (and not its identification number or comment or negation part), the access function is fact_prop(FactStruc,Proposition).

The operations on knowledge items also follow a name convention. The client accessing the knowledge base uses the following sets of predicates:

- mobal_get_< *Item* > (ItemStruc) returns stored items. For facts, the corresponding call is mobal_get_fact(FactStruc)

- **mobal_query_**$< Item >$ **(ItemStruc)** returns inferrable items, i.e., if necessary performs inferences to find an answer; this group of procedures is defined for facts, metafacts, and metametafacts only

- **mobal_new_**$< Item >$ **(ItemStruc)** adds new items

- **mobal_delete_**$< Item >$ **(ItemStruc)** deletes the item that is given as an argument

In this table, **ItemStruc** refers to the internal format of a representation item, not to the presentation format that was defined in the preceding section. The internal format is not documented in this book, but can be found in [Sommer *et al.*, 1993b].

Event callback predicates are available so that a MOBAL client can stay informed about changes in the knowledge base. These callbacks are called by MOBAL whenever an event occurred, e.g., a new fact has been entered or derived, or a new rule has been entered or learned. All callback predicates have an empty dummy definition that can be overridden by client-specific code. The programmer uses the callback predicates to react to the events generated by MOBAL. The event callback predicates have the following names:

- **mobal_**$< Item >$**_stored (ItemStruc)** is called whenever MOBAL has stored a particular item

- **mobal_**$< Item >$**_deleted (ItemStruc)** is called whenever a particular item is deleted from the knowledge base;

- **mobal_**$< Item >$**_changed (ItemStruc)** is called whenever the ItemStruc changes in the knowledge base.

The coupling of MOBAL with another system is easy because of the predicates of the programmer's interface and because of the encapsulated access to its knowledge structures which insulates clients from MOBAL internals. Through the PI, MOBAL can interact with expert system shells, databases, or any other software system. Through Prolog's "C" interface, MOBAL can be integrated any software module or existing system that can be linked in to "C".

For more details on the PI, please refer to MOBAL's user guide [Sommer *et al.*, 1993b].

Chapter 3

The Inference Engine IM-2

This chapter describes the underlying knowledge representation system of MOBAL (and BLIP) focusing on the implemented inference engine IM-2. Having presented our representation formalism on the knowledge level, we now have a closer look at its operationalization. IM-2 provides services to the user as well as to system tools. It is responsible for drawing the inferences by applying the rules which were entered by the user or which were constructed by one of the inductive components (RDT or CLT). A reason maintenance subsystem integrated into the inference engine takes care of updating the knowledge base if the input of facts, rules, and metapredicates is withdrawn by the user or the knowledge revision component (KRT) of the system.

In this chapter, we present the knowledge structures and inference mechanisms of IM-2, with a particular focus on how these mechanisms are used to operationalize MOBAL's knowledge representation as we have described it in the preceding chapter. We start by describing the goals that have led to the design of IM-2 and give a brief overview of the system (section 3.1). We then proceed to a description of the various representation constructs offered by the inference engine, and show how MOBAL's knowledge representation maps to these constructs (section 3.2). After that, the inference mechanism for forward and backward inferences is detailed (section 3.3). Following the description of reason maintenance (section 3.4), we conclude with a discussion (section 3.5).

3.1 Introduction

3.1.1 Design Goals

In the MOBAL system the inference engine has to fulfill a number of requirements stemming from two different sources. First, as the knowledge representation component of a knowledge acquisition system IM-2 contributes to fulfilling the design goals underlying the knowledge acquisition environment (see chapter 2). Second, the inference engine has to support the inductive modeling process of the rule discovery, concept formation, and knowledge revision components.

In order to support the knowledge acquisition process as understood in the sloppy modeling paradigm (see section 1.2.4, [Morik, 1989]), the inference engine is involved in fulfilling at least four of the design goals of the knowledge acquisition environment discussed in section 2.3 [Wrobel, 1988a], and which are as follows.

Immediate Feedback The consequences of modeling decisions should immediately be computed and displayed for the user, e.g., when a user or a inductive component incorporates a new rule into the model, inferences should be made in order to help the user to check whether the newly established rule has the intended effects.

Revisability It must be possible to revise modeling decisions and the knowledge representation system has to check which of the inferred statements are no longer valid and delete them from the knowledge base.

Integrity and Consistency Maintenance the modeling process by employing integrity maintenance procedures between various knowledge sources and consistency checks.

Inspectability contents of the knowledge base, e.g., the system should be able to describe how a fact was inferred.

From the above general requirements of the sloppy modeling paradigm, more specialized requirements for the inference component of a sloppy modeling system can be derived. These requirements are independent of demands posed by the domain and the expressiveness of the representation language[1],

[1] A more detailed discussion of such requirements can be found in [Emde, 1989].

and are a consequence of the incremental closed-loop nature of learning processes in a sloppy modeling system.

Knowledge Revision Support The knowledge representation *formalism* should support the revision of induced knowledge by providing various facilities to modify knowledge entities and in particular by enabling the explicit representation of modifications that later on can be subject to further improvements (see [Emde *et al.*, 1983], [Michalski and Winston, 1986], [Emde, 1991], [Wrobel, 1989], [Wrobel, 1994]). Furthermore, the dependencies between rules and derived facts must be represented in a way that this knowledge is accessible by the learning component. If contradictory facts are derived or if new data contradict derived facts, then a knowledge revision component must be able to analyze the origin of the contradictions (see section 7.4).

Reason Maintenance A reason maintenance sub-component should support the automatic revision of knowledge by propagation of changes.

Contradictory Knowledge As discussed in section 2.2.6, the representation system should allow the explicit representation of contradictory knowledge, so that contradictions can stored and resolved later at a convenient time when the necessary system resources are available.

Organization of Knowledge It is important that the representation formalism offer constructs for structuring and grouping knowledge base entries. For example, usually it is helpful to separate domain-independent knowledge from domain-dependent knowledge.

The design of the inference engine IM-2, which provides inference services in the MOBAL system, was based upon the set of requirements discussed above. IM-2 was designed not only to serve as the knowledge representation subsystem of the MOBAL system, but as a general inference component useful for different types of closed-loop learning systems. Its predecessor has already been used as the inference component of METAXA [Emde, 1987; Emde, 1991] which inspired many of the features of IM-2. Beyond the capabilities necessary to operationalize MOBAL's current knowledge representation, IM-2 therefore offers additional services that are not currently exploited in the MOBAL system, but may be made available in future releases of the system. In this chapter, we therefore use MOBAL's knowledge representation as described in section 2.1 as a starting point, and first identify how these representation structures are operationalized in IM-2. Wherever appropriate, we then point out which additional capabilities are offered beyond those used in MOBAL.

3.1.2 An overview of IM-2

The inference engine IM-2 provides a uniform representation formalism consisting of attributed assertions and rules. "Uniform representation" means that, first, only few representational constructs are used to fulfill the various requirements stated above, and second, that there is no pre-supplied distinction in IM-2 between the different representation levels of MOBAL, i.e., object level, metalevel, and metametalevel. As described below, these levels instead are implemented using different IM-2 *worlds*. The *world* mechanism allows the convenient structuring of knowledge into different "partitions".

The representation formalism of the inference engine allows the representation of uncertain and contradictory knowledge via the attached *evidence points*. The inference mechanism[2] of the inference engine allows both forward inferences (in order to be able to compute the consequences of modeling decisions for the user) and backward inferences (to answer queries posed by the user or the learning component). Integrated reason maintenance procedures propagate changes made by the user or the knowledge revision component KRT to all dependent entries, and ensure integrity maintenance between the different knowledge sources.

The general task of the inference engine is to receive and store knowledge base entries (facts and rules) and to perform inferences with these entries to answer queries. If an assertion or a rule that was entered is retracted, or if a new input results in contradictions which invalidate previous inferences, the assertional and inferential knowledge is to be updated accordingly.

In this way, the inference engine serves as a knowledge representation system. IM-2 does not provide the usual constructs known from programming languages, e.g., for manipulating or specifying control mechanisms, or for supporting debugging. Such constructs are offered in AI programming languages (e.g., in CONNIVER [McDermott, 1983] or MULTILOG [Kauffman and Grumbach, 1987]), logic-oriented programming and inference systems (e.g., in PROLOG, MRS [Russell, 1985] and RUP [McAllester, 1982]), and

[2]With respect to the inference mechanism and the reason maintenance procedures, the inference engine IM-2 can be considered to be the successor of the inference engine IM-1 designed to be used in a text-understanding system with an interest-driven processing of uncertain and incomplete knowledge [Emde and Schmiedel, 1983].

various metalevel extensions of PROLOG (see [Bowen, 1985]). In contrast to most of the representation systems (RUP, MRS, etc.) IM-2 allows the representation of higher-order concepts such as "transitivity" (see [Habel and Rollinger, 1982])[3] and the use of such concepts to reason about inferential knowledge. Various autoepistemic operators allow the formulation of (non-monotonic) rules, whose application result depends on the current state of the system's knowledge, and which can be invalidated by new data. Such dependencies are maintained by the reason maintenance procedures. A system (TMS or ATMS) which automatically resolves contradictions that can result from default inferences is not part of the inference engine.

3.2 The Knowledge Representation in IM-2

In this section, we describe the representational constructs offered by IM-2 for the representation of facts and rules, and show how MOBAL's knowledge representation as defined in chapter 2 maps to these constructs. Since IM-2 uses a slightly different syntax for its entries, we use a `typewriter` font for IM-2 constructs so they can easily be distinguished from MOBAL constructs that are written in sans serif font. We will begin by describing how factual knowledge is represented in IM-2, and then proceed to inferential knowledge. The examples in this section and the rest of the chapter are taken either from the TRAFFIC-LAW domain described in section 9.1, or from a domain model that represented the voting behavior of US senators (see [Emde *et al.*, 1989]).

3.2.1 Factual Knowledge

In IM-2, the central knowledge structure for the representation of factual knowledge is an *assertion*. An assertion can most easily be understood as proposition (positive literal) that is annotated with a high-dimensional attribute set. The proposition is simply an arbitary predicate symbol with one or more arguments which are terms (see below). The most important attribute is the *evidence point* that we already introduced in section 2.1.1. Thus, assertions very directly correspond to the annotated format of the generally Horn clauses that were defined in section 2.2.7. Here are some examples of how MOBAL facts are represented in IM-2:

---

[3]The representation of high-level (second-order) concepts is also supported by the system OMEGA [Attardi and Simi, 1984] and the CYC system [Lenat and Guha, 1990, p. 36].

large(cadillac)	`large(cadillac) --- ep:[1000,0]`
not(small(cadillac))	`small(cadillac) --- ep:[0,1000]`
both(medium(ford))	`medium(ford) --- ep:[1000,1000]`

When statements are entered into IM-2 or returned as the result of a query, attributes are attached to the core of the statement with the symbol "`---`", as in the preceding examples. Each attribute is specified by giving its name and its value, which must be a Prolog term, separated by "`:`"; different attributes are separated by "`,`". The inference engine allow arbitrary attributes to be attached to statements, but possesses a number of built-in attributes which have a fixed meaning. Here, we have used the built-in `ep` attribute to specify evidence points for the respective propositions. As an example of a free attribute, the MOBAL system uses a comment attribute `c` to store user-given comments, as in:

```
large(cadillac) --- ep:[1000,0], c:'Cadillacs are
large cars.'
```

One important capability of IM-2 that is not presently made accessible in MOBAL is the larger range of terms that can be used as arguments of propositions. Whereas in the representation defined in chapter 2, we defined terms to be only constants and numbers, IM-2 is capable of handling terms that are constructed with arbitrary function symbols. Thus,

```
manufacturer(cadillac)
```

is a valid term that could be used in an assertion:

```
location(manufacturer(cadillac),usa)
```

Here, we have followed the general IM-2 convention that the `ep` attribute can be omitted whenever its value is `[1000,0]`. It is also possible in IM-2 to use predicates symbols or entire propositions as arguments in another proposition, i.e., predicates may be used as constants or as function symbols when desired. This powerful feature allows the representation of information about statements. The formal basis for this flexible use of terms is developed in [Emde, 1989] and [Emde, 1991]; it is based on the concepts of *term-constructing* and *formula-constructing operators*, which are generalizations of functions and predicates, and are specified by associating with them a so-called *degree* (see [Kalish and Montague, 1964, p. 271ff], [Habel, 1986], [Rollinger, 1984]). The function symbols "`,`", "`;`", "`all_of`", "`all`", "`[]`", and "`excl`" have a special meaning when they are used in the description of support sets (see section 3.2.3).

As pointed out above, IM-2 uses a flat representation of knowledge, i.e., does not have a predefined notion of object-, meta-, or metametalevel. Consequently, metafacts and metafacts are also represented by assertions. To distinguish the different levels from one another, the *world* mechanism of IM-2 is exploited. A world is a set of statements grouped together under a common name that is attached to these statements as the predefined "`w`" attribute. In MOBAL, all facts and rules are stored in the world called `object_level1`, all metafacts and metarules are stored in the world `meta_level`, and all metametafacts are stored in the world `meta_meta_level`. Thus, to be precise, the fact

large(cadillac)

corresponds to the assertion (as usual omitting the `ep:[1000,0]` attribute)

```
large(cadillac) --- w:object_level1
```

whereas the metafact

opposite(large,small)

corresponds to

```
opposite(large,small,all) --- w:meta_level
```

The third argument above is the *support set* of the metafact that is not represented as an attribute, but carried along as an additional argument when translating to the IM-2 representation. We will describe the exact format of possible support set descriptions in IM-2 in section 3.2.3. As pointed out in section 2.1.8, metarules and metametafacts do not have associated support sets in the current version of MOBAL, so so the metametafact

m_symmetrical(opposite)

simply translates to

```
m_symmetrical(opposite) --- w:meta_meta_level
```

Besides the `ep` and `w` attributes, assertions carry a number of other predefined attributes that are used for internal bookkeeping purposes of the inference engine; these are described in detail in section 3.2.4.

This describes the basic constructs used to represent assertional knowledge in IM-2. As neither logic operators such as $\wedge$, $\vee$, $\forall$, and $\exists$ used to produce complex propositions are predefined, nor are variables admitted as arguments of assertions, more general information about the world must be represented as inferential knowledge.

3.2.2 Inferential Knowledge

Inferential knowledge is represented in IM-2 by rules which are also annotated with various attributes. A rule consists of a list of premises and a conclusion, separated by the symbol "`-->`". An important difference between the rule representation defined in section 2.1.4 and the inference engine form is that the latter uses an explicit variable list that precedes the rule. Thus, the MOBAL rule

small(X) → not(large(X))

is represented in the inference engine as

```
x elem (all excl []) excl [] ::
small(x)-->not(large(x)) --- w:object_level1
```

The expression following the variable `x` until the `::` separator is the *support set* of the rule which in this example allows all possible values for `x`. As a convention, unrestricted support sets are often simply omitted when writing down rules. The syntax of the support expression is fully described in section 3.2.3 below. To specify the desired evidence points for rule premises and conclusions, premises and conclusions may be written with the evidence point modifiers `not` and `both` which represent `[0,1000]` and `[1000,1000]`. A premise is considered satisfied if an assertion in the knowledge base matches its so specified *target evidence point* (see section 3.2.4).

Again, since IM-2 does not *per se* distinguish between the different representational levels of MOBAL, a world attribute is used for this purpose. The symbol "`&`" is used to connect premises, so the rule

temperature(Person,T) & gt(T,37) → fever(Person)

is represented in IM-2 as (omitting the support set):

```
person,t :: temperature(person,t) & gt(t,37) -->
fever(person) --- w:object_level1
```

Metarules can be used to reason about inferential knowledge (see [Lenat and Guha, 1990, p. 36]). Since IM-2 allows predicates and entire propositions as arguments in literals, they can be represented in the same rule formalism as object level rules, but are entered into the world `meta_level`. Thus, the metarule

opposite(P,Q) → opposite(Q,P)

is represented in IM-2 by

```
p,q,supset ::
opposite(p,q,supset)-->opposite(q,p,supset) ---
w:meta_level
```

Just as metametafacts, metarules do not have a support set in the current implementation. They do, however, need to carry around the extra support set argument in the literals of their rule schema, because, as described above, the support set of a metafact is represented by an extra argument in IM-2. Note that IM-2checks support set descriptions whenever a rule is applied, but is incapable of comparing different support sets for generality or inclusion. Therefore, all support set arguments in metarules must match exactly, and it is thus not possible to specify general rules about *metafacts* with different support set descriptions.

3.2.3 Built-in Predicates and Auto-epistemic Operators

`eq(_,_)`	equal
`ne(_,_)`	not equal
`lt(_,_)`	lower than
`gt(_,_)`	greater than
`ge(_,_)`	greater than or equal
`le(_,_)`	lower than or equal
`add(_,_,_)`	addition
`sub(_,_,_)`	subtraction
`prod(_,_,_)`	multiplication
`div(_,_,_)`	division

Table 3.1: Built-in Predicates of the Inference Engine

In general, all predicates can be used to build premises and conclusions. To further enhance the representational power of rules, there are also a number of additional predicates whose meaning is predefined by the inference mechanism of IM-2. These predicates come in two groups, namely *built-in predicates* for arithmetic computations, and predicates which are so-called *autoepistemic operators*. Above, we already saw an example of the use of the built-in predicate `gt` in the rule about body temperature. Table 3.1 gives a complete listing of all the arithmetic predicates that are available.

While the arithmetic built-in predicates are a relatively straightforward extension of the rule formalism familiar from many PROLOG dialects, the predicates representing autoepistemic operators (see table 3.2 for a complete list) are an important extension that greatly enhances the range of knowledge that can be expressed in IM-2. Generally speaking, an autoepistemic operator is a predicate the evaluation of which depends on the current state of the knowledge base. This means that the use of these premises results in a *non-monotonic* behavior of the system, i.e., existing inferences may become invalid when new statements are added to the knowledge base. A premise using the operator `unknown` evaluates to true if and only if the

```
count(!<proposition>,?<number>)
max_of(!<variable>,!<proposition>,?<maximum>)
min_of(!<variable>,!<proposition>,?<minimum>)
sum_of(!<variable>,!<proposition>,?<sum>)
unknown(!<proposition>)
```

Table 3.2: Autoepistemic Operators in IM-2

proposition that is given as argument cannot be proved from the current knowledge base. A premise built with `count` will bind its output argument (marked with a `?` in table 3.2) to the number of propositions in the knowledge base that match its first argument (an input argument marked with `!`). The proposition can be any formula with rule variables and terms appearing as arguments. The extreme values of numerical object attributes can be determined with the operators `max_of` and `min_of`. They require a variable as first argument which also appears in the embedded proposition. The evaluation of a premise built with `max_of` returns the maximum value of the (numeric) ground terms substituted for the variable unifying the embedded proposition with the assertions in the knowledge base. The operator `min_of` computes the minimum of these values. The operator `sum_of` can be used to perform summations over the variable instances. Premises built with the operators `max_of`, `min_of`, and `sum_of` require that there is at least one assertion in the knowledge base which can be unified with the embedded proposition. Otherwise, the attempt to confirm the premise fails.

The evaluation of premises built with autoepistemic operators takes into account the assertions already stored in the knowledge base but also includes an attempt to deduce additional assertions through backward-chaining (see section 3.3). Usually, the embedded propositions contain one or more variables (in addition to the variables which possibly appear as the first argument of the autoepistemic operator). These variables may already be bound to a ground term before the premise is evaluated either by previously evaluated premises or (within a backward-chaining inference) by the conclusion. If a variable which also appears somewhere else in the rule (in another premise or in the conclusion) is not bound to a ground term, then the variable is bound during the evaluation of the premise. On backtracking these variables can be bound to other ground terms. More details about the evaluation of premises with autoepistemic operators can be found in section 3.3.3.

The autoepistemic operators are a powerful feature of IM-2, and have been used in many applications of the MOBAL system, e.g. in the ICTERUS domain where `unknown` was used to derive a list of input values still needed from the user (see section 9.2.2 and below for examples). Autoepistemic operators can also be used to derive additional information about input examples for learning, such as the number of objects in a scene as proposed in [Michalski, 1983] or the extreme values of numerical object attributes as used in IDS [Langley and Nordhausen, 1987]. Table 3.3 shows a few examples of how autoepistemic operators are used. Rule (1) in table 3.3, when applied, counts assertions which list the senators of the various US states and stores the result as the number of the (known) senators. The variables in the embedded propositions of the premise do not occur somewhere else in the rule. Therefore, all assertions with the predicate "`senator_of`" that are stored in the knowledge base or that can be deduced with the help of rules are included in the count. Rule (2) infers the highest income of a senator using the assertions about his individual incomes. Since the variable `sen` occurs in the conclusion, this rule, as described above, will generate not one `max_individual_income` fact, but several (one per senator). This will

```
x,y,n ::  count(senator_of(x,y),n)
      --> number_senators(n)                                    (1)
sen,ee,max ::  max_of(ee,individual_income(sen,ee),max)
      --> max_individual_income(sen,max)                        (2)
sen,ee,sum,t ::  sum_of(ee,individual_income(sen,ee),sum) &
   threshold_income(t) & gt(sum,t)
      --> prosperous(sen)                                       (3)
p,g ::  variable_parameter(p) &
   unknown(parameter_validity(p,g))
      --> current_validity(p,2)                                 (4)
p,g ::  variable_laboratory_parameter(p) &
   unknown(parameter_validity(p,g))
      --> not(current_validity(p,2))                            (5)
p,g ::  variable_parameter(p) &
   unknown(variable_laboratory_parameter(p)) &
   unknown(parameter_validity(p,g))
      --> current_validity(p,2)                                 (6)
```

Table 3.3: Autoepistemic Operators in Rules

happen for both backward and forward inferences[4]. If `sen` did not occur in the conclusion, only one fact giving the maximum income across *all* senators would be derived. The application of rule (3) will compute the overall income of a senator and lead to assertions describing the senator as prosperous if his/her overall income exceeds a certain threshold. Rule (4) infers a default value representing the currently valid application range of parameter values in the ICTERUS domain if the general validity of a parameter is not known. Rule (5) is quite interesting when compared to rule (4), because the two rules represent *interacting defaults* (see [Reiter and Criscuolo, 1981]). Such rules may lead to contradictions in the knowledge base, which can then be used to trigger a refinement of existing rules. In this example, rule (4) might

[4]In general, rules are used in forward-chaining inferences, if the evaluation of the premises can instantiate all variables in the conclusion (see section 3.3.1). If the MOBAL/IM-2 parameter `embedded_propositions_as_entry_points` is set to no, then the propositions which occur as arguments of the autoepistemic operators are not used to trigger forward-chaining inferences.

be replaced by rule (6).

Since inferences with rules containing an autoepistemic operator may become invalid with changes to the assertional knowledge, the reason maintenance component makes special provisions for keeping track of the nonmonotonic dependencies resulting from autoepistemic operators. This requires in particular to not only delete dependent inferences when a statement is deleted, but to also draw new inferences that are possible due to the deletion of a statement. By maintaining both of these dependencies, IM-2 offers the same level of reason maintenance services for inferences with autoepistemic predicates as for inferences with regular knowledge base assertions.

Support Sets

In the preceding sections, we already gave some examples of how support sets are incorporated into rules and added as an additional argument to assertions that represent metafacts. In this section, we will precisely define the range of expressions that are allowed as support set specifications of rules and metafacts. The support set concept used in IM-2 is based on an idea by Habel and Rollinger (1982), who suggested using explicit descriptions of the valid application range (support sets) to represent particular rule-like relations whose validity is (locally) restricted, e.g. the transitivity of predicates such as "west_of". Their solution introduces support sets as an annotation of higher-order assertions (metafacts) which refer to higher cognitive concepts such as "linearity" or "on-a-circle". Later on, Emde, Habel, and Rollinger (1983) recommended the support set concept as a basis for concept formation. upports sets took their present form as part of the work on concept formation in BLIP [Emde, 1989; Wrobel, 1989].

The syntax of support sets in IM-2 corresponds very closely to the support set syntax defined in section 7.3.2. Recall from section 7.3.2 that a support set for rule with n variables is an n-dimensional Cartesian product of *domain descriptions* from which an extensional list of *global exceptions* can be excluded. The correspondence between the two representations can most easily be seen by considering some examples. So consider the rule

> involved_vehicle(X,Y) & owner(Y,Z) → responsible(X,Z)
> – ((minor_violation × (all \ {sw,md}) × all)
> \ {(event1, smith, car1),(event2,dole,car2)})

the support set of which exhibits the entire range of support set restrictions that are possible: the entire support set is restricted by a list of global exceptions at the end, the first domain is specified as all instances of the predicate minor_violation, the second domain is restricted by a list of local exceptions, and the third domain is unrestricted. In IM-2, this rule would be stated as

```
x,y,z elem (minor_violation excl [], all excl
(sw;md), all excl []) excl (ev1,cd ,car1 ;
ev2,ef,car2) ::  involved_vehicle(x,y) & owner(z,y)
--> responsible(x,z) --- w:  object_level1
```

Here, we can see that the operator `elem` is used to connect the variable list of the rule with the support set description proper. The latter consists of the n dimensional tuple of domains and the list of global exceptions connected by `excl`. The `excl` operator is also used to specify the local exceptions of domains. As usual, `all` denotes the set of all terms, i.e., an unrestricted domain, the term `[]` refers to the empty set. An empty exception list can also be omitted.

Note that the above operators used to refer to sets of objects in assertions do not have any predefined semantics in the current implementation of IM-2. This means that syntactically different terms are treated as references to different objects, even if their extension is identical. In the current implementation the symbols mentioned have the above predefined meaning only for the description of the valid application range of rules (see section 3.2.3).

The processing of support set descriptions in IM-2 differs from that of corresponding additional premises. When a new assertion is unifiable with the premise of a rule, the new assertion can trigger a forward inference. In contrast, a rule is not triggered if the extension of an intensionally described support set increases, i.e. rules are only applied in order to explicate the meaning of new assertions which are unifiable with the premises of the rule. If, for example, a new assertion with the predicate `minor_violation` is added to the assertional knowledge, then the above example rule is not automatically triggered. Reason maintenance does ensure, however, that when facts about a predicate used in a support set are removed, all inferences with the corresponding rule are checked and removed if necessary.

Note that in contrast to the *rule censors* approach described in [Michalski and Winston, 1986], support set descriptions unlike *rule censors* cannot be ignored in case of restricted resources, if, for example, a fast reaction of the system is required. Rule censors (a predicate or disjunction of predicates) are intended to represent rare exceptions to the rule, whereas support sets are an integral part of the rule.

Rule-generating Rules

The careful reader may have noticed that from the representation items defined in section 2.1, we have so far left out metapredicates and metametapredicates which are the means by which metafacts and metametafacts can be translated into rules and metarules. Such a construct can only be represented in an inference engine if the declarative representation of inferential knowledge is linked to the corresponding rules. In the METAXA learning programs (see [Emde, 1987]), which can be considered to be the predecessors of RDT, the inference processes trigger attached procedures designed to generate and purge rules. This solution required an ingenious manipulation of the reason maintenance procedures in the inference engine IM-1, which was used in the METAXA programs. For this reason, IM-2's representation formalism for rules has been extended to admit not only propositions, but also rules as conclusions of rules[5]. Rules which infer other rules are referred to as *rule-generating rules.* As an example of how a metapredicate is represented by a rule-generating rule, consider the metapredicate

opposite(P,Q): P(X) $\rightarrow$ not(Q(X))

from section 2.1.7 which is represented in IM-2 by

```
p,q,supset,theory ::  opposite(p,q,supset) &
subtheory(theory) --> (x elem supset ::  p(x) -->
not(q(x)) --- w:theory) --- w:mp
```

This complicated rules exhibits many of the powerful features of IM-2's representation, and prototypically shows how the world concept of IM-2 is used to represented MOBAL's metaknowledge. First of all, all rule-generating rules are stored in the world `mp`, which is expressed by the `w` attribute of the entire rule. Now note that in IM-2, it is possible to enter the rule that is generated by a rule-generating rule into a *different* world. This can be done simply by specifying a separate `w` attribute for the rule that forms the conclusion of the rule-generating rule. In the current implementation, the world into which a rule is to be entered is not hard-coded, but specified by the special predicate `subtheory`, which binds the variable `theory` that then specifies the target world (see section 3.2.4). Also note that the support set

[5]Other approaches (not) to integrate higher-order statements into the representation are referred to in section 2.2.9 and 3.1.

argument from the metafact is properly asserted in front of the generated rule.

For metametapredicates, the situation is very similar, except that they do not need have their own support sets. Thus, the metametapredicate

m_symmetrical(mp): mp(P,Q) → mp(Q,P)

is represented in IM-2 by

```
mp,t :: m_symmetrical(mp) & subtheory(t) --> (p,q ::
mp(p,q) --> mp(q,p) --- w:t) --- w:mmp
```

in the world mmp.

This concludes the description of the constructs used to represent assertional and inferential knowledge. The next section deals with the attributions of formulae and rules which provide the possibility to represent negated statements, uncertain and contradictory knowledge, and to organize the knowledge.

3.2.4 Attributes of Assertions and Rules

In the preceding sections, we have introduced assertions and rules as statements that are annotated with a high-dimensional attribute set. We also briefly presented examples of the two most prominent user-visible attributes, namely evidence points (for assertions) and world identifiers (for assertions and rules). In this section, we will have a more detailed look at the attribute concept of IM-2, and present in detail the attributes that are used for assertions and rules. The concept of attributed formulae and rules in IM-2 is adopted from the (more general) approach of attributed knowledge entities in SRL [Habel, 1986, p. 87f]. The concept of attributions resembles the concept of qualified facts and rules in the PROLOG meta-interpreter AQUALOG [Paredis, 1988]. The attributes are also similar to the "fields" of slots in CYC [Lenat and Guha, 1990, p. 39].

The following attributes can currently be used in IM-2 for assertions:

A-ATT = A-ATT-1 × A-ATT-2
A-ATT-1 = ID × EP × KT × UR × W

The set A-ATT-1 comprises all the fixed attributes of assertions that are predefined by the inference engine, whereas A-ATT-2 is a set of arbitrary attributes that can be specified by the user. In MOBAL, comments are stored in such a user-specified attribute. The system-defined attributes are the following: an internal identifier for the assertion (ID), an evidence point (EP), a knowledge trace (KT), a use record (UR) and an identifier of a world (W).

Rules can be annotated with the following attribute set:

$$\text{R-ATT} = \text{R-ATT-1} \times \text{R-ATT-2}$$
$$\text{R-ATT-1} = \text{ID} \times \text{KT} \times \text{UR} \times \text{W} \times \text{F}$$

where again a distinction has been made between system-defined attributes (R-ATT-1) and user-specified attributes (R-ATT-2). The former consist of the following: an internal identifier for the rule (ID), a knowledge trace (KT), a use record (UR), an identifier of an IM-2 world and an identifier of an evidence transfer function (F).

The following sections describe and explain the attributes of assertions and rules predefined in IM-2.

Evidence Points

Instead of a binary truth value or a one-dimensional evidence rating, the formulae in IM-2 have as attributes an *evidence point* "`ep`" of a two-dimensional *evidence space* which is formed by the dimensions *"evidence-for"* and *"evidence-against"* a proposition. The two-dimensional evidence rating was proposed by Rollinger as an alternative to the one-dimensional evidence rating as it is used in most AI systems to represent and apply uncertain knowledge (see [Rollinger, 1983], [Rollinger, 1984])[6].

The evidence point of a formula is determined by the positive and negative evidences that were entered by a user or the overall system and/or inferred using rules. The maximum value for the positive and the negative evidences is 1000, while the minimum value is 0:

$$\text{EP} = [1000,0] \times [1000,0]$$

The cornerpoints of the evidence space, i.e., the evidence points `[1000,0]`, `[0,1000]`, `[1000,1000]` and `[0,0]`, correspond to the epistemic truth values T (told true), F (told false), BOTH (told both true and false) and NONE (told neither true nor false) that were introduced by Belnap (1976); in most MOBAL domain models, only these cornerpoints are used.

[6]This approach is (partially) implemented in IM-1 (see [Emde and Schmiedel, 1983], [Morik and Rollinger, 1985]).

The interpretation of the evidence points is determined by three parameters that correspond to the threshold parameter used in MYCIN ([Shortliffe, 1976, p. 102]). The parameter `min_confirm_evidence` specifies the minimum positive (negative) evidence that is necessary for an assertion to be interpreted as being true (or false). The parameter `max_counter_evidence` determines the maximum negative (positive) evidence for an assertion still to be interpreted as being true (or false). An evidence point is a contradiction if both the positive and negative evidences are greater than the value of the parameter `contradiction_threshold`. The default values of these parameters are `1000` for `min_confirm_evidence`, `0` for `max_counter_evidence` and `1000` for `contradiction_threshold`.

The values of these parameters are not only used to answer queries posed to the inference engine but also in inference processes to determine whether a premise with a given target evidence point (see section 3.2.2). If the target evidence point is `[1000,0]` (`[0,1000]`), the matching assertion's positive (negative) evidence must be at least `min_confirm_evidence`, and its negative (positive) negative evidence must not be greater than `max_counter_evidence`. If the premise target point is `[1000,1000]`, both the positive and negative evidence of the matching assertion must be greater than `contradiction_threshold`.

The parameter `max_counter_evidence` influences the inference behavior of IM-2 in quite an important way, since it can be used to decide whether *blocking* is to be used or not. As introduced in section 2.2.8, blocking means that the inference engine will not use contradictory statements for inferences. If the parameter `max_counter_evidence` is set to `0`, as is the default in MOBAL, a contradictory assertion will satisfy neither a premise with target point `[1000,0]` nor one with target point `[0,1000]`, since in both cases, the threshold for counter evidence is exceeded. This is exactly the behavior required for blocking of inferences with contradictory information. If, on the other hand, `max_counterevidence` is set to `1000`, both positive and negated premises will be satisfied by a contradictory assertion, and the resulting behavior corresponds exactly to the monotonic multi-valued semantics described in section 2.2.7.

Whether or not blocking is desired depends largely on pragmatic considerations. If blocking is not used, the inference behavior of IM-2 is monotonic and matches the formal multi-valued semantics. On the other hand, without blocking, faulty information can be propagated quite far throughout the knowledge base. This can reduce in a large number of derived contradictions which all depend on the single initial piece of faulty information, and may make it difficult for the user as well as for the knowledge revision component KRT to track down the origin of the problem. The consequences would be even more disasterous if facts derived from contradictory information were used in the induction of further rules.

Worlds

To support the organization of knowledge in IM-2, a *world*-attribute has been introduced in IM-2. This attribute offers the possibility to separate the general knowledge from the specific knowledge of a domain, to separate background knowledge from induced knowledge, to separate different types of knowledge (e.g. *constructive* metarules from *restrictive* metarules [Thieme, 1989]) and to separate procedurally oriented representations from declaratively oriented ones (e.g. rules from their corresponding metafacts). This kind of knowledge organization is particularly advantageous if the various knowledge entities are of a global type or domain-independent, because general knowledge can be stored in a separate world and then inherited into several different worlds. This kind of knowledge organization also enables the representation of alternative models [Emde, 1989]. Currently, however, worlds are used in MOBAL only to implement the different metalevels; they are not made accessible directly.

All assertions and rules which have the same term as the *world-attribute* (with the identifier "w") form a *world*. Others will be created, as soon as assertions or rules with a new world name are entered or inferred. Every world can be extended by new assertions (or rules) and modified by deletions (e.g. the change of an evidence point to [0,0]). The information that is stored in one world is in general only accessible within this world. This enables the representation of different and incompatible domain models. For example, the two following assertions belong to different worlds and thus do not represent contradictory statements:

```
senator_of(wallop,wyoming) --- ep:[1000,0], w:model1
senator_of(wallop,wyoming) --- ep:[0,1000], w:model2
```

Each world can have its own specific threshold values to interpret evidence points. In addition, it is possible to specify for each world the maximum forward- and backward-chaining inference depths (see section 3.2.5).

The organization of knowledge is supported by the possibility to define inheritance relations between worlds (see section 3.2.5) and the possibility

```
mmp
mp1,sw::m_symmetrical(mp1) & subtheory(sw) -->
        (p,q,s::mp1(p,q,s) --> (mp1(q,p,s)---w:sw))

meta_meta_level
subtheory(meta_level)
m_symmetrical(inverse_2)

mp
p,q,subset,sw::inverse_2(p,q,subset) &
    subtheory(sw) -->
  ((x,y elem subset ::
        p(x,y) --> q(y,x))---w:sw)

p,q,subset,sw::inclusive(p,q,subset) &
    subtheory(sw) -->
  ((x elem subset ::
        p(x) --> q(x))---w:sw)

meta_level
subtheory(object_level1)
inclusive(from_south_west,for_star_wars,all)
p,q,s:: inverse_2(p,q,s) -->
        inverse_2(q,p,s)

object_level1
from_south_west(gregor)
for_star_wars(gregor)
x elem all::from_south_west(x) -->
   for_star_wars(x)

---> Transformation
---> Inheritance
```

Figure 3.1: Knowledge Organization in MOBAL

to specify a *selective transfer* of knowledge. For example, MOBAL uses inheritance relations to separate domain-independent knowledge (metapredicate definitions) from domain-dependent knowledge (metafacts built with metapredicates). While metapredicate definitions are stored as rule-generating rules in the world `mp`, *metafacts* (and *metarules*) are stored in the world `meta_level`.

As introduced in section 3.2.3, a *selective transfer* of assertions and rules from one world into another one is possible in IM-2 by rules whose conclusions have world-attributes, and is used in MOBAL to represent metapredicates as rule-generating rules that are kept in a separate world. Through inheritance, it is possible for the following rule-generating rule to be stored in the world `mp` and to be known in the world `meta_level`.

```
p,q,s,t :: inclusive(p,q,s) & subtheory(t)
     --> ((x elem s::p(x) --> q(x))--- w:t)--- w:mp
```

The application of the rule to the following assertion in the world `meta_level`:

```
subtheory(object_level1) --- w: meta_level
inclusive(from_south_west,
            for_star_wars,all) --- w: meta_level
```

creates the following rule in the world `object_level1`

```
x elem all :: from_south_west(x)
     --> for_star_wars(x) --- w: object_level.
```

The same organization is used in MOBAL for *metametafacts* and *metarules*. Figure 3.1 illustrates the current organization of knowledge in MOBAL, with inferred assertions and rules being printed in italics. *Metametafacts* are stored in the world `meta_meta_level`, *metametapredicate definitions* in the world `mmp` and the *facts* and *rules* used to describe the objects of a domain in the world `object_level1`.

The concept of worlds is nothing more but an indexing of knowledge entities, which is supported by different AI systems in a similar form. The world mechanism in IM-2 is somehow similar to the context mechanism in AI programming languages such as QA4 or CONNIVER [McDermott, 1983]. The most important difference is the fact that in IM-2 several worlds can be accessed at the same time without requiring specific operations which switch from one context to the next one. IM-2 *worlds* are also similar to the *viewpoints* of OMEGA [Attardi and Simi, 1984]. The main difference is that information can only be be added to OMEGA *viewpoints*. If a knowledge entity in OMEGA is modified, a new viewpoint needs to be created. This allows keeping track of previous states of the knowledge, but it also takes up a lot of resources (execution time and/or storage capacity). In IM-2, worlds may be changed and the overall system (or user) is responsible for ensuring that previous knowledge states can be recovered, e.g. by making copies of a world.

The IM-2 world mechanism has much more in common with the *theory* or *world concept* of the logical programming systems MRS ([Russell, 1985]) and MULTILOG ([Kauffman and Grumbach, 1987]). The main difference, however, is not so much the inference mechanisms it provides or the possibilities of knowledge organization it offers but the fact that in IM-2 the EP-attribute allows also the representation of contradictory knowledge in one world if this is necessary.

Although it is possible to dynamically change the inheritance relations in IM-2, the IM-2 world concept is primarily geared to a static knowledge organization. An approach which deals with dynamic access conditions is described in [Wachsmuth and Gängler, 1991].

Internal Identifiers

All assertions and rules in IM-2 have an internal identifier as an attribution named "id". It is used to represent reason maintenance information, but it can also serve as a reference to the assertions and rules involved in particular operations performed on the knowledge base (e.g. deletions). These internal identifiers are also used in knowledge trace attributions and use record attributions, which are explained in the following sections. The identifiers for assertions are composed of the character "f" and an integer generated by IM-2. Identifiers of rules begin with the character "r".

```
from_south_west(gregor) --- id:  f17
for_star_wars(gregor) --- id:  f18
x ::  from_south_west(x)
    --> for_star_wars(x) --- id:  r5
```

Knowledge Traces

Knowledge traces are internal attributes of assertions and rules in the inference engine that fulfill a central role in meeting the design goals of immediate feedback, revisability, reason maintenance, and knowledge revision support discussed in section 3.1.1. All of the above functionalities require that the inference engine be able always to tell how an entry in the knowledge base originated, i.e., whether it was input by the user or derived from other entries in the knowledge base. The purpose of the knowledge trace attribute "`kt`" is to store this kind of information for assertions and rules.

The values of the knowledge trace attribute consist of a list of data items pointing to the origin of the positive and negative evidences for assertions or to the origin of rules. In contrast to evidence point and world attributes, knowledge trace attributes are interanl data structures that can only be queried, not entered. The following assertion shows an example of a knowledge trace attribute:

```
for_star_wars(gregor) --- id:  f18
                kt:  [[[1000,0],[r5,[f17]]],
                   [[1000,0],input]]
```

The attribute means that rule `r5` was used to infer the assertion `f18` from assertion `f17`, and additionally `f18` was explicitly entered by a user or the overall system. The data revealing the origin of an inferred evidence point in assertions consist of two pieces of information: the evidence point that resulted from an inference and a tuple consisting of a reference to the rule, and a list containing the identifiers of assertions that were used in the inference to confirm premises and support set descriptions. The symbol "`input`" occurs if the evidence point has been entered by the user.

The origin of rules is described with a reference to the rule-generating rule that was used to infer the rule, and a list containing identifiers of assertions that were used to confirm the premises of the rule-generating rule. The symbol "`input`" occurs if the rule has been entered by the user. If a *built-in* predicate or operator was used to confirm a premise, the symbol "`built_in`" serves to mark this. Each source of an inferred evidence point leads to precisely one entry in the knowledge trace attribution. A renewed user input of an evidence point overrides the previous input. The inference of an evidence point replaces an entry of a previous inference with the same rule from the same assertions.

```
x,c ::  count(for_star_wars(x),c)
     --> number_star_wars_advocates(c) --- id:r17,
             kt:  [input]
number_star_wars_advocates(123) --- ep:  [1000,1000],
```

```
kt:  [[[1000,0],[r17,[built_in]]],
      [[0,1000],input]], id:  f44
```

The above assertion was inferred with rule `r17` and the negation has been entered by the user. The evidence point `[1000,1000]` of the assertion marks the resulting contradiction.

The Use Record

The maintenance and revision of knowledge requires not only information about the orign of knowledge entities, but also about the use of the entities. This information is provided by IM-2 with the *use record attribute*. The use record is a list containing references to assertions and rules which were inferred using the corresponding knowledge item (assertion or rule). The use record attribute is used by the reason maintenance component of IM-2 to propagate changes through the knowledge base. The rule and the assertions of the last paragraph may have following use records:

```
x,c :: count(for_star_wars(x),c)
     --> number_star_wars_advocates(c) --- ur:  [f44]
number_star_wars_advocates(123) --- ur:  [], id:  f44
from_south_west(gregor) --- ur:  [f18,f22], id:  f17
```

The rule was used to infer an evidence point for `f44`. This assertion was not used to infer other assertions. Assertion `f17`, however, was used to infer evidences for `f18` and `f22`.

The Evidence Transfer Function

Whenever all premises of a rule are satisfied by matching assertions in the knowledge base, the resulting evidence point of the conclusion must be computed. By default, this is done using a minimum function, i.e., the conclusion evidence point is the minimum of all matching premise evidence points. A maximum function is then used to combine the evidence points from different inferences leading to the same conclusion (see section 3.3.1). Although the use of these functions makes sense in many cases, one may wish in other cases to rely on other functions, e.g. in order to represent flexible (imprecise) concepts (see [Michalski, 1990]) or some other kind of probabilistic inference. In these cases, the (optional) the evidence transfer function attribute "`f`" may be used to specify a user-defined evidence transfer function. allows to replace the minimum functions used to compute inferred evidence points of conclusions by a user-specified function.

As an example of the usefulness of such specialized evidence transfer functions, consider the ICTERUS domain described in section 9.2. In this model, the confidence model for diagnoses has been implemented at the level of facts and rules by relying on built-in arithmetic predicates in rules. An alternative would have been to perform these computations directly in the evidence transfer functions of individual rules in order to avoid burdening the domain model with these details[7].

Suppose it makes sense to use a summation function to compute the overall *evidence* of a diagnosis from the individual *evidences* provided by various laboratory and clinical parameters to come to a diagnosis. This relation could be represented by the following rule:

```
p,d ::  clinical_diagnosis(p,d) & lab_diagnosis(p,d)
     --> diagnosis(p,d) --- f:  ev_sum(999),
```

which computes the evidence point of the conclusion using a user-specified PROLOG procedure `ev_sum` taking an additional argument (999). An application of this rule to the assertions:

```
clinical_diagnosis(anne,hepatitis) --- ep:  [300,20]
lab_diagnosis(anne,hepatitis) --- ep:  [177,0]
```

would compute a particular evidence for a hepatitis diagnosis, for example:

```
diagnosis(anne,hepatitis) --- ep:  [477,0],
```

provided `ev_sum` is implemented as shown in table 3.4.

The inference engine requires the definition of a PROLOG procedure with four parameters as the evidence transfer function. The procedure receives as first parameter the value of the argument that was specified in the evidence transfer function attribute of the rule. The second parameter is a PROLOG list containing numerical ratings that describe how well the various premises are confirmed[8]. The third parameter passes the target point attached to the conclusion. The last argument returns the result of the computation (an evidence point) to the inference engine.

---

[7]Such a representation was chosen in the initial ICTERUS model developed by Stollmann GmbH in the expert system shell TWAICE.

[8]The exact meaning of these values (≥ 0, ≤ 1000) is explained in section 3.3.3.

```
ev_sum(Max,[Confirm_degree1,Confirm_degree2],
          [1000,0],[Sum,0]):-
    Sum is Confirm_degree1 + Confirm_degree2,
    Sum =< Max,
    !.
ev_sum(Max,_,[1000,0],[Max,0]).
ev_sum(Max,[Confirm_degree1,Confirm_degree2],
          [0,1000],[0,Sum]):-
    Sum is Confirm_degree1 + Confirm_degree2,
    Sum =< Max,
    !.
ev_sum(Max,_,[0,1000],[0,Max]).
```

Table 3.4: Implementation of an Evidence Transfer Function

3.2.5 The Meaning of Assertions in the World System

Predicates in the world **system** have particular meanings. The two-place predicate **inheritance** serves to describe inheritance relations between worlds. The assertions with this predicate cause the inference engine to use the assertions and rules of superordinate worlds to answer queries and to confirm premises. The assertion

```
inheritance(mp,meta_level)--- w:  system
```

for example, defines an inheritance relation between the worlds mp and meta_level. When metafacts are entered or inferred, the rule-generating rules in the world mp are regarded as rules that are stored in the world meta_level.

The two-place predicates contradiction_threshold, max_counter-evidence, and min_confirm_evidence can be used to specify for each world the parameters described in section 3.2.4 that interpret evidence points. For example, the following assertions may serve in the world meta_level to confirm premises using assertions which have a positive evidence point of at least 900 and which do not have a negative evidence of more than 100 points:

```
min_confirm_evidence(meta_level,900)--- w:system
max_counter_evidence(meta_level,100)--- w:system
```

The assertion

```
contradiction_threshold(object_level1,900)---
              w:system
```

allows the confirmation of premises in the world `object_level1` that have the symbol "`both`" using assertions which have a positive and a negative evidence value of more than 900 points. If these threshold values are not specified for a world, then the default values illustrated in Table 3.5 will be used.

```
min_confirm_evidence = 1000
max_counter_evidence = 0
contradiction_threshold = 1000

max_forward_search_depth = 5
max_backward_search_depth = 10
```

Table 3.5: Default Values in MOBAL

The predicates `max_forward_search_depth` and `max_backward_search-depth` can be used to specify the search depth in inference processes. In MOBAL, for example, the world `object_level1` has by default a maximum forward inference depth of 5 inferences. By default, the world `object_level1` has a maximum backward-chaining inference depth of 10 inferences[9]. The following assertions define these threshold values:

```
max_forward_search_depth(object_level1,5) ---
              w:  system
max_backward_search_depth(object_level1,10) ---
              w:  system
```

The assertions used to interpret evidence points and to restrict inference processes are very specific not only because of the impact they have on the result of inference processes but also because the procedure that adds them

[9]The forward and backward inference depths are restricted (relatively) independently of one another. Forward inferences that have reached the maximum forward inference depth can still trigger backward inferences if the current inference depth is less than or equal to the restrictions on backward inference processes.

to the world `system` is special. In general, a new input leads to a new (additional) assertion if the arguments in the proposition differ syntactically from the arguments of stored assertions. New assertions built with the predicates described above, however, overwrite assertions that already exist, if they refer to the same world.

3.3 The Inference Mechanism

The next sections explain the inference strategies for forward and backward inferences implemented in the IM-2 inference engine, which as in other systems can interact (KEE, ART, etc.) (see [Mettrey, 1987]). The inference strategies in IM-2 can only be manipulated by a modification of the parameters used to impose a maximum inference depth.[10]

3.3.1 Forward-chaining Inference

The inference engine attempts to perform forward inferences with an assertion, when the evidence point of the assertion has changed (to an EP other than `[0,0]`) as a consequence of an input, an inference, or reason maintenance. The input of a new rule triggers no forward-chaining inference[11]. Forward-chaining is performed using the following depth-restricted *breadth-first* strategy.

- First, a check is made if the current inference depth is less than or equal to the maximum forward-chaining inference depth.
- Then, all *applicable rules* are determined and each applicable rule is:
  - unified with the assertion, and
  - an attempt is made to confirm the (partially or completely instantiated) remaining premises of the rule (see section 3.3.3);

[10] In IM-2 it is not possible to specify conflict resolution strategies which select some of the applicable rules. In IM-2 rules are applied according to the order in which they are internally stored in the knowledge base. Future versions should at least use the number and the complexity of the premises to determine the order.

[11] The computation of consequences of a new rule as feedback for the user is triggered in the MOBAL system by queries for ground instances of the conclusion from the IM-2-MOBAL interface.

  - if this attempt is successful, the system checks whether the variable bindings correspond to the support set description of the rule (see section 3.3.3), and
  - whether the inference (directly or indirectly) provides evidence to an assertion which was used to confirm a premise (see section 3.4.3), and only if this is not the case,
  - the system will use a minimum-function to compute the evidence point of the conclusion (according to the degree to which the individual premises were confirmed, see section 3.3.3), and the inferred conclusion (or the new knowledge trace to the known assertion/rule) is added to the knowledge base,
  - if other instantiations of the premises are possible, the system will try to infer other assertions or rules.

- Finally, reason maintenance is invoked in order to propagate changes to evidence points made during the inference process to dependent knowledge entities.

- This strategy is applied to all inferred assertions, i.e., forward-chaining is continued on the next inference level.

A rule is called *applicable* if the rule contains a premise unifiable with the proposition part of the assertion, and if all variables of the conclusion can be instantiated by the confirmation of the premises. The latter condition results from the fact that assertions are not allowed to have variables as arguments. To give an example, the following rule will not be used to make forward inferences because the premise with the built-in predicate `ne` will not cause the instantition of the variable `x` in the conclusion:

```
person,p_a,x ::  age(person,p_a) & ne(p_a,x)
     --> not(age(person,x)).
```

This rule is only applicable in backward inferences, for example, in order to check whether an entry about a person's age is consistent with the assertional knowledge.

If the assertions that are stored in the knowledge base cannot help to confirm a premise, an attempt is made to infer an assertion with a corresponding evidence point. Backward inferences are also triggered in order to find alternative instantiations of variables. The results of all forward and backward inferences are stored in the knowledge base, even if the results of backward inferences could not be used to perform forward inferences. Only those inferences that have led to the evidence point of [0,0] will not be stored in the knowledge base.

If the result of an inference consists of a new evidence point for an assertion that is already stored in the knowledge base, the system will check whether this assertion was used to confirm the premises. Only if this is not the case will the result be stored in the knowledge base. This prevents circular inferences which are discussed thoroughly in section 3.4.3. Every modification of the assertional and inferential knowledge is propagated by the reason maintenance to the dependent assertions and rules.

3.3.2 Backward-chaining Inference

The inference engine triggers backward inferences if the stored assertions do not allow a query to be answered or a premise to be confirmed, i.e, if there is no attributed formula that can be unified with the proposition part of the query or if the evidence point of an assertion is not sufficient. The starting point of a backward inference is a proposition which can take variables as arguments, and which is attributed with a particular target evidence point. The goal of a backward inference is to infer an assertion that can be unified with the given proposition. The evidence point of this assertion must equal the target evidence point or lie within an area around the target point which is determined by the corresponding threshold values. The following (depth-restricted) *depth-first* strategy is applied in order to perform backward inferences:

- First, the system checks whether the same or a more general proposition[12] is the goal of a superordinate backward inference process (thus preventing nonterminating recursions).

- If this is not the case, the system will check whether the current inference depth is less than or equal to the maximum backward inference depth.

- Then, it will compute a list of *applicable* rules, and process this list sequentially until the inference goal is achieved (or until there are no more applicable rules). In order to apply a rule

  - the proposition is unified with the conclusion, and

[12] A proposition is regarded to be "more general", if it contains fewer bound variables.

- then the system tries to confirm the (partially or completely instantiated) premises of the rules;
- if all premises were confirmed, the system checks whether a) all variables in the conclusion are instantiated and b) the variable bindings meet the support set description of the rule, and
- whether c) the inference (directly or indirectly) delivers evidences for an assertion that was used to confirm a premise (see section 3.4.3);
- only if the condition a) and b) are met and c) is not the case a minimum function will be used to compute the evidence point of the conclusion from the degree of confirmation of the various premises, and the conclusion (or new knowledge trace of a known assertion/rule) will be added to the knowledge base. Then, the evidence point of the assertion is recomputed using the updated knowledge trace attribute;
- if the evidence point of the assertion has changed an attempt is made to use the new or modified assertion to perform forward inferences.

• Finally, the reason maintenance is invoked to propagate modifications to assertions brought about by the inference process to dependent knowledge entities.

A rule can be used to perform backward inferences if it is possible to unify its conclusion with the proposition part of the query, and if the required evidence point is equal to or at least in the range of the target evidence point of the conclusion as defined by the corresponding threshold values.

3.3.3 The Confirmation of Premises

The premises of rules are processed in the order in which they appear in the rule. In the case of forward inferences, the variables of the premises are partially or completely bound by the assertion which triggered the forward inference. In the case of backward inferences, the variables of the premises are partially or completely bound by the conclusion[13]. Premises with a *built-*

[13]The human-computer interface of MOBAL sorts premises with *built-in* predicates to the end of the premise list to ensure that variables in these premises are bound before the premises are evaluated.

in predicate of the inference engine are evaluated by a call of a corresponding PROLOG function.

In order to confirm a premise with a formula-making operator (i.e., not a *built-in* predicate or autoepistemic operator) the system will first search in the knowledge base for an assertion whose proposition part can be unified with the premise and whose evidence point corresponds to the target point of the premise (or which is in the range that is formed by the evidence threshold value parameters). If an assertion is found, this means that there is enough evidence to confirm the premise and no counter evidence has been inferred so far, which would prevent the premise to be become confirmed (see section 3.2.4). As the system performs only depth-restricted inferences, it may be the case that in the actual situation it is possible to deduce additional counter evidence for the premise. Therefore, the system tries to deduce contrary evidence for the assertion by backward-chaining inference (section 3.3.2) within the current search depth limit. The premise becomes confirmed if this attempt fails or delivers not more contrary evidence than allowed by the corresponding evidence threshold parameter (section 3.2.4). In this case, all variables in the premise (which may also appear in other premises or the conclusion) are bound to the corresponding terms in the assertion. The positive evidence of the assertion is attached to the premise as degree of confirmation. The negative evidence is attached to the premise if the premise is negated. The minimum of positive and negative evidence of the assertion is used as degree of confirmation if the premise is marked with the symbol "`both`". If too much counter evidence is deduced, the system searches for another assertion in the knowledge base whose proposistion part can be unified with the premise.

If a corresponding assertion is not stored in the knowledge base, the system tries to deduce confirmative evidence for the premise by backward chaining inference. If an assertion has been deduced whose evidence point corresponds to the target point of the premise, then the system tries also to deduce contrary evidence for the assertion. The premise is confirmed if this attempt fails or delivers not more contrary evidence than allowed by the evidence threshold parameter. The variables in the premise are instantiated and the confirmation degree of the premise is computed as described above. If backward chaining inference is not able to deliver an assertion with an appropiate evidence point the attempt to confirm the premise is abandoned and the system backtracks to a previously confirmed premise in order to find a different instantiation of variables in the premise.

The confirmation of premises with an autoepistemic operator is divided into two steps. In the first step a (depth-restricted) backward inference process is triggered using the nested proposition as goal. Except for premises with `unknown` this backward inference process is repeated until no more assertions can be inferred (within the corresponding search depth restriction). In the second step, the set of (stored) assertions matching the nested proposition is evaluated according to the meaning of the autoepistemic operators (see section 3.2.3).

If *built-in* predicates and autoepistemic operators are used, we distinguish two cases: either the evaluation of the premise is successful (the comparison operation leads to a positive result, the arithmetic operation produces the desired result, or the system does not come up with any assertion for a proposition with the `unknown` operator, etc.) or the evaluation fails. In the first case, the premise is confirmed and receives a confirmation degree of 1000. In addition, the variables in the remaining premises and the conclusion will be instantiated accordingly, if necessary. In the second case, the attempt to confirm the premise fails, thus prompting the system to search for other instantiations of variables in previous premises that enable an inference[14]. If there are no other possibilities to confirm previous premises, the rule application fails and is stopped.

3.3.4 Evaluating Support Set Descriptions

After all premises of a rule were confirmed, the systems checks if the variables of the rule are instantiated according to the support set description. This is done using the procedure described in the last section which is straightforward because the support set description of a rule is internally represented as separate premise list.

3.4 Reason Maintenance

The reason maintenance component of IM-2 is responsible for propagating modifications to dependent assertions and rules. In contrast to systems using a TMS or ATMS (see [Doyle, 1979], [De Kleer, 1986] and [Filman, 1988]) reason maintenance is not an independent subsystem. Instead, this component uses procedures of the inference mechanism to recompute the evidence points of conclusions and to verify the results of nonmonotonic

[14]In the case of forward inferences the system will not search for alternative ways to confirm the premise which had triggered the inference process.

inferences. It directly uses and manipulates the internal inference engine representation of the knowledge trace and use record attributions of the assertions and rules, i.e. it does not have data-dependency structures of its own.

Reason maintenance in IM-2 is *not* based on a data dependency maintenance concept using so-called *data-dependency nodes*[15], which can be "IN" and "OUT" and which provide the basis of most well-known approaches of reason maintenance. The meaning of these *labels* can roughly be described as follows. Knowledge entities that have a data dependency node labeled "IN" have a justification; hence, they are part of the current belief state of the system. Knowledge entities whose data dependency node is labeled "OUT' do not have a valid justification, i.e. they are no part of the current belief state. These labels provides very elegant means to realize hypothetical reasoning and to realize the exploration of alternative problem solving solutions. In order to explore an alternative, the label of nodes can be changed to "OUT" without losing any information. The retraction of a modifications only requires the corresponding labels to be restored. This means that it is not necessary to recompute the corresponding knowledge entities.

Reason maintenance in IM-2 is oriented towards *permanent* modifications in the knowledge base, including the *refinement* of the rule knowledge, in order to meet the requirements posed by the knowledge acquisition and machine learning framework. Although it can sometimes make sense to recover a previous knowledge state, it is usually not necessary to fall back onto a rule once it has be rejected. The use of the retraction operation in IM-2 (or the use of the corresponding operations offered by MOBAL) leads to the complete removal of assertions and rules (assuming that there is no other knowledge trace justifying the knowledge item). If the assertion/rule is entered again, all previously made inferences have to be recomputed[16].

In contrast to forward and backward inference processes no depth restrictions are imposed on reason maintenance, i.e. modifications of the assertional or inferential knowledge are propagated through the entire knowledge base.

[15] As, e.g., [Charniak and McDermott, 1984], [Reinfrank, 1985], [Doyle, 1979] and [Filman, 1988].

[16] Nevertheless, IM-2 is also able to support hypothetical reasoning and the delevopment of modeling alternatives by offering the world attribution concept [Emde, 1991]. Of course, the exploration of alternatives using the world attribute may require a lot of storage capacity, but the effort to restore the original state is very low. Thus, it is not suitable for exploring many different alternatives. ATMS approaches are much better suited to this task, especially if the various alternatives do not differ very much (see [De Kleer, 1986]).

The reason maintenance process is divided into two steps: any modification of the assertional and inferential knowledge immediately causes the system to compute which inferences have to be recomputed. When the forward or backward inference process which caused the modification is finished, all necessary recomputations are made (see sections 3.3.1 and 3.3.2).

3.4.1 Determining Inferences that are to be Recomputed

We distinguish two cases in determining inferences which need to be recomputed. The determination of the inferences performed without autoepistemic operators is supported by the use record attribute of assertions and rules. For all assertions and rules listed in the use record attribute of a modified assertion or deleted rule, the system has to check the corresponding knowledge traces. Each single knowledge trace containing a reference to the modified knowledge item describes definitely and completely the inference which has to be recomputed.

The nonmonotonic inferences with autoepistemic operators are processed differently, since the use record attribute of an assertion does not show whether it was used to evaluate premises with autoepistemic operators (see section 3.2.3), and also since *new* assertions can invalidate non-monotonic inferences.

The determination of the nonmonotonic inferences which could be affected by a new or modified assertion is supported by specific data entries which are automatically stored in the PROLOG knowledge base when a rule is added to the knowledge base. The form of these entries is the same for all autoepistemic operators. The procedure used to maintain nonmonotonic inferences is therefore very general and can also be applied to new autoepistemic operators. The entries have the following form:

```
nm(<proposition 1>,<proposition 2>,<rule id>)
```

The first proposition describes the proposition that is used as an argument of the autoepistemic operator in the nonmonotonic inference rule. The second proposition describes the conclusion of the rule. The arguments of these propositions are terms and (possibly identical) PROLOG variables computed from the original rule. The input of following rule `r1`:

```
drug,component::  count(contains(drug,component),1)
     --> monodrug(drug)
```

leads to following `nm`-entry:

```
nm(contains(X,Y),monodrug(X),r1).
```

Whenever the evidence point of an assertion is modified (e.g. by an input), these entries are used to determine the set of the nonmonotonic inferences that could be affected by the modified (new) assertion. The propositional part of the modified assertions is matched against the first proposition of all `nm`-entries. If the propositions are unifiable, the second proposition will be used to determine the assertions that could be affected by the modified assertion. The rule identifier serves to determine the knowledge trace which is to be recomputed. The meaning of the above entry for rule `r1` is as follows. If a new assertion about a component Y of a drug X is entered or inferred (or if the evidence point of such an assertion has changed), then look in the knowledge trace of the assertion describing X as monodrug for an inference based on the rule `r1`. If such a knowledge trace is found apply the rule once more for the drug X.

3.4.2 Recomputing Inferences due to Modificiations

The recomputation of inferences uses a *breadth-first* strategy based on the scheme described in section 3.3.3 for the confirmation of premises. The recomputation of inferences differs from the normal confirmation procedure in so far as the premises of the inferences to be recomputed can only be confirmed by the assertions that are noted in the knowledge trace (and in so far as no backward inference processes are triggered). If during the recomputation a premise cannot be confirmed any more, because, for example, the corresponding assertion is purged, the new evidence point of [0,0] that results from the inference will be assigned to the conclusion. This leads to the knowledge trace being purged. If it was the last one, the assertion (or rule) will be deleted, which in this case may lead to further recomputations.

The recomputation of inferences is necessary in IM-2 for two reasons. First, the knowledge trace attribute contains no information about how well the various premises were confirmed, but this information is necessary in order to determine the evidence point of the conclusion. Second, the knowledge trace of assertions inferred with rules containing autoepistemic operators includes no reference to assertions which have been matched against the embedded propositions. Therefore, the premises with autoepistemic operators have to be re-evaluated.

3.4.3 Problems caused by Circularities

Before the result of an inference is added to the knowledge base, the system checks whether the inference is part of a circular inference chain. On the one hand, this prevents nonterminating program loops in the reason maintenance procedures, and on the other hand this precludes assertions from becoming their own evidence source.

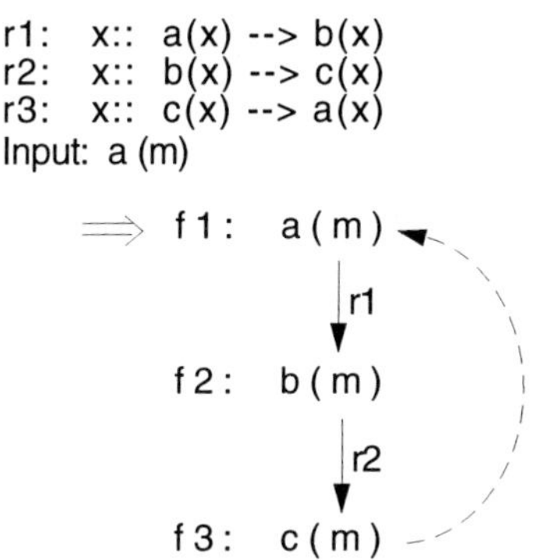
r1: x:: a(x) --> b(x)
r2: x:: b(x) --> c(x)
r3: x:: c(x) --> a(x)
Input: a (m)
⟹ f1: a(m)
r1
f2: b(m)
r2
f3: c(m)

Figure 3.2: The Circular Inference of a Positive Evidence

Figure 3.2 illustrates what would happen if assertions delivered evidence to themselves. It shows a circular inference chain inferred after an input of assertion `f1`. If in this situation the entered evidence point for assertion `f1` is retracted, the inferred evidence points for the inferred assertions and the entered assertion will not be modified because they support each other. Consequently, these assertions can only be purged by retracting one of the applied rules.

Less severe are the consequences when the system does not prevent the inference of a negative (positive) evidence for assertions that provide their positive (or negative) evidence to enable the verification of a premise. Figure 3.3 shows an example. It demonstrates the situation after the input of an assertion and a few forward inferences. Rule `r3` could be use assertion `f3` that to infer negative evidence for the entered assertion in another forward inference process. This would invalidate the inferences made with the entered assertion because the premise of the first rule is no longer confirmed.

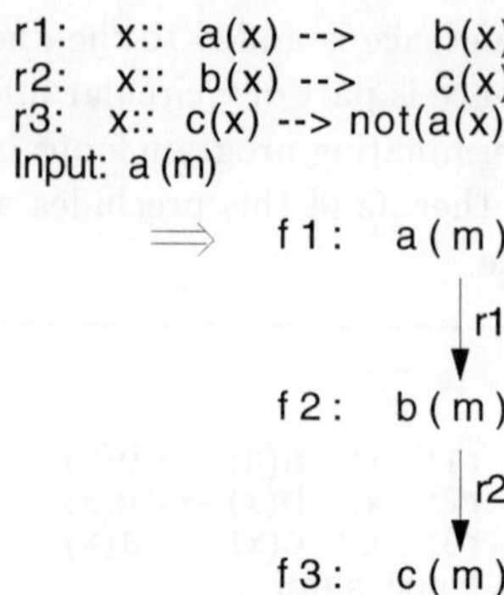
r1: x:: a(x) --> b(x)
r2: x:: b(x) --> c(x)
r3: x:: c(x) --> not(a(x))
Input: a (m)
f1: a(m)
r1
f2: b(m)
r2
f3: c(m)

Figure 3.3: The Circular Inference of a Negative Evidence

The reason maintenance component would then retract all forward inferences made including the inference of a negative evidence for the entered assertion. Only the (entered) positive evidence for the assertion would remain and this would lead to the retraction of all other assertions[17].

Both kinds of circular reasoning are prevented in IM-2 by the test described in section 3.3.3. Unfortunately, this solution to the problem has two drawbacks. On the one hand, the system does not perform inferences that later on could turn out to be of some importance, and on the other hand rules that are capable of producing a contradiction are not applied if their application leads to inference cycles. Hence, such rules cannot be discovered by a knowledge revision component without the user's help if the component is only triggered by contradictions in the assertional knowledge, as is the case in KRT.

Let us take as an example a state of the system's body of knowledge illustrated in figure 3.4 in order to explain the first point. An entered assertion `f1` is used to infer the assertions `f2` and `f3`. After that, assertion `f3` is entered. The inference of evidence from assertion `f3` to justify assertion `f1` is blocked as described above. Retracting the evidence that is entered

[17] As the reason maintenance does not trigger any forward inferences, i.e. no further attempt is made to make a forward inference using `f1`, when the inference of a negative evidence for the entered assertion is retracted, there is no risk of a never-ending series of inferences and retractions.

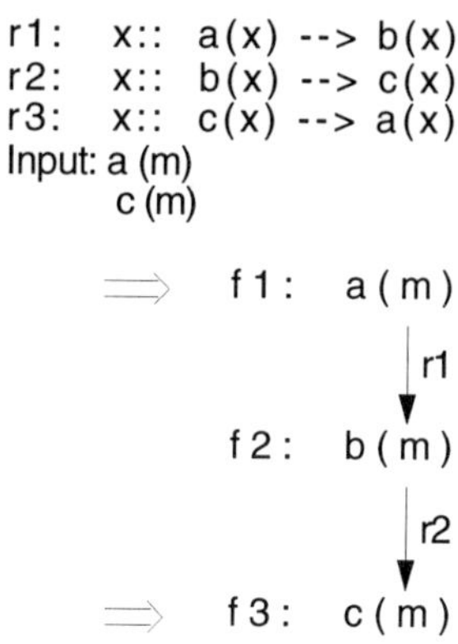
r1: x:: a(x) --> b(x)
r2: x:: b(x) --> c(x)
r3: x:: c(x) --> a(x)
Input: a (m)
c (m)
f1: a(m)
r1
f2: b(m)
r2
f3: c(m)

Figure 3.4: Disadvantages of Preventing Cycles

for `f1` would therefore lead to the retraction of `f1` and `f2`, because other no evidences for these assertions are stored in the knowledge base.

In most cases this will not have any serious consequences, because a query can prompt the system to use rule `r3` in order to infer the deleted assertions. A new inference will only fail if the maximum backward inference depth is reached.

The other negative aspect of the above procedure is the following. A set of rules allowing circular inferences like those shown in figure 3.3 can point to a weakness (or fault) in a domain model. If a knowledge revision component needs a contradiction in the assertional knowledge in order to become active, such circular inferences should not be blocked as it is done in Im-2. In Mobal, the rule knowledge is represented on the metalevel as metafacts. The input or induction of rules leads to a metalevel consistency check on the basis of *metarules*. An inconsistent set of rules can only be added to the knowledge base if metarules able to detect the inconsistency of the corresponding metafacts are missing (or if the support set is restricted) (see section 3.2.3).

A simple alternative to the above method of preventing circular inferences would be to prohibit the use of rule sets that can lead to such inferences. This idea was suggested by Falkenhainer with his *Belief Maintenance System* Bms [Falkenhainer, 1987]. This solution is not appropriate if a system has to support the (sloppy) modeling of a domain.

3.5 Discussion

The IM-2 inference engine offers a relatively uniform representation formalism that combines a number of different concepts to represent uncertain and contradictory knowledge, to organize knowledge, to perform uncertain and nonmonotonic inferences, and to support knowledge revision processes. Thus, it fulfills the requirements stated at the beginning of this chapter. Other systems such as MRS, OMEGA, MULTILOG, RUP, and BMS are partially based on similar concepts, but they fulfill only a subset of these requirements. Of course, we do not claim that IM-2 fulfills all requirements that may arise in an inductive learning and/or knowledge acquisition system. For example, it is clear the knowledge representation formalism is very restrictive. Among other things, it might be necessary to represent existential quantified statements. The "Annotated Predicate Calculus" APC, described by Michalski [Michalski, 1983], is more powerful with respect to the representation of learning results. In this chapter we were primarily interested in the fact that a learning and knowledge acquisition task forces particular requirements to be fulfilled independently of the kinds of statement which must be representable in a model of a domain.

For this reason, the work described in this chapter is closely related to the work of Brazdil [Brazdil, 1986], [Brazdil, 1987], who proposed to use a metalevel extension of PROLOG in order to to represent the epistemic knowledge in a teaching/learning system.

Chapter 4

The Sort Taxonomy

4.1 Introduction

One of the prerequisites for building up a domain model is the specification of a description language. For a logic-oriented representation, as used in MOBAL, domain-specific predicates have to be declared along with their admissible arguments. If a many-sorted logic is used for representing the domain model, the sorts of the arguments, the compatibility of the sorts, and the mapping of terms to sorts have to be declared as well. This specification can be viewed as a knowledge acquisition task in itself [Kietz, 1988].

In this chapter, a general approach to support this acquisition process and automatically to build a sort taxonomy is presented. The sort taxonomy is used to specify the well-sorted expressions in a many-sorted logic, i.e. to specify the logic description language for a particular domain model.

The taxonomy is constructed on the basis of facts input by the user. It is assumed that the user inputs only semantically well-formed expressions, even though he is not forced to specify the description-language beforehand. Nevertheless this approach supports users in entering and revising language specifications as they want. These specifications from users are fully integrated into the process of the automatic acquisition of the language specification on the basis of meaningful facts, which the users enter into the system. From this integrated language specification the criterion for the well-sortedness of language expressions, i.e. facts and rules, is derived.

The taxonomy evolves incrementally as more and more facts and declarations are typed in. Revisions in the set of facts and declarations produce revisions in the taxonomy. If a new fact or rule input is not well-sorted with respect to the taxonomy acquired so far (e.g. if the user has forgotten how he used a certain predicate before), this is indicated to the user. The system does not, however, prevent the user from revising the taxonomy. In contrast, the resulting changes are computed by the system automatically, so that the user need not be concerned with the changes of the taxonomy implied by changes of the domain model. The taxonomy construction is achieved by structuring the known term sets for each sort in the given predicates according to set theory, i.e. we take the set theoretical relations between the extensions of sorts for determining the relations between sorts. Therefore, an inductive step would be necessary to use the taxonomy for predictions. So far, this step is not performed by our system in order to preserve the incrementality and reversibility of the approach. Instead, the user can initiate this inductive step, i.e. can transfer the acquired relations between sorts into fixed description language specifications, which are nevertheless further maintained in the taxonomy.

The hypothesis space of MOBAL's model-based learning procedure can also be pruned by the use of a sorted logic. Automatic sort processing ensures that only those parts of the hypothesis space are pruned that contain hypotheses that cannot successfully be tested against the fact basis.

4.1.1 An Example

To illustrate the acquisition of a sort taxonomy we would like to give an example from the *side-effects of drugs* domain. In figures 4.1 - 4.4 and 4.6, we use meaningful class names[1] for the classes, which are represented by nodes. The subclass relation between classes is represented by links. In figure 4.5 the equivalence classes of sorts themselves and their known extensions are shown.

We would like to start the domain modeling with the relations between symptom and disease. These relations can be expressed by the two predicates, indicate and cause. By inputting the facts

indicate(sore_throat,flu)
cause(flu,sore_throat)

into the system, the sort taxonomy shown in figure 4.1 is created. Here, nodes represent class names and links represent subclass relations between classes. The class name symptom represents the equivalence class [arg_1_indicate,

[1] The system generates only class names like class_1, but in the sort graphic user given sortnames are used as node label if they are known to the system.

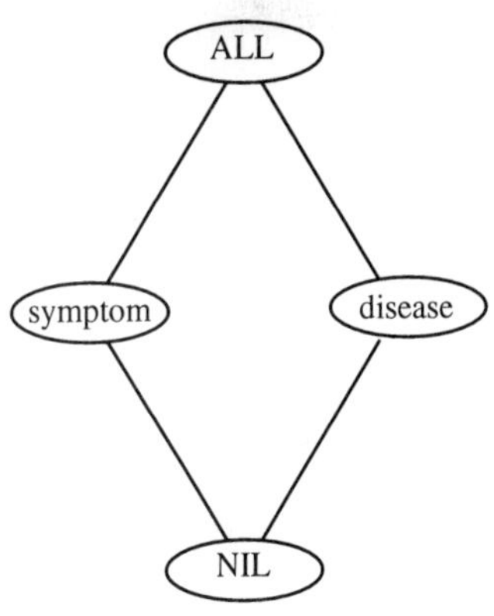

Figure 4.1: Sort Taxonomy of indicate and cause

arg_2_cause] and the class name disease represents the equivalence class [arg_2_indicate, arg_1_cause]. The system has thus established the equivalence of the argument sorts of the first argument of the predicate indicate and the second argument of cause as well as the equivalence of the argument sorts of the second argument of indicate and the first argument of cause. The known extension of class symptom is {sore_throat}. The known extension of class disease is {flu}. Therefore it establishes the two classes to be disjoint, i.e. the system does not know any term which belongs to the extensions of both classes.

The system so far knows only ALL as a mutual superclass. This is changed when the system receives facts about positive effects of substances, like

affect_pos(inspirol,sore_throat)
affect_pos(aspirin,flu)
affect_pos(benzethoniumchloride,sore_throat)
affect_pos(acetylsalicyl_acid,flu)

The system builds two new equivalence classes, one for each argument of the predicate affect_pos. In figure 4.2, they are called substance, containing the argument sort of the first argument of affects_pos, and irritation, containing the argument sort of the second argument. The system finds out that the extension of symptom as well as the extension of disease are subsets of the extension of irritation, i.e. that substances affect diseases as well as symptoms.

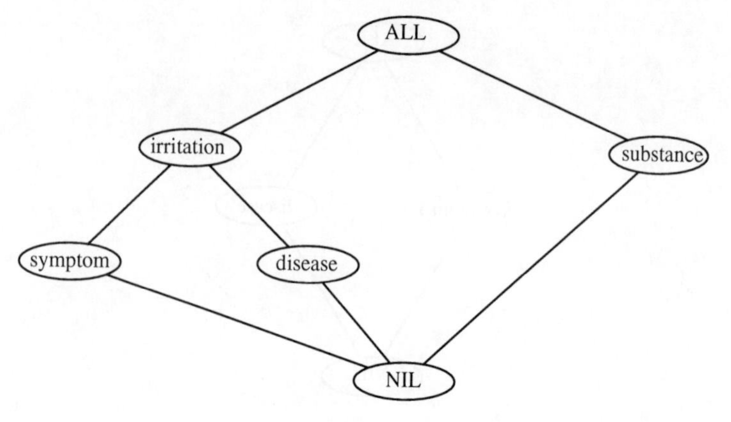

Figure 4.2: Sort Taxonomy that includes Facts about affect_pos

Therefore, it not only creates substance as a new equivalence class disjoint to all other classes within the taxonomy, but also irritation as a generalization of symptom and disease.

Specialization of equivalence classes is also performed by the system. The facts

contains(inspirol,benzethoniumchloride)
contains(aspirin,acetylsalicyl_acid)

lead to the creation of the equivalence classes with the names act._agent (with the argument sort arg_2_contains) and drug (with the argument sort arg_1_contains) as specializations of substance. The resulting taxonomy is shown in figure 4.3.

Two new equivalence classes named person (with the argument sort arg_1_suck) and dragée (with the argument sort arg_2_suck) are introduced by giving the fact

suck(fred,vivil)

They are completely disjoint from all other existing equivalence classes as shown in figure 4.4.

If we input the fact

suck(john,inspirol)

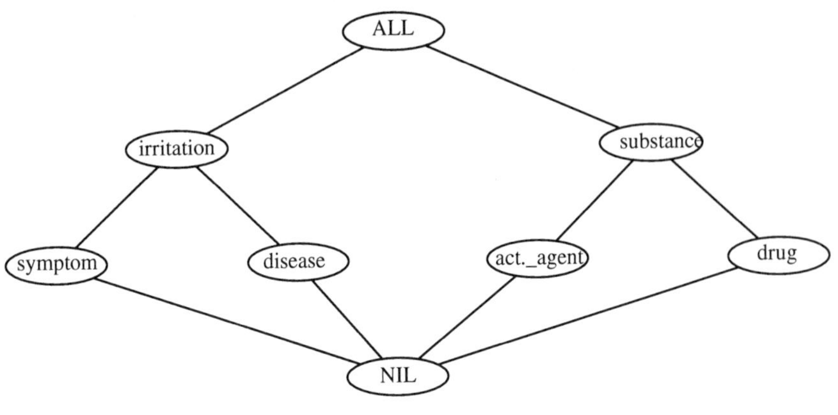

Figure 4.3: Sort Taxonomy after entering Facts about **contains**

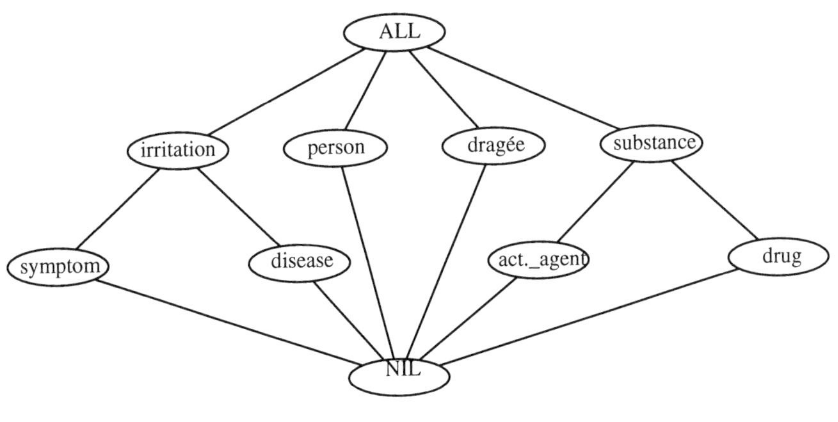

Figure 4.4: Sort Taxonomy after the First Fact about taking **dragées**

the system will diagnose overlaps between dragée and drug and between dragée and substance, both consisting of the term inspirol. For each overlap, an intersection sort representing this overlap is built. Both intersection sorts (int(dragée, drug) and int(dragée, substance)) have the extension inspirol. They are integrated into the taxonomy by building the new equivalence class named pill as a mutual subclass of dragée and drug. The resulting taxonomy is shown in figure 4.5. In this figure, all equivalence classes are shown precisely as represented within the system. For each class, the contained argument sorts and the current extension are shown.

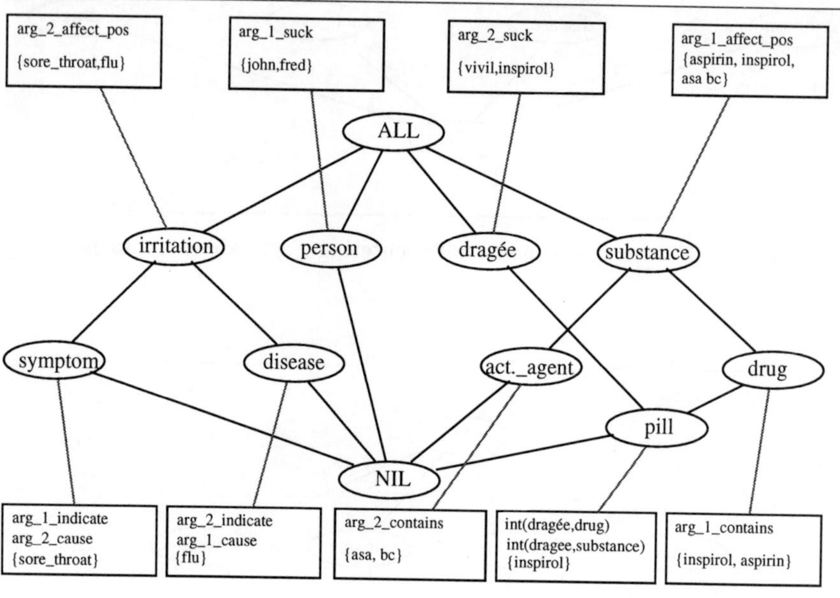

Figure 4.5: Acquired Taxonomy with Argument Sorts and Extensions

The created taxonomy is independent of the sequence of input: the facts of our example may be given in any order. To demonstrate this, we swap the order of input for the last two facts. If

suck(john,inspirol)

were input in the situation of figure 4.3, the taxonomy of figure 4.6 would be the result. All terms of the equivalence class named dragée are now known

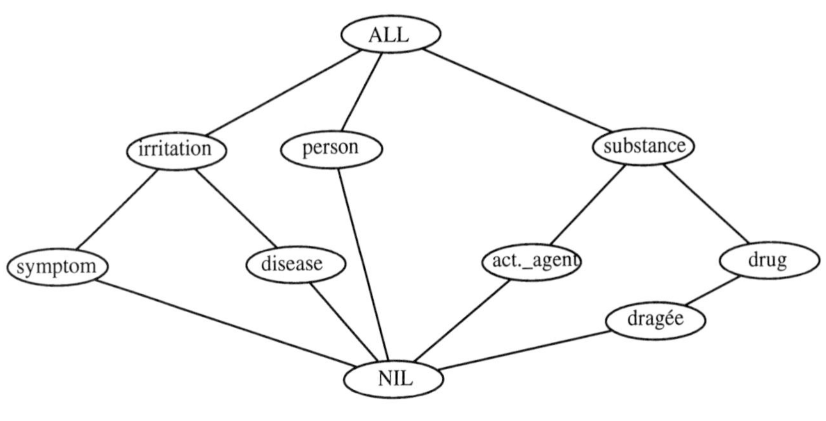

Figure 4.6: Intermediate Stage after the Exchange of Entries

to be drugs, so the class is integrated into the taxonomy as a specialization of **drug**. For the input

suck(fred,vivil)

this condition is no longer true: **dragée** is no longer a specialization of **drug**. For this reason, **dragée** becomes a new equivalence class at the level of **substance**. The old class now precisely describes the intersection sorts between **drug** and **dragée** and **substance** and **dragée**. If it is named **pill**, the taxonomy of figure 4.5 is reached again[2].

The changes in the taxonomy caused by the revision of facts are computed similarly. The result of revisions is independent of sequence, too.

The automatically acquired sort taxonomy in figure 4.5 is equivalent to the set of predicate declarations and relations between sorts shown in table 4.1[3].

[2]The system will number the classes according to the order in which they show up. Given the different order of the facts, the taxonomies generated by the system - which correspond to figure 4.5 - differ in so far as the names of dragée and pill that are generated by the system are exchanged. This is because the order of the facts determines the order in which the classes are generated.

[3]The used formalism is defined in section 4.2.2.

Whereas most systems which use a sort logic require this specification beforehand, it can be automatically acquired in MOBAL with the approach presented in this chapter.

```
indicate(<symptom>,<disease>).
cause(<disease>,<symptom>).
affect_pos(<substance>,<irritation>).
suck(<person>,<dragée>).
contains(<drug>,<act_agent>).

symptom :< irritation.
disease :< irritation.
act_agent :< substance.
drug :< substance.
pill := dragée, drug.
NIL := irritation, person.
NIL := irritation, dragée.
NIL := irritation, substance.
NIL := person, dragée.
NIL := person, substance.
NIL := act_agent,drug.
```

Table 4.1: User Sort Specifications

4.1.2 Overview

In section 4.2, we describe the way we get from a set of facts and user sort specifications to a sort taxonomy. The terms are mapped into sorts corresponding to the argument places of the used predicates. For every argument place of every predicate, a unique argument sort is generated. This can be done automatically by the system without making *a priori*predicate declarations. Using this nonintuitive definition of sorts, we can compute an adequate representation of sorts by dividing the set of sorts into equivalence classes of sorts. These classes represent what is normally called a sort: a unique name for argument places with the same extension. These classes are arranged along a partial ordering representing the compatibility-relation between sorts. The partial ordering is derived from the subset-relation between the extensions of the sorts. Finally, we determine the overlapping between sorts and represent them in the taxonomy to distinguish between overlapping and disjoint sorts. By doing this, we get a lattice of equivalence classes of sorts.

In section 4.3, we present transformations of the sort lattice which make an incremental and reversible acquisition of the sort lattice possible. These transformations describe the changes in the sort lattice corresponding to changes in the set of facts and in the user sort specifications. This enables the incremental and reversible acquisition of the sort lattice by adding new facts and user sort specifications, beginning with no facts, no user sort specifications, and the empty lattice.

In section 4.4, the sort lattice is used to specify the description language of the domain models acquired with MOBAL. In particular, we describe how the acquired sort lattice is used to check the well-sortedness of facts and rules. This well-sortedness of rules is also used to prune the hypothesis space of RDT.

In section 4.5, we describe some implementation details of the sort taxonomy tool (STT) within MOBAL.

4.2 The Sort Lattice

In this section, we present the taxonomy of sorts computed from the user given sort specifications and/or the set of known facts. First we define the correspondence between argument places and sorts. With this correspondence, we can compute the extensions of the argument sorts, i.e the sets of terms that belong to these kinds of sorts. Based on these argument sorts and their extensions, we define user sorts and their extensions and the formalism in which sort specifications can be entered into the system.

Using the extensions of the sorts, we can compute the most important relations between sorts:

- the equivalence of sorts,
- the inclusion of sorts,
- the overlapping of sorts, and
- the disjointness of sorts.

It can be shown that a sort lattice representing these relations can be constructed from the sort information residing within the user-given sort specifications and the set of facts. From this lattice, a bijective extension function to a complete infimum-homomorph lattice of the lattice of the power set of all terms (pset(TERM)) exists. This function transports into the sort lattice part of the valid laws of the boolean algebra (pset(TERM),$\cap$,$\cup$,$\neg$,{},TERM) with the partial ordering $\subseteq$, being expected intuitively. The partial ordering (subset relation) and the infimum operation (intersection) are transported from the extensions into the sort lattice. We can define the supremum operation so that it is as similar as possible to the union of sets.

4.2.1 The Automatically Built Argument Sorts

In a many-sorted logic, all predicates must be declared before use. In predicate declarations for each argument, a sort to which the used arguments must belong is specified. So as not to trouble the user, the system itself generates the declarations of predicates when a predicate is used for the first time. Normally, arguments with equal sorts are declared with identical sort names, but trying to do this automatically from the first fact for this predicate is like guessing the user's intention.

In our approach, a new unique sort is invented for each argument place of each predicate. By collecting all terms used in facts for one argument place of a predicate, we then derive the set of terms belonging to the argument sort (the extension of the argument sort). For each argument sort generated for an argument place of a predicate, an extension can be derived by doing this collection. These extensions are the base for calculating the relations between the argument sorts. Based on these extensions, the system then automatically calculates the equality of argument sorts within the sort taxonomy by building equivalence classes of sorts. This method produces the finest sort taxonomy based on the current set of facts. For this reason, the set of well-sorted formulae is restricted as much as possible to formulae supported by facts, e.g. two argument sorts are equal only if they are mapped to the same extension.

Let us now assign a unique sort name to each argument position of each predicate. As all the predicate names are unique, we can form a unique sort name for each argument position of each predicate using the predicate name and the argument position number.

Definition 4.1 (Argument sort) *Let PN be the set of the predicate names, I a number that denotes a legal argument position in a predicate,*

and SN a set of unique sort names. Then we can define a function
arg_sort: I, PN $\longrightarrow$ *SN*
which uses the predicate name and the argument position number to provide a unique sort name for each argument sort.

We can now define the sorting, i.e., the function that assigns to each sort name the set of the terms that belong to this sort. Consequently, a sort consists of a name and a set of terms - its extension - assigned to it.

Definition 4.2 (Extension function ext for argument sorts) *Let SN be the set of unique sort names, TERM the set of all terms, and FB (fact basis) the set of the facts that are known to the system. Then the function ext: SN* $\longrightarrow$ pset*(TERM), with* $t_i \in ext(arg\_sort(i,p)) \Leftrightarrow$
$p(t_1, \ldots, t_i, \ldots, t_n) \in FB \vee \neg p(t_1, \ldots, t_i, \ldots, t_n) \in FB$
assigns to each sort name an extension based on the current fact basis.

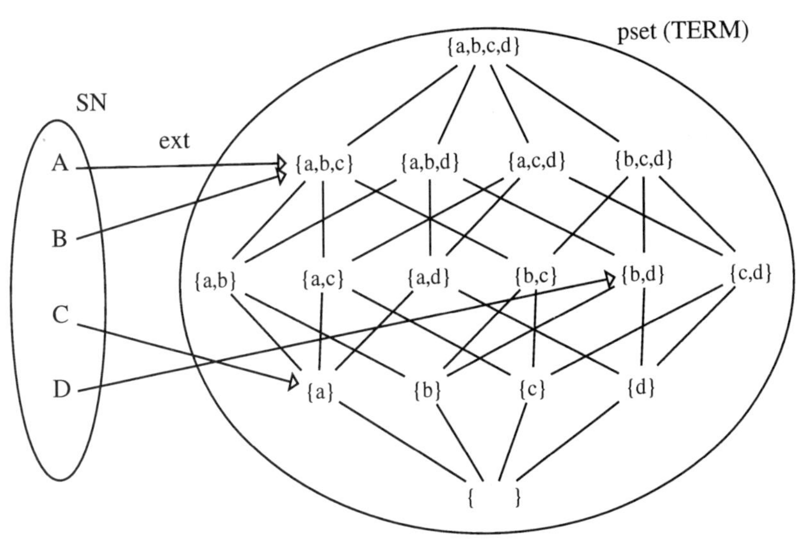

Figure 4.7: An Example Demonstrating the Function of ext

Let us have a look at an example. When the system knows the facts
FB = {p(a,b),p(b,c),¬ p(c,a),r(a,b),¬ r(a,d)}

with SN = {A,B,C,D}, the following sorting

A = ext(arg_sort(1,p)) = {a,b,c}
B = ext(arg_sort(2,p))= {a,b,c}
C = ext(arg_sort(1,r)) = {a}
D = ext(arg_sort(2,r)) = {b,d}

and the entire set of all terms TERM = {a,b,c,d} will be the result. Figure 4.7 illustrates this example graphically.

4.2.2 User-given Sort Specifications

In contrast to the system-generated argument sorts, which are descriptive, i.e. they describe what is in the knowledge base and not necessarily what a user wants to be in the knowledge base, user-given sort specifications are prescriptive, i.e. they specify what should be in the knowledge base and not necessarily what is in the knowledge base.

User-given sort specifications can be used for several purposes

- They introduce meaningful names into the sort taxonomy and therefore increase the understandability of the sort taxonomy.
- They enable the user to introduce the sort information he knows.
- As the incrementally and reversibly acquired sort information is in flux to reflect the current fact base, the user sort formalism can be used to freeze an archived state of modeling.

To follow the balanced cooperative modeling paradigm, the formalism for user sort specifications should be as expressive as the formalism for system computed sort specifications. Therefore there are four kinds of sort specification that users can give:

- sort declarations for argument places of predicates,
- sort inclusions of single sorts and intersections of sorts,
- definition of sorts as intersection of other sorts, and
- sort disjointness.

User sort specifications must not be violated by facts[4] and rules[5] (see section

[4]Two user sorts specified as disjoint must not have a common term.

[5]A variable must not occur at argument places declared with disjoint sorts.

4.4), and they are used by the system for inferences[6] (see the definition of ext for user sorts).

The declaration of sorts for argument places of predicates can be given in predicate declarations. Predicate declarations are syntactically similar to positive facts but the arguments are not terms: rather they are user sort names enclosed in < and > or - if this place should not have a user sort - <>, e.g.:

```
owner(<person>,<>)
```

This says, that all terms occurring in facts at the first argument of the predicate owner belong to the sort person, i.e. only persons can own things, whereas the sort of the second argument is not specified, i.e. everything can be owned.

Definition 4.3 (User sort) *Let PN be the set of the predicate names, PB the set of user predicate declarations, I a number that denotes a legal argument position in a predicate, and SN the set of unique sort names. Then we can define a function user_sort: I, PN $\longrightarrow$ SN, with*

$$user\_sort(i,p)) = s_i \Leftrightarrow p(< s_1 >, \ldots, < s_i >, \ldots, < s_n >) \in PB$$

which uses the predicate name and the argument position number to access the user sort names for predicate declarations.

In addition, the user can specify required inclusions of user sorts. This is done using the relation :< between sorts. As a shortcut it is allowed using multiple sorts at the right-hand side. This states that the left sort is a subsort of each of the sorts at the right-hand side, e.g.:

```
child :< person.
woman :< person,female.
```

The second is equivalent to

```
woman :< person.
woman :< female.
```

This says, that the sort at the left side is a subsort of all sorts at the right side, i.e. that all children must be also persons and that all women must also be persons as well as females.

The system handles :< as a partial ordering, i.e. it uses

[6]If a term belongs to a sort specified as subsort of another sort, then the system infers that it also belongs to the supersort.

- reflexivity: a :< a,
- transitivity: a :< b and b :< c implies a :< c, and
- antisymmetry: a :< b and b :< a implies a := b

to complete the user-given specifications.

In fact, all persons which are also females are women. This can be expressed in the user sort formalism by the definition of a sort as the intersection of two other sorts, e.g.:

```
man := person,male.
woman := person,female.
```

Finally, the user can specify the disjointness of user sorts using the empty sort NIL by defining the intersection to be NIL, e.g.:

```
NIL := male,female.
NIL := man,woman.
```

Now, let us define the extension of user sorts.

Definition 4.4 (Extension function ext extended for user sorts) *Let SN be the set of unique sort names, including the special sorts* ALL *and* NIL*, TERM the set of all terms, FB (fact basis) the set of facts that are known to the system, PB the set of user predicate declarations, and SB the set of subsort and defined sort specifications. Then the function*

$$ext\text{: } SN \longrightarrow \text{pset}(TERM)$$
$$\text{with } t_i \in ext(s) \Leftrightarrow$$
$$(s = \mathsf{ALL} \wedge t_i \in TERM) \vee$$
$$(s = user\_sort(i,p) \wedge (p(t_1,\ldots,t_i,\ldots,t_n) \in FB \vee \neg p(t_1,\ldots,t_i,\ldots,t_n) \in FB)\ )\vee$$
$$(s = arg\_sort(i,p)) \wedge (p(t_1,\ldots,t_i,\ldots,t_n) \in FB \vee \neg p(t_1,\ldots,t_i,\ldots,t_n) \in FB)\ )\vee$$
$$(s_0 :< s_1,\ldots,s,\ldots,s_n \in SB \wedge t_i \in ext(s_0)\ )\vee$$
$$(s_0 := s_1,\ldots,s,\ldots,s_n \in SB \wedge t_i \in ext(s_0)\ )\vee$$
$$(s := s_1,\ldots,s_j,\ldots,s_n \in SB \wedge \forall j \in 1,\ldots,n\text{: } t_i \in ext(s_j)\ )$$

assigns to each user sort name an extension based on the current fact basis and set of sort specifications.

Let us conclude this section with a definition of consistency of user sort specifications. It is clear that inconsistencies could only occur on the basis of disjoint requirements. Let us look at an example:

man :< human
NIL := man,human

This could be considered as inconsistent in itself, because man is required to be a subsort of human as well as required to be disjoint from human. But in fact, there is no contradiction as long as no term is known for man, i.e. it is consistent as long as ext(man) = {}. This fits perfectly into the overall behavior of MOBAL (see chapter 3 for rule set inconsistencies).

Definition 4.5 (Consistency of user sort specifications) *The set of user sort specifications is consistent if and only if ext(NIL) = {}.*

4.2.3 The Equivalence Classes of Sorts

In our approach the most important relation between sorts is their equality. This relation is handled by the decomposition of the set of argument sorts as well as user sorts into equivalence classes of sorts. Sorts are mapped into the same equivalence class if they have the same extension. This causes an injective function between the equivalence classes and the extensions. From now on we will speak about the extensions of classes, meaning the equal extension of the contained sorts. The classes represent what is normally named a sort: the equality of arguments. The computation of equivalence classes shows which argument and user sorts have an equal extension. Consequently, we need an equivalence relation that groups the sorts with the same extension into classes. For further use, these equivalence classes are named by unique names. Since we do not want to deal with the form of the class names here, we will also introduce a class construction operator which provides us with the classes the sorts belong to.

Definition 4.6 (Equivalence classes of sorts) *The relation* $\approx \subseteq SN \times SN$ *defined by*

$\forall\, s_1, s_2 \in SN: s_1 \approx s_2 \Leftrightarrow ext(s_1) = ext(s_2)$

is an equivalence relation, as = is one. Let $SN/\approx$ *denote the set of classes of sorts with the same extension. Let CLASS denote a set of unique class names and let cn:* $SN/\approx \longrightarrow CLASS$ *be a bijective function that assigns to each equivalence class such a unique name.*

Finally, let class: $SN \longrightarrow CLASS$ *with*

$\forall\, s_1, s_2 \in SN: class(s_1) = class(s_2) \Leftrightarrow s_1 \approx s_2 \Leftrightarrow ext(s_1) = ext(s_2)$

be the function that computes to each sort the class it belongs to.

In the following we will not further distinguish the classes and their names, but later we will use these class names to define a representation of intersection sorts. Using the above definition we can conclude that all classes have at least one sort that belongs to the class name:

$\forall$ c $\in$ CLASS: $\exists$ s $\in$ SN: class(s) = c

Consequently, if we want to prove something for the classes, we have to show that this is true of all the elements of SN being arguments of class.

Definition 4.7 (Extension of equivalence classes)
Let cext: CLASS $\longrightarrow$ pset*(TERM) be the function that assigns to the classes their extensions:* $\forall$ *s* $\in$ *SN: cext(class(s)) = ext(s).*

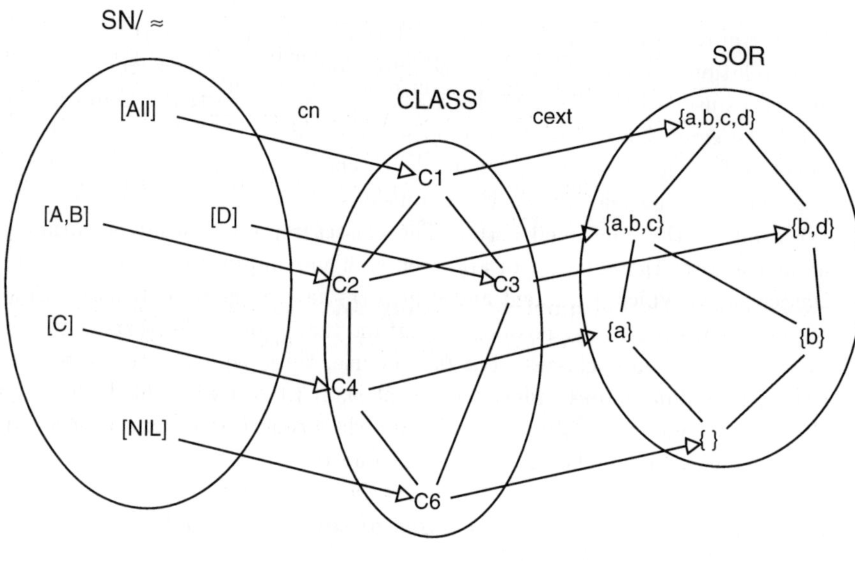

Figure 4.8: Example of the Function cext

Lemma 4.1 *cext is an injective function:*

$\forall$ $c_1,c_2 \in$ *CLASS*: $cext(c_1) = cext(c_2) \Rightarrow c_1 = c_2$

$cext(class(s_1)) = cext(class(s_2))$

$\Leftrightarrow ext(s_1) = ext(s_2)$

$\Leftrightarrow s_1 \approx s_2$
$\Leftrightarrow class(s_1) = class(s_2)$

Figure 4.8 illustrates for our example the equivalence classes resulting from SN and the function cext resulting from ext together with cn. cext is a function suitable as morphism between pset(TERM) and our sort structure CLASS, i.e., cext is the function which we require to transfer some laws of the boolean algebra pset(TERM) into our sort structure.

4.2.4 The Compatibility Partial Ordering between Classes

After determining which sorts are equivalent, we must determine which sorts are compatible. Compatibility is used to decide the sort-correctness of variable bindings in formulas. Compatibility between classes induces compatibility between the sorts contained in the classes. As a minimal requirement, this relation must be a partial ordering [Oberschelp, 1962]. In our case, the compatibility partial ordering is determined by the subset partial ordering between the extensions of the classes. A class c_1 is a subclass of a class c_2 iff the extension of c_1 is a subset of the extension of c_2, i.e. a class c_1 is a subclass of c_2 if all terms belonging to c_1 also belong to c_2. This corresponds to the usual understanding of subclass.

Definition 4.8 (The partial ordering over the equivalence classes)
$\leq \subseteq CLASS \times CLASS$ *with* $c_1 \leq c_2 \Leftrightarrow cext(c_1) \subseteq cext(c_2)$

(CLASS,$\leq$) is a partial ordering, as cext is injective and (pset(TERM),$\subseteq$) is a partial ordering, i.e. cext is an order-morphism from CLASS to pset(TERM).

$\leq$ can be used to define the following functions and relations:
subclass-relation:
subclass $\subseteq$ CLASS $\times$ CLASS
subclass(c_1,c_2) $\Leftrightarrow (c_1 \leq c_2) \wedge \neg (c_2 \leq c_1)$
predecessor:
subs: CLASS $\longrightarrow$ pset(CLASS) with
subs(c_1) := { c$\in$ CLASS c $\leq c_1 \wedge$ c $\neq c_1$ }
successor:
supers: CLASS $\longrightarrow$ pset(CLASS) with
supers(c_1) := { c $\in$ CLASS $c_1 \leq$ c $\wedge$ c $\neq c_1$ }
The following relation, between subclass, subs and supers holds:

subclass(c_1,c_2) $\Leftrightarrow c_1 \in$ subs(c_2) $\Leftrightarrow c_2 \in$ supers(c_1)
d-subclass-relation:
d-subclass $\subseteq$ CLASS $\times$ CLASS
d-subclass(c_1,c_2) $\Leftrightarrow (c_1 \leq c_2) \wedge (\neg$ c3 : $(c_1 \leq$ c3 $\wedge$ c3 $\leq c_2))$
direct predecessors:
d-subs: CLASS $\longrightarrow$ pset(CLASS) with
d-subs(c_1) := {c $\in$ subs(c_1) | $\neg$ $c_2 \in$ subs(c_1): c $\leq c_2$ }
direct successors:
d-supers: CLASS $\longrightarrow$ pset(CLASS) with
d-supers(c_1) := {c $\in$ supers(c_1) | $\neg$ $c_2 \in$ supers(c_1): $c_2 \leq$ c }
The following relation, between d-subclass, d-subs and d-supers holds:
d-subclass(c_1,c_2) $\Leftrightarrow c_1 \in$ d-subs(c_2) $\Leftrightarrow c_2 \in$ d-supers(c_1)

It is also possible to specify the subclass relation or the d-subclass relation between the sorts so as to define our partial ordering. It will then evolve through the definition of the reflexive or reflexive and transitive closure. But it has to be made sure that the closure that has been defined is antisymmetrical, i.e that there are no cycles.

A nonempty, finite partial ordering (H,$\leq$) or directed acyclic graph (DAG) can be easily graphically displayed as an order diagram.

This diagram represents the elements of H as nodes. In the case of two elements e_1 and e_2 of H, with e_1 directly preceding e_2, node Ne_1 that corresponds to e_1 is located below (or to the left of) node Ne_2 that corresponds to e_2, and it is linked to Ne_2 by an arc.

It is easy to see that x $\leq$ y for any two elements of H if in an order diagram that represents H Nx is located below (or to the left of) Ny and linked to Ay by an upward (right) directed arc chain.

This property of partial orderings is used to provide the user with a graphic representation of the sort structure.

An example of an order diagram is the representation of pset(TERM) illustrated in figure 4.7.

4.2.5 Building Intersection Sorts

Often, there are overlaps between two or more classes without any one class being a subclass of any of the others. To distinguish these overlapping classes from disjoint classes, we need a mutual subclass of the overlapping classes. In our side-effects of drugs example, the classes containing **liquid** and **drug** illustrate such an overlap. A mutual subclass of these classes would be the class containing **serum**. To represent the relation between these classes within our sort lattice, the system can generate additional sorts representing the overlaps between classes. For this purpose, we define intersection sorts as the named intersections of class extensions. This means that intersection sorts are artificial and do not represent arguments of predicates, but as we see in section 4.4.2, they represent possible sorts of variables.

Definition 4.9 (Intersection sorts IS) *Intersection sorts IS are all two-element sets of classes which overlap and which are not subclasses of each other:*

$$IS = \{ \{c_1,c_2\} \subseteq CLASS \mid \neg(c_1 \leq c_2) \wedge \neg(c_2 \leq c_1)) \wedge \neg(cext(c_1) \cap cext(c_2) = \{\}) \}$$

The extension function iext: IS $\longrightarrow$ pset*(TERM) of IS looks as follows:*

$$\forall \{c_1,c_2\} \in IS: iext(\{c_1,c_2\}) = cext(c_1) \cap cext(c_2)$$

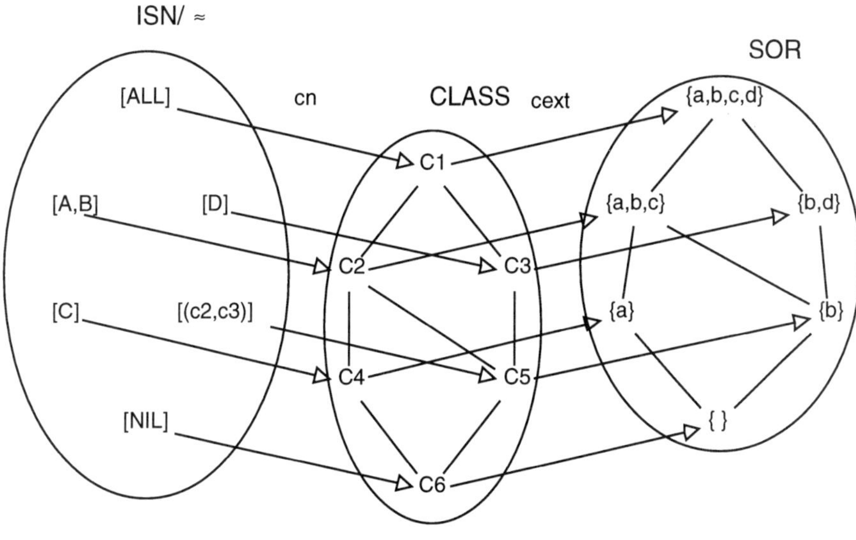

Figure 4.9: An Example of IS and SN

If $\approx$, class, cn and cext are extended to ISN = SN $\cup$ IS, the union of SN and IS, this definition will recursively generate intersection sorts for all overlapping classes. Clearly, this can be a computationally expensive operation as there are in the worst case 2^n intersections to be built for n classes. Therefore it is the choice of the user (see section 4.5) if intersections are built or not. In figure 4.9 we illustrate the intersection sorts IS with our example.

Definition 4.10 (Intersecting classes of a class) *The function inters computes for each class all the classes that form an intersection sort with that class.*

$inters: CLASS \Longrightarrow \text{pset}(CLASS)$ *with*

$inters(c) = \{ c_1 \in CLASS \mid \{c,c_1\} \in IS \}$

4.2.6 The Lattice of the Equivalence Classes

In order to obtain a surjective extension function cext we will use the subset of pset(TERM), which only contains the extensions of sorts (from SN) and all intersections of these extensions.

Definition 4.11 (Set of sort extensions SOR)
Let $SOR \subseteq \text{pset}(TERM)$ *be with*
(a) $\{\} \in SOR,\ TERM \in SOR,\ \forall\ s \in SN: ext(s) \in SOR$
(b) $m_1,m_2 \in SOR \Rightarrow m_1 \cap m_2 \in SOR$
(c) There are no other $m \in SOR$

As we now show, SOR is exactly the subset of pset(TERM) which contains all and only the extensions of ISN as elements.

Lemma 4.2 *cext is surjective for SOR, and therefore a bijective function between CN and SOR (seeLemma 4.1):*

$\forall\ m \in SOR : \exists\ c \in CLASS : cext(c) = m$

bf Proof: by complete induction:
(a) $m = TERM \Rightarrow c = class(\mathsf{All})$
(b) $m = \{\} \Rightarrow c = class(\mathsf{NIL})$
(c) $m = ext(s) \Rightarrow c = class(s)$
(d) $m = m_1 \cap m_2$*: With the inductive assumption:*

$c_1,c_2 \in CLASS: cext(c_1) = m_1 \wedge cext(c_2) = m_2$

$\Rightarrow m = cext(class(\{c_1,c_2\}))$

As cext is a bijective function, its inverse function $cext^{-1}$ *is well defined.*

It is known from lattice theory [Hermes, 1967, pp.27-28], that a subset of a complete lattice closed against the meet-operation is a lattice in its own right and also a meet-sublattice of the original lattice. As SOR is closed against the meet-operation by definition 4.11, SOR is a lattice

(SOR,$\subseteq$,$\cap$,$\sqcup$) and a meet-sublattice of (pset(TERM),$\subseteq$,$\cap$,$\cup$). The same holds for (CLASS,$\leq$,$\sqcap$,$\sqcup$), because SOR and CLASS are isomorphic.

Thus, the order and the meet operation of our sort structure are equivalent to the subset ordering and the intersection operation. And the join of sorts is the smallest element of the sort structure which is larger than the union of the sort extensions.

Lemma 4.3 *Two elements in SOR and CLASS have a definite meet:*
$\forall\ m_1,m_2 \in SOR$: $m_1 \sqcap m_2 = m_1 \cap m_2$
$\forall\ c_1,c_2 \in CLASS$: $c_1 \sqcap c_2 = class(\{c_1,c_2\})$
$= cext^{-1})(cext(c_1) \cap cext(c_2))$
SOR and CLASS are two isomorphic meet-semilattices.

Lemma 4.4 *SOR and CLASS have each a definite join:*
$\forall\ m_1,m_2 \in SOR$: $m_1 \sqcup m_2 = \bigsqcap(supers(m_1) \cap supers(m_2))$
$\forall\ c_1,c_2 \in CLASS$: $c_1 \sqcup c_2 = \bigsqcap(supers(c_1) \cap supers(c_2))$
$= cext^{-1}(cext(c_1) \sqcup cext(c_2))$
SOR and CLASS are two isomorphic join-semilattices.

The partial ordering, the meet and the join constitute a lattice. The partial ordering and the meet operation in SOR are equivalent to the subset ordering and the intersection operation in pset(TERM). Thus, we can summarize as follows:

Theorem 4.1 *CLASS and SOR are two isomorphic complete lattices, with SOR being a meet-sublattice of* pset*(TERM) and cext thus a meet-morphism from CLASS to* pset*(TERM).*

This theorem holds independently of how SN and ext are modeled, the decisive factor being the complete formation of intersection sorts and the subsequent formation of equivalence classes, i.e. we are always able to use the information the user gives about SN and ext to construct such a complete meet-sublattice with the above theorems valid in it. How this lattice is best represented, and how it can be adjusted to accommodate modifications of SN and/or ext will be the subject of the next section.

4.3 Computing the Sort Lattice

Having discussed in the last section how the sort lattice is related to the current knowledge base, the topic in this section is, how to build this lattice in an incremental and reversible way, i.e. how to reflect changes in the knowledge base within the sort lattice. In order to make the acquisition of the sort lattice incremental and reversible, we have to define operations transforming a sort lattice according to knowledge base changes, i.e. transforming the sort lattice from its old state into a new one corresponding to the current knowledge base.

Not all changes of the knowledge base are relevant for the sort lattice. Changes of the knowledge base which affect the sort lattice are:

- adding/deleting a fact by the user or the inference engine,
- adding/deleting a predicate declaration, and
- adding/deleting a subsort relation.

We have to define operations for each of these changes. The operations affect only the function ext between some sorts and their extensions. Based on the definition of ext in sections 4.2.1 and 4.2.2 all these operations can be reduced to two basic operations:

- adding a set of terms to the extension of a sort,
- deleting a set of terms from the extension of a sort.

Before we can specify these two operations in detail, we give an overview of them and specify the representation of the sort lattice.

4.3.1 Representation of the Sort Lattice

As specified in the last section the partial ordering and the intersection sorts are represented using the names of equivalence classes instead of the names of sorts. This yields a highly modular representation for the operations to be specified. We can simply hold the function between class names and extensions constant. Only the membership of sorts to classes changes if the sort's extensions change. The existing partial ordering and the existing intersection sorts remain unchanged. All we have to do is to compute a new class for the changed sort and possibly purge the old class, if it no longer contains any sort.

If a changed sort fits into another existing class, we must only add the sort to the class. If the changed sort does not fit into any existing class, a new class with a new class name has to be created. The position of the new class within the lattice has to be determined, and all of its intersection sorts have to be built and integrated into the class hierarchy. The position in the lattice can be determined from the position of the old class of the changed sort. Intersection sorts with the new class can also be built and integrated into the lattice using the intersection sorts of the old class. Integration of the new intersection sorts can be done by applying this method recursively. The old class must be deleted if it is empty after integrating the changed argument sort and the new intersection sorts. When a class is deleted, all of its intersection sorts and all information concerning its former place within the lattice have to be deleted as well. If this produces more empty classes, these must also be deleted.

The average expense of this approach is lower than computing the relations directly between the sorts since it is easier to determine what remains unchanged and what has to be changed.

Let us recall what determines the position of a class c in the sort lattice. There is

- the set of all superclasses of c (computed by supers(c)),
- the set of all subclasses of c (subs(c)),
- the set of all classes which intersect with c (inters(c)), and finally
- all other classes which are disjoint to c
  (dis(c) = CLASS / ({c} ∪ supers(c) ∪ subs(c) ∪ inters(c))).

These sets will be the basis for a precise specification of the changes to a sort lattice when the assignment of terms to sorts changes.

The first three of these functions completely specify the relations of classes within the sort lattice. Additionally, the system has to know what sorts are in a given class ($cn^{-1}(c)$) and which extension the class has (cext(c)). This gives the following set of 6-tuples as a complete representation of the sort lattice.

Definition 4.12 (Representation of the sort structure SORT)
SORT = { (c,cn^{-1}(c),cext(c),inters(c),subs(c),supers(c)) | c ∈ CLASS }

Each 6-tuple represents the class name, the equivalence class of sorts and intersection sorts, the extension of the class, the set of the classes that have an intersection with this class and the set of the superclasses of this class.

The following is an example of SORT.

SORT = {
 (c_1, {all}, {a,b,c,d}, {}, {c_2,c_3,c_4,c_5,c_6}, {}),

$(c_2, \{A,B\}, \quad \{a,b,c\}, \{c_4\}, \{c_3,c_5,c_6\}, \qquad \{c_1\} \qquad),$
$(c_3, \{C\}, \quad \{a\}, \quad \{\}, \{c_6\}, \qquad \{c_1,c_2\} \qquad),$
$(c_4, \{D\}, \quad \{b,d\}, \{c_2\}, \{c_5,c_6\}, \qquad \{c_1\} \qquad),$
$(c_5, \{(c_2,c_4)\}, \{b\}, \quad \{\}, \{c_6\}, \qquad \{c_1,c_2,c_4\} \qquad),$
$(c_6, \{nil\}, \quad \{\}, \quad \{\}, \{\}, \qquad \{c_1,c_2,c_3,c_4,c_5\})$
$\}$

It is true that this representation is redundant, as it specifies inters, subs and supers separately for each class, thus increasing the efforts involved in maintaining consistency. Nevertheless, it contains the relevant information about the sort lattice which has to be provided for the user and the system, and which enables a relatively simple definition and rapid computation of the transformations that the sort lattice undergoes.

Definition 4.13 (The empty sort lattice SORT0) *The initial sort lattice SORT0, i.e. the sort lattice without any sorts, which initiates the modeling process, is defined as::*

$SORT0 = \{$
$(c_1, \{all\}, TERM, \{\}, \{c_2\}, \{\} \quad),$
$(c_2, \{nil\}, \{\}, \qquad \{\}, \{\}, \quad \{c_1\})$
$\}$

4.3.2 Changing the Sorts Extension

In order to specify the relations of the new equivalence class we will use the former equivalence class, which differs from the new class in the set of changed terms. For the former class, all the relations with the other classes of the sort lattice are already determined. This means that in the case of the former class (fc) we already know the division of all classes (CLASS) into superclasses of the former class (supers(fc)), subclasses of the former class (subs(fc)), intersection classes with the former class (inters(fc)) and classes disjoint from the former class (dis(fc) = CLASS / ({fc} ∪ supers(fc) ∪ subs(fc) ∪ inters(fc))). The relations of the former class can then be used to determine the relations of the new class.

The relations of the new class also depend on whether the related classes contain all the changed terms, none of the changed terms, or a subset of the changed terms. Consequently, we still need to subdivide all classes into classes with all the changed terms (A), classes with none of these changed terms (N), and classes with only some of these changed terms (S).

These two partitions are complete for all classes except the former. By means of cross-classification of these two partitions we get twelve sets of classes. For all classes c ∈ CLASS we determine the relations of c to the new class, based on the membership of c in one of these twelve sets. Additionally, we have to specify the relation of the former class to the new class. By doing this, we have entirely computed the position of the new class within the sort lattice.

Adding a Set of Terms to a Sort

Given: s, the sort with the changed extension,

t, the terms, that should be added to s,

fc, the former class of s,

supers(fc), subs(fc), inters(fc), dis(fc), the position of the former class within the lattice, and

A, S, N, the partition of all classes into classes with all new terms, some new terms, and no new terms.

Desired: nc, the new class of s,

supers(nc), the superclasses of the new class nc,

subs(nc), the subclasses of the new class nc,

inters(nc), the classes intersecting with the new class nc, and

dis(nc), the classes disjoint to the new class nc.

$c = fc \Rightarrow c \in subs(nc)$
The former class is a subclass of the new class, as the extension of the new class contains all terms of the former one.

$c \in (supers(fc) \cap A) \Rightarrow c \in supers(nc)$
The superclasses of the former class, which also contain all the new terms, are also superclasses of the new class, as their extension contains both the extension of the former class and all the new terms.

$c \in (supers(fc) \cap N) \Rightarrow c \in inters(nc) \wedge c \sqcap nc = fc$
The superclasses of the former class, which do not contain any new term, are no superclasses of the new class, but all other elements of the extension of the new class are also contained in their extensions. Consequently, they are to be used to form a new intersection whose

extension is identical with the extension of the former class, i.e, the intersection sorts to be formed anew with them belong to the former class. Hence, the former class should only be purged, if it is still empty after the integration of the new class and its intersections.

$c \in (\text{supers}(fc) \cap S) \Rightarrow c \in \text{inters}(nc) \wedge \text{cext}(c \sqcap nc) = \text{cext}(fc) \cup (t \cap \text{cext}(c))$
The superclasses of the former class, which contain only some of the new terms, are not superclasses of the new class, but all other elements of the extension of the new class and some new terms are also contained in their extensions. Consequently, they are to be used to form a new intersection whose extension is the union of the extension of the former class and the common new terms.

$\text{subs}(fc) \cap (A \cup S) = \{\}$
There can be no subclass of the former class that contains any of the new terms, as the former class does not contain any one.

$c \in (\text{subs}(fc) \cap N) \Rightarrow c \in \text{subs}(nc)$
The subclasses of the former class are also subclasses of the new class, as the extension of the new class also comprises the extension of the former class.

$c \in (\text{inters}(fc) \cap (A \cup S))$
The classes that form an intersection with the former class and that contain all or some of the new terms must normally be used to form a new intersection whose extension additionally contains all/part of the new terms in contrast to the intersection with the former class. However, the new terms could also contain all the terms that c misses to be a subclass of nc. Therefore, we have to distinguish between two cases:

$c \subseteq (\text{cext}(fc) \cup t) \Rightarrow c \in \text{subs}(nc)$
If the intersection to be formed falls into the class that is to be used to form the intersection, this class represents another subclass of the new class, and the intersection need not be formed and represented.

$c \not\subseteq (\text{cext}(fc) \cup t) \Rightarrow c \in \text{inters}(nc) \wedge \text{cext}(c \sqcap nc) = \text{cext}(c \sqcap fc) \cup (t \cap \text{cext}(c))$
A new intersection sort has to be built. This new intersection sort is integrated into the sort lattice by the recursive application of

this technique by adding the set of all the new terms, which are also in the intersection class, to the intersection with the former class.

$c \in (\text{inters}(fc) \cap N) \Rightarrow c \in \text{inters}(nc) \wedge c \sqcap nc = c \sqcap fc$

If the intersecting class does not contain any of the new terms, then the intersection to be formed with the new class falls into the same class as the intersection formed with the former class. This is because none of the new terms is contained in the newly formed intersection.

$c \in (\text{dis}(fc) \cap (A \cup S))$

The classes disjoint with the former class that contain all or some of the new terms must normally be used to form a new intersection whose extension additionally contains all/part of the new terms in contrast to the intersection with the former class. But, if the extensions of these classes are subsets of the new terms, they become subclasses of the new class. Therefore, we have to distinguish between two cases:

$\text{cext}(c) \subseteq t \Rightarrow c \in \text{subs}(nc)$

A class that is disjoint from the former class and that has only all/parts of the new terms as its extension becomes another subclass of the new class.

$\text{cext}(c) \not\subseteq t \Rightarrow c \in \text{inters}(nc) \wedge \text{cext}(c \sqcap nc) = t \cap \text{cext}(c)$

All the other classes that are disjoint from the former class and that contain all/parts of the new terms have to be used to form new intersections which have all/parts of the new terms as their extension. Our technique can also recursively create the class that contains these new intersections by adding the new terms to NIL.

$c \in (\text{dis}(fc) \cap N) \Rightarrow c \in \text{dis}(nc)$

The classes disjoint from the former class that do not contain any of the new terms are also disjoint from the new class.

The recursive application of our technique needs to be modified in that it only integrates the new intersection into the new class and will not purge the sort that triggers the procedure from its former class.

The division of all classes into A, S and N need not be recomputed for the recursive application of the procedure, as it is the same t or a subset of t that is added to the existing classes. Only some classes from S are moved to A if only a subset is added.

Removing a set of terms from a sort

Given: s, the sort with the changed extension,

t, the terms, that should be removed in s,

fc, the former class of s,

supers(fc), subs(fc), inter(fc), dis(fc), the position of the former class within the lattice, and

A, S, N, the partition of all classes into classes with all of the deleted terms, some of the deleted terms, and none of the deleted terms.

Desired: nc, the new class of s,

supers(nc), the superclasses of the new class nc,

subs(nc), the subclasses of the new class nc,

inter(nc), the classes intersecting with the new class nc, and

dis(nc), the classes disjoint to the new class nc.

$c = fc \Rightarrow c \in supers(nc)$

When a set of terms is removed, the former class becomes a superclass of the new class, as it additionally contains these terms.

$c \in (supers(fc) \cap A) \Rightarrow c \in supers(nc)$

The superclasses of the former class with all the removed terms are also superclasses of the new class.

$supers(fc) \cap (S \cup N) = \{\}$

All superclasses of the former class must contain the removed terms, otherwise they would not be superclasses of the former class, i.e this case is impossible.

$c \in (subs(fc) \cap (A \cup S))$

For the subclasses of the former class which contain all or some of the removed terms, we have to distinguish two cases:

$cext(c) \subseteq t \Rightarrow c \in dis(nc)$

If the extension of the subclass of the former class is only a subset of the removed terms, it will become a disjoint class of the new class.

$\text{cext}(c) \not\subseteq t \Rightarrow c \in \text{inters}(nc) \land \text{cext}(c \sqcap nc) = \text{cext}(c) / t$
If the extensions of the subclasses of the former class contains more than the removed terms, new intersection sorts must be built. They can be recursively integrated into the sort lattice by removing the terms from the classes which were used to form the intersection.

$c \in (\text{subs}(fc) \cap N) \Rightarrow c \in \text{subs}(nc)$
The subclasses of the former class that do not contain any removed term are also subclasses of the new class.

$c \in (\text{inters}(fc) \cap (A \cup S))$
For the classes that form an intersection with the former class which contain all or some of the removed terms, we have to distinguish two cases:

$\text{cext}(c \sqcap fc) \subseteq t \Rightarrow c \in \text{dis}(nc)$
If the intersection with the former class contains only a subset of the removed terms, the intersection with the new class will be empty. These classes are thus disjoint from the new class.

$\text{cext}(c \sqcap fc) \not\subseteq t \Rightarrow c \in \text{inters}(nc) \land \text{cext}(c \sqcap nc) = \text{cext}(c \sqcap fc) / t$
If the intersection with the former class contains more than the removed terms, a new intersection sort has to be built. The extension of the new intersection sort corresponds to the intersection with the former class less the removed terms. It can be formed and then integrated into the sort lattice by recursively removing the terms from the intersection with the former class.

$c \in (\text{inters}(fc) \cap N) \Rightarrow c \in \text{inters}(nc) \land c \sqcap nc = c \sqcap fc$
The classes that form an intersection with the former class and that do not contain any of the removed terms also form an intersection with the new class, with the intersection falling into the same class as the intersection with the former class.

$\text{dis}(fc) \cap (A \cup S) = \{\}$
There are no classes that are disjoint from the former class and containing any of the removed terms.

$c \in (\text{dis}(fc) \cap N) \Rightarrow c \in \text{dis}(nc)$ All classes that are disjoint from the former class are also disjoint from the new class.

4.4 The Many Sorted Logic

We present the application in MOBAL as an example of how this technique can be applied and used to develop and update a taxonomy, even though, of course, we can think of other possible applications such as the the development of an object taxonomy for an expert system based on case data. The relations represented in the sort taxonomy are equivalent to a zero-order Horn logic. Thus, another possible application is to use the sort taxonomy for the data-driven generation of zero-order Horn rule hypotheses that do not contradict the fact base.

In MOBAL the sort taxonomy provides the user with an overview of the current state of the model, i.e. of the relations between the predicates based on the facts currently known to the system. The sort taxonomy that reflects the present model is graphically presented to the user in the form of an order diagram. This eases the inspection of a knowledge base.

The sort taxonomy is also used in MOBAL to define a sort logic that represents the domain model. In contrast to the use of a normal logic the use of a sort logic in MOBAL has several advantages. It is possible to check and ensure that the user input is sort-correct, and the space consisting of the hypotheses made by the system is pruned by the use of the sort logic to contain only hypotheses that can be tested against the current knowledge base.

The sort taxonomy represents the extent to which the argument sorts are compatible, i.e., it states whether:

- argument sorts are identical, i.e., whether they are in the same equivalence class and have thus the same extension,
- one argument sort is a subsort of another one, i.e., whether the equivalence classes in which they are contained are in an order relation, and their extension is thus a subset of the other one's extension,
- argument sorts overlap, i.e., whether the equivalence classes in which they are contained have a common meet unequal to NIL, and thus terms that belong to both of them are known, namely the extension of the meet,
- argument sorts are disjoint, i.e., whether the equivalence classes in which they are contained have NIL as the meet, and there are thus no known common terms.

In addition, it stores the so far known extensions of all sorts that can be represented by the taxonomy, i.e. the assignment of terms to sorts.

This sort taxonomy and the assignment of argument positions of predicates to sorts represented in the sort taxonomy serves to restrict the set of the well-formed object-level formulae (i.e. object-level facts and object-level rules) to sort-correct formulae. Together with a sort-correct inference relation, i.e. an inference relation that makes sure that only sort-correct formulae are deduced from sort-correct formulae, the taxonomy provides a sort logic to represent the domain models.

However when defining the sort logic (i.e. the sort-correctness of facts, rules and inferences) we have to take into consideration that the relations represented in the sort taxonomy and, above all, the known extensions have to be incrementally acquired first, and that they are possibly not yet correct. The sort taxonomy is only correct in relation to the facts known so far, but it can always be modified by the input of new facts. These new facts that lead to a modification of the sort taxonomy, as they do not correspond to the sort taxonomy, can be rejected in a normal (not incrementally acquired) sort logic for not being sort-correct. But we want to use them to acquire our sort lattice. Consequently, we cannot reject all of them. Hence, we need to pursue a strategy that is slightly different from, say, [Oberschelp, 1962], when defining sort-correctness. This sort-correctness will then be used to check the user input, but the final decision as to whether an input is sort-correct or not has to be made by the user. Thus, it is possible to enter facts and rules that contradict the currently used sort taxonomy. These facts will modify the taxonomy, so that it corresponds again to all facts, and all facts in the system are sort-correct. Rules which according to the current taxonomy are not sort-correct do not prompt a modification of the taxonomy directly but only by means of facts deduced by it. Thus, the rules can result in inferences which are not sort-correct according to the current sort taxonomy. Such inferences are not possible in a normal sort logic, but they should be made in our case, if the user has insisted that they are sort-correct and thus enhance the taxonomy.

We now summarize the requirements our sort logic has to meet:

- Facts and rules that have been entered are to be checked whether they are sort-correct.

- Facts and rules that are regarded as being sort-correct by the system are to produce sort-correct inferences only.

- If the user insists that an input not considered to be sort-correct by the system is sort-correct, it has to be accepted by the system, and the sort taxonomy needs to be adjusted to accommodate the input and the inferences of the input.

4.4.1 Sort-correctness of Facts

In order to define the sort-correctness of facts we need to define the incompatibility of a term with a sort. The fact is sort-correct, iff all terms of the fact are compatible with the corresponding argument position sorts:

$$\text{sort-correct}(\text{p}(t_1,\ldots,t_n)) \Leftrightarrow \forall\ i_{1..n}\text{: compatible}(t_i,\text{arg\_sort}(\text{i},\text{p}))$$

This, of course, also applies to negated facts, as the negation does not influence sort-correctness.

Usually, the compatibility of a term with a sort is defined by means of the term's extensional membership in this sort. This, however, is a piece of information that is first to be acquired by MOBAL, and that as a result cannot be used for the purpose of a definition. Instead, we want to define compatibility by taking into account the fact that it is consistent with the current sort taxonomy: that the term belongs to the sort. This means, we ask whether relevant changes of the relations between the sorts will result when the extension of the sort additionally contains this term.

If a term is added to a sort, the following relations of the sort taxonomy can change (see section 4.3.2):

(a) The changed sort becomes equivalent with a current supersort.

(b) The as yet equivalent sorts become subsorts of the changed sort.

(c) Current supersorts can become sorts that will only overlap with the changed sort.

(d) The intersections with other sorts will become larger.

(e) Disjoint sorts can become subsorts or sorts which have an intersection with the changed sort.

The cases (a) and (b) are not relevant changes of the taxonomy. If a current supersort does not contain the new term (case (c)), it will then no longer be a supersort; and it is likely either that the term does not belong to the sort, i.e., that the fact is really not sort-correct, or that the term should also belong to the supersort but has not been used yet in the predicates that belong to the supersorts. This case should be monitored by the system and notified to the user. Case (d) should be monitored to see whether there are relevant changes of the taxonomy as a result of the changed intersection sort, i.e., the compatibility of the term with the intersection sort should be checked. When the term already belongs to a currently disjoint sort (case (e)), the compatibility of these two sorts will change. This case, too, should be monitored by the system.

This enables us to define the compatibility of a term with a sort as follows.

A term t is compatible with a sort s, if and only if t does not belong to a sort disjoint from s, when t belongs to all supersorts of s, and when the term is compatible with all intersections of s that change.

$$\begin{aligned} \text{compatible(t,s)} \Leftrightarrow \neg\, \exists\text{c: } & (\text{class(s)} \in \text{dis(c)} \land \text{t} \in \text{cext(c))} \lor \\ & (\text{c} \in \text{supers(class(s))} \land \text{t} \notin \text{cext(c))} \lor \\ & (\text{c} \in \text{inters(class(s))} \land \text{t} \in \text{cext(c)} \land \\ & \neg\, \text{compatible(t,\{c,class(s)\})}) \end{aligned}$$

4.4.2 The Sort-correctness of Rules and Inferences

As in the case of the sort-correctness of facts where the compatibility of terms with the argument sorts is used for the definition, the compatibility of variables with argument sorts is used to define the sort-correctness of rules. To this end, a class from the sort lattice is assigned to each variable.

Let V be the set of all variables, then the function

$$\text{var\_sort: V} \longrightarrow \text{pset(SN)}$$

assigns to each variable the set of sorts to which the variable belongs. This means that terms substituted for this variable must belong to all these sorts, i.e. to the intersection of these sorts. Let us extend class accordingly:

$$\begin{aligned} &\text{class}(\{\}) = \text{class(TERM)} \\ &\text{class}(\{s_1, s_2, \ldots, s_n\}) = \text{class}(s_1) \sqcap \text{class}(\{s_2, \ldots, s_n\}) \end{aligned}$$

This sort of variables will then provide the quantification domain of the variable, i.e. a rule in which the variable occurs can only be applied to the terms that belong to the sort of the variable. When, say, cough syrup is the sort of the variable X, the following rule holds for cough syrup but not for pill:

∀ X:take(P,X) ⇒ drink(P,X)

A variable may only be replaced by terms that belong to the sort of variables. A substitution $\sigma = \{V_1/t_1,\ldots,V_n/t_n\}$ is sort-correct, iff all terms belong to the sorts of the variables they are substituted for:

$$\text{sort-correct}(\ \{V_1/t_1,\ldots,V_n/t_n\}\ ) \Leftrightarrow \forall\ i_{1..n} : t_i \in \text{cext}(\text{class}(\text{var\_sort}(V_i)))$$

For all substitutions in a formula to produce sort-correct formulae the sort of the argument position where the variable occurs must be a supersort of the variable sort. When a variable occurs in several argument positions in a formula, the sort of the variable must be smaller than any of the argument sorts. In the rule

contains(A,W) & affect_pos(W,K) → affect_pos(A,K),

for example, the sort of the variable W must be both a subsort of the argument sort of the second argument of **contains** and a subsort of the argument sort of the first argument of **affect_pos**; and the variable A must be both a subsort of the argument sort of the first argument of **contains** and a subsort of the argument sort of the first argument of **affect_pos**. Our sort lattice has exactly one largest sort which is smaller than a set of sorts, namely the meet of the set of sorts. In our sort lattice this is the intersection sort of the set of sorts. Consequently, a variable sort must be smaller than or equal to the intersection sort of the respective argument position sorts.

In order to define sort-correctness we need a function which provides for a variable V and a formula F the set of all argument sorts:

$$\text{oc: V,F} \longrightarrow \text{pset(SN)}$$

Using the extended class function as above, this is the intersection of the argument sorts to which the variable in the formula is bound, for example:

$$\text{oc}(v,p(v,w) \wedge q(v,v)) = \{\text{arg\_sort}(1,p),\text{arg\_sort}(1,q),\text{arg\_sort}(2,q)\}$$

A formula F with the variables $V_1, \ldots, V_n$ is sort-correct when every variable sort is not empty and smaller or equal to the intersection sort of the argument sorts where the variable occurs:

$$\text{sort-correct(F)} \Leftrightarrow \forall\ V_{1..n}\text{: class}(\text{var\_sort}(V_i)) \neq \text{class}(\mathsf{NIL}) \wedge \\ \text{class}(\text{var\_sort}(V_i)) \leq \text{class}(\text{oc}(V_i,\text{F}))$$

As the intersection sort of sorts is always represented in our lattice, the system can use it as a sort for a variable in a rule where there is no explicitly assigned variable. Then, we have:

$$\text{sort-correct}(R) \Leftrightarrow \forall\, V_{1..n}\text{: class}(\text{oc}(V_i,R)) \neq \text{class}(\mathsf{NIL}) \wedge \\ \text{var\_sort}(V_i) = \text{oc}(V_i,R)$$

When this definition of the variable sort in rules is used, and sort-correct substitutions are made in inference processes, then inferences will always be in harmony with the current sort taxonomy. However, rules that are not sort-correct, i.e. rules where the sort of a variable is in the same class as NIL, are no longer used to infer facts when sort-correct substitutions are made in inference processes as there are no terms that can be substituted for this variable. This confronts us with the problem that inferences cannot help improve the taxonomy, as substitutions are based on the sort membership of terms that are still to be acquired. Consequently, we will resort to the normal substitution in inference processes. Then, however, we are faced with the problem that it is possible to use sort-correct rules and facts to infer not sort-correct facts, for example, the sort-correct fact `not (take(fred,aspirin))` and the sort-correct rule

$$\mathsf{not(take(}V_1,V_2\mathsf{))} \rightarrow \mathsf{not(drink(}V_1,V_2\mathsf{))}$$

can be used to infer the fact `not(drink(fred,aspirin)` that is not sort-correct. This fact would transfer aspirin into the sort liquid, something which should not happen. Consequently, we restrict the sort-correctness of rules to ensure that such cases are excluded.

A rule $\mathsf{P} \rightarrow \mathsf{K}$ with variables $V_i, \ldots, V_n$ is sort-correct, iff both premise P and conclusion C are sort-correct according to the former definition; and the intersection sorts of the argument position sorts that result for the variables of the premise are subsorts of the intersection sorts of the argument sorts that result for the variables of the conclusion. This means that the intersection sorts of the premise are smaller than the corresponding intersection sorts of the conclusion:

$$\begin{aligned} \text{sort-correct}(\mathsf{P} \rightarrow \mathsf{K}) \Leftrightarrow \forall\, V_{i..n} :\ & \text{class}(\text{oc}(V_i,\text{P})) \neq \text{class}(\text{NIL}) \wedge \\ & \text{class}(\text{oc}(V_i,\text{P})) \leq \text{class}(\text{oc}(V_i,\text{C}) \wedge \\ & \text{var\_sort}(V_i) = \text{oc}(V_i,\text{P}) \wedge \\ & \text{class}(\text{oc}(V_i,\text{P})) = \text{class}(\text{oc}(V_i,\mathsf{P} \rightarrow \mathsf{K})) \end{aligned}$$

This definition of sort-correct rules and sort-correct facts can only be used to infer sort-correct facts (they are in harmony with the taxonomy) given a normal substitution. Rules and facts that are not sort-correct but requested by the user are also used to make inferences entailing a modification of the taxonomy.

4.4.3 Monitoring the User Input

The definitions of sort-correct facts and rules enable the system the check whether the user inputs sort-correct facts and rules. This can help to avoid errors such as those that arise from the exchanging of arguments. Let us, for example, assume that given the state of the model as illustrated in figure 4.5 the user enters the fact

contains(ass,alka_seltzar)

The system knows from previous facts that ass is a term of the sort active_agent and that active_agent and drug are so far disjoint sorts. In this fact, however, ass issued as a term of the sort drug. The system alerts the user that this fact conflicts with the current model, but that it can be in harmony with the current model when the arguments are exchanged. However, if the user insists on the fact being correct, the input will be accepted and the model will be modified accordingly.

Similarly, the system recognizes a rule that is not sort-correct. The user is then alerted that this rule can lead to the inference of facts that contradict the current sort lattice. However, if the user insists on the rule being correct, the inferences will be made and the sort lattice will be adjusted to accommodate the inferred facts.

However, monitoring only ensures the sort-correctness of rules and facts in relation to the current sort lattice. Rules that were sort-correct on input can, for example, become not sort-correct when conflicting facts are entered and the user insists on them being sort-correct. Then the old rules can serve to infer facts that are no longer sort-correct. Such a case is usually difficult for the user to realize but can hardly be avoided owing to the incrementality of the acquisition. Of course, it is possible only to recognize what conflicts with the current sort taxonomy, and not with the user's intentions.

4.4.4 Pruning the Hypothesis Space Through Sort-correctness

The definition of sort-correct rules can also be used to avoid making rule hypotheses that are not sort-correct. The important reason that such a hypothesis should not be made is that according to the first definition of sort-correctness of rules it is not possible to verify rules that are not sort-correct using the current fact knowledge.

The sort taxonomy and thus sort-correctness results from the sorting of the terms of all facts in the knowledge base. If a rule is not sort-correct, the knowledge base cannot have any conjunction of facts which can be counted as an instance of the rule. For a rule which has a variable that is bound to incompatible argument positions, i.e., the meet of these argument positions is NIL, there can be no facts as instances of this rule. The reason for this is that there are no facts which have a term that occurs in all the argument positions that were bound to this variable, since otherwise the intersection of these argument positions would contain at least this term. Consequently, fact knowledge cannot be used to verify these hypotheses.

We give an example (see section 4.1.1) to illustrate the pruning of the hypothesis space by sort-correctness. When we take the metapredicate w_transitive(P,Q,R): P(X,Y) & Q(Y,Z) $\rightarrow$ R(X,Z), we obtain 5^3 =125 hypotheses with this three-place metapredicate and 5 two-place predicates without a sort logic. When the automatically acquired argument-sort-lattice illustrated in figure 4.5 is used, only three hypotheses are possible:

w_transitive(affect_pos,indicate,affect_pos)
w_transitive(affect_pos,cause,affect_pos)
w_transitive(contains,affect_pos,affect_pos)

This illustrates how much computation is saved by the automatically built sort-taxonomy. User specified sorts regularly save less hypotheses as they do not reflect the current state of the fact base but its intended state.

4.5 The Sort Taxonomy Tool

4.5.1 Operation Modes of the Sort Taxonomy

The sort taxonomy tool STT is the implementation within MOBAL of what is formally described in this chapter. For efficiency reasons, STT works in three different modes, which can be set in its parameter sort_processing_mode:

- off: No sorts are precomputed. A change from update or delay to this mode clears the sort taxonomy immediately. Queries from other tools, e.g. a hypothesis sort compatibility query from RDT are computed on the fly.

- **update**: This is the incremental mode in which the sort taxonomy is continuously updated as new knowledge items are entered into the system. A change from **delay** or **off** to this mode causes immediate update/computation of the sort taxonomy.

- **delay**: This the non-incremental mode in which modifications of the knowledge base are collected, but the taxonomy is not adjusted to them. In this mode, the user may explicitly call for an update (Update Sorts in the Call menu). This mode was introduced for efficiency reasons. From the specification of the basic update operations in section 4.3.2 it is easy to see that the computational effort of changing the sorts extensions is nearly independent from the number of terms changed. So it is much faster to delay STT, make several knowledge base changes and then update STT for all changes together, than to update STT for each change.

The sort taxonomy, calculated by STT, gives an overview of the actual state of the fact base (in the sorts window, accessed via MOBAL's Windows menu). A graphical presentation, as shown in figure 4.10, is also available (double-click on a sort in the sorts window). The taxonomy is used by the user for inspection and by the system to check the sort compatibility of new facts and rules (rule hypotheses). If a sort taxonomy has been calculated and the STT parameter **check_for_well_sortedness** is set to **on**, the arguments of new facts will be checked for compatibility with the current taxonomy. If an input causes two previously disjunct sort classes to intersect, or a term to be entered into a class even though it is not a member of the superclass, then MOBAL issues a warning to that effect.

As we have already noted (see section 4.2.5), the most time consuming part and, in the worst case, even intractable part of the algorithm is the generation of intersection sorts. Therefore the user can select whether intersection sorts are to be built or not with the parameter **generate_intersection_sorts**.

The user can also specify which sorts are maintained by STT via two parameters (**argument_sorts** and **user_sorts**). They can specify whether argument sorts should be always maintained, maintained only if there is no user sort specified for this argument position, or not maintained at all. The maintenance of user sort specification can also be turned on or off. If these parameters are changed, the involved sorts are added to or deleted from the sort taxonomy.

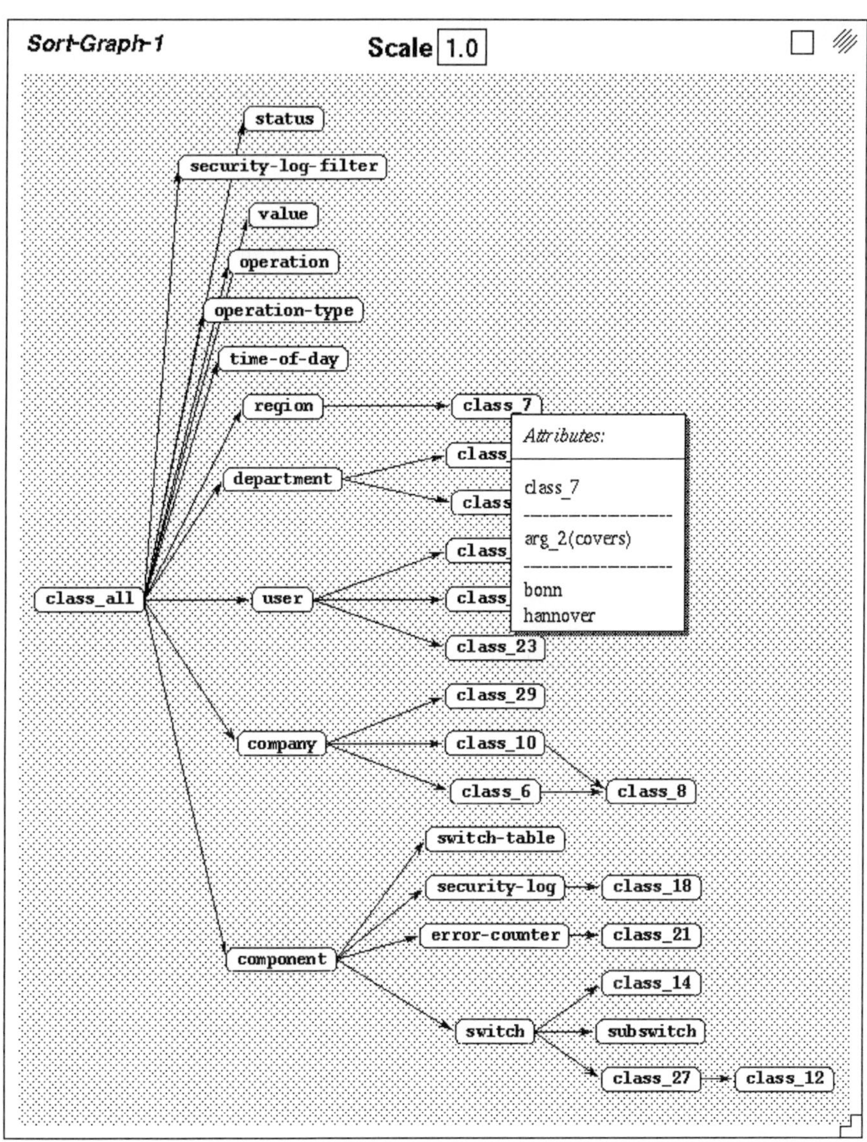

Figure 4.10: The Graphical Interface for STT

4.5.2 Generating User Sort Specifications

STT enables the user to transfer the automatically acquired and maintained sort taxonomy into the user sort formalism. This operation is useful for freezing an archived state of domain modeling. As the automatically built relations between sorts are based on the current fact knowledge, the acquired sort taxonomy changes if new facts are acquired. But, this is possibly not the users intention if the taxonomy has reached a "correct" state. Therefore, the system enables the user to transfer the acquired descriptive taxonomy of argument sorts into the prescriptive user sort formalism. This operation asks the user for a user sort name for each equivalence class[7], builds predicate declarations with these acquired user sort names, transfers the d-subclass relation between classes into the :< relations between the acquired user sort names, and intersection sorts within classes into sort definition using the := relation.

[7]If an equivalence class already contains a user sort this name is proposed.

Chapter 5

The Predicate Structure

5.1 The Tasks of the PST

This chapter describes predicate topologies and the predicate structuring tool, PST, which builds and manages topologies. As its main task, it allows the user better inspection of the knowledge base, since to understand a knowledge base, the user must see its overall structure. There exist multiple types of data, which can be structured; in MOBAL, one of these types is the objects, which are structured into a taxonomy by STT (chapter 4). Additionally, the predicates can be structured: this is the task of PST. A simple kind of presentation of a structure of the predicates is to draw a rule graph of the knowledge base, but in large knowledge bases, it is not possible to present the whole graph on the screen at once. Normally, the user has to focus on a small part of the graph, thus losing the survey of the knowledge und its structure. A mechanism to focus is therefore not sufficient.

We search for another way to handle this problem by using *abstraction*. The goal of the abstraction is to neglect local dependencies of the rule graph by merging similar predicates to classes. Then, the nodes of an abstract rule graph represent a class of predicates. The links of the graph are abstracted inferential dependencies. In MOBAL, such a graph is called *topology*. It supports users in inspecting large knowledge bases.

The described merge reduces the number of nodes of a rule graph as well as the number of links. If the abstraction is well chosen, the abstract graph can be drawn on the screen at once and it presents an understandable structure of the knowledge base. It is one goal of this chapter is to describe algorithms for building a topology by abstraction (section 5.3).

KADS [Wielinga and Breuker, 1986] handles the problem of structuring in a comparable way. In this approach, the inference structure is represented by the inference layer. Meta-classes heap up concepts and relations, the dependencies between meta-classes are described by knowledge sources. Since in MOBAL, concepts and relations are represented by predicates, the nodes of a topology correspond to meta-classes. Because MOBAL uses rules to describe the dependencies of predicates, the links of a topology, representing possible rules, correspond to the knowledge sources of KADS.

However, inspection is not the only task of the predicate structuring tool. Like the other tools of MOBAL, it allows not only the automatic generation of topologies, but also the users to enter topologies manually, so they can also define the inference structure. This follows from the balanced cooperative modeling paradigm. Since they know about the semantics of the predicates, they are able to define the depedencies of sets of predicates in terms of a topology graph. Users can do so, even if they do not know the particular rules. The learning algorithm of MOBAL uses this information to restrict the hypothesis space to those rules which are semantically sensible. So the performance increases and the learning of senseless rules is restricted. Both mechanisms, the abstraction of rule graphs and the reduction of the hypothesis space are decribed in section 5.4.

A third problem, that could be solved by the predicate structuring tool is the representation of a task structure. Clancey [Clancey, 1986] demands that the definition of tasks and subtasks control the problem-solving mechanism. KADS follows this idea with the *task layer*. The user may interpret the topology as a task structure. The top node contains the solution predicates; the bottom nodes contain the input predicates. The links, from bottom to top, are inference steps of classifications. So, all tasks can be modeled as a sequence of classifications where the ranges of the classifications are described by the topology. However, problem-solving strategies such as heuristic classification or divide-and-conquer, cannot be discriminated by topologies. Moreover, the inference strategy of IM-2 is fixed and cannot be guided by a topology. Therefore, a topology is only a reduced mechanism for describing the task layer.

The predicate structuring tool supports the user as well as other tools in various ways:

Inspectability: The user must be able to get an overview of the knowledge base, and realize more global structures. This is supported by the PST.

Modularization: The user can define modules of the knowledge base, the interfaces of two modules being described by edges between nodes of the modules. To do so is provided by PST.

Task-oriented representation: The user can give a task structure by using PST. This structure can differ from the given rule base.

Reduction of the hypothesis space: The rule discovery tool (RDT) uses the PST to restrict the learnable rules to those rules which are compatible with the topology.

Focusing the learning: The difference between the user-given task oriented topology and a system-generated topology can be used for focusing the learning on interesting rules.

Automatic generation of a topology: PST generates the overall inference structure of the knowledge base by abstracting the rule graph.

5.2 PST: Representation and Operations

In MOBAL it is possible to create as many topologies as the user likes[1]. Every topology is a directed acyclic graph, a DAG. All predicates of the knowledge base are attached to the nodes of the graph. The edges of a topology define possible or desired inferences, depending on the purpose of this topology. Every topology contains an special node, which is assumed to be adjacent to all of the others. It is called *basic node*. All unclassified predicates are attached to this node.

The nodes of the topologies are described by the six-ary Prolog-predicate

tnode (ID, Nodename, Comment, Predicates, Links, Topologyname)

ID: The ID is a unique internal number for access by the system. The exception is the basic node of a topology, it has the ID Topologyname:basic_node.

Nodename: The name serves for access by the user and must be given by him.

Comment: Additional information given by the user.

---

[1]At least one topology must exist, that is normally called `system`.

Predicates: A list of predicates of the knowledge base attached to this node.

Links: A list of the predecessors of this node. The predecessors are represented by their ID.

Topologyname: This argument determines the topology to which the node belongs.

5.2.1 The Interface of the PST

The topology of predicates can be inspected and modified by the user. The interface to the topology provides the following operations to the user:

- the presentation of a topology,
- commands for adding and deleting nodes,
- commands for adding and deleting links,
- commands for attaching and deattaching predicates to or from nodes,
- a command for creating new topologies, and
- a command for generating a topology as an abstract rule graph.

The MOBAL-menu contains an item **New Topology Window** to open such a window. MOBAL asks the user for the topology he wants to open if more than one exists. Then MOBAL opens a window like the one shown in the lower part of figure 5.1.

The nodes in this window have the following form:

NodeName/TopologyName
- $[Pred_1, \ldots, Pred_n]$
<- $[Link_1, \ldots, Link_m]$

The topology name will not be printed if it is the standart topology system and the links will not be printed if the set is empty. The links will be printed by their nodenames instead of their IDs.

Entering and Deleting Topology Nodes Topology nodes are entered via the MOBAL-scratchpad. The scratchpad format is the same as the format of the presentation of nodes, only the keyword **tnode**: should precede the entry. A comment can precede the input.

The user is subject to the following restrictions:

- The names of nodes must be unique relative to all topologies. If a node with the same name exists, the system appends the first number n to the name of the new node, that makes the nodename unique.
- The input of comment is optional; if it is not given, the comment of the node stays uninstantiated.
- The input of Preds and Links are also optional.
- If the set of predicates is not empty, the system attaches these predicates to the new node and removes them from all other nodes of this topology. Unknown predicates are ignored.
- If the set of links is not empty, all links that imply no cycles are added. If a link implies a cycle, the system asks the user whether it should shrink this cycle to one node or ignore this link. Unknown predecessors produce entries in the agenda of MOBAL (described in section 5.2.3).

Deleting of nodes can be forced by clicking the button **Delete** of the command-stack of this node. The predicates of this node will be classified to the basic node of this topology by the system.

Entering and Deleting of Links The user can add new links to a node by clicking **Add Link**. He can enter a single predecessor or a list of predecessors that will be added to the topology. The predecessors must be given by the nodename or by the ID. If the new link creates cycles the same procedure as for entering new nodes will proceed.

By clicking **Remove Link** the user can delete a single link or a set of links.

Adding and Removing Predicates This is analogous to adding links, if the user clicks **Add Preds**. The specified predicates are removed from the old nodes they are attached to and are then attached to the given node.

Clicking **Remove Pred** and entering a single predicate or a list of predicates will force an attaching of these predicates to the basic node of the topology.

Creating New Topologies The user can create an additional topology by choosing the item **Create New Topology** of the MOBAL-menu. He must enter a new name for this topology. The created topology consists of a single node, the basic node. All predicates of the knowledge base are attached to this node.

Generating an Abstraction of the Inference Structure If the user clicks the menu item *Generate Topology*, the system offers several algorithms amon which the user can choose. A detailed description of the algorithms follows in section 5.3.

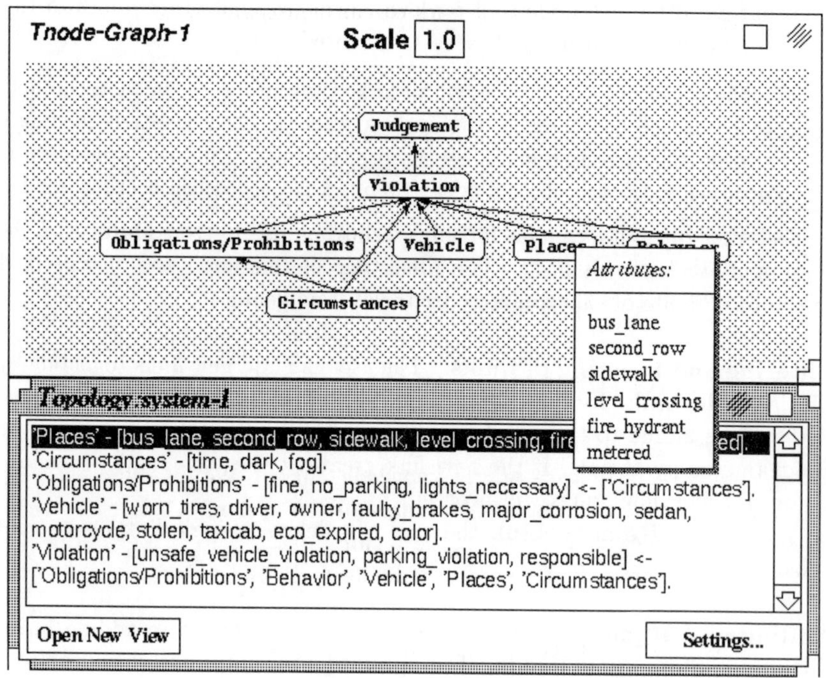

Figure 5.1: The User-Given Topology of the Domain TRAFFIC-LAW

5.2.2 The Graphic Interface

There is also a graphical presentation of the topology. The user is not able to change the topology itself by this interface, but may inspect the topology. It is possible to create as many graphics as the user likes, each in its own window. The graphic will be displayed when the user clicks the button **Graphic** on the command-stack of a node. He has to distinguish two cases:

- The chosen node is the basic node. In this case, the whole topology will be displayed. Isolated nodes like the basic node will not be displayed because they are not relevant for the structure of the knowledge base. Figure 5.1 shows such an output.

- The chosen node is not the basic node. This node and all adjacent nodes with the connecting edges will be displayed. This is a focused presentation of the topology, which can be expanded.

5.2.3 The Agenda

The agenda of open ends handles tasks that the user has still to do. For all open ends the system generates an agenda entry that marks this task. For PST there exists only one kind of agenda entry. If the user enters a link to a not yet existing node, MOBAL produces an entry to mark that the user has to define that node. After inserting the missing node, the system automatically creates the edge and removes the agenda entry.

5.3 The Automatic Generation of a Topology

This section is about the automatic generation of a topology by abstracting the inference structure of the knowledge base. We introduce several techniques to build such an abstraction, and the user may select the technique that is to be applied. All of the techniques use the rule graph of the knowledge base: thus, first we have to define and build this rule graph.

5.3.1 Building the Rule Graph

In our context, the *rule graph* is a directed, possibly cyclic graph with exactly one node for every predicate that occurs in a rule. Two nodes are linked by an edge, if there is a rule with the predicate of the start node in the list of premises of that rule and the predicate of the target node as the conclusion. A recursive occurrence of a predicate, i.e. both as a premise and as a conclusion of a rule, will not cause an edge. Figure 5.2 shows the graphs of two rules.

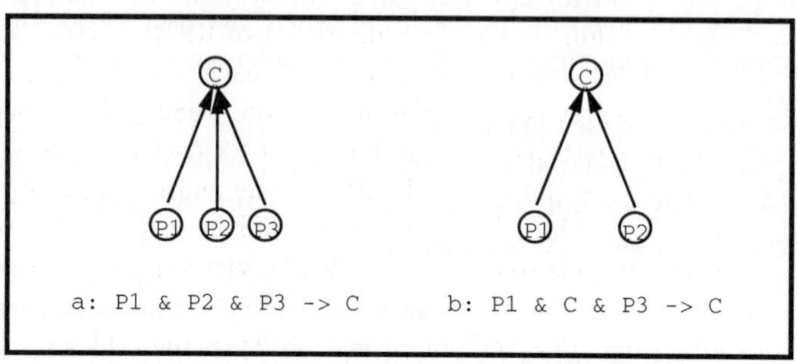

Figure 5.2: Rules and their Resulting Graphs

In MOBAL, it is possible to use special predicates. These are autoepistemic operators[2], built-in-operators[3] and the operator `not`. For all these operators, the operator itself is not used in the rule graph. Instead, the arguments of the operator are checked to see whether they are predicates of the knowledge base, and if this is the case, these arguments are used to build the rule graph.

Thus, the algorithm for each rule is:

1. Collect all premises of this rule.

2. Generate for every premise a topology node, if it does not yet exist.

3. Generate also for the conclusion a node, if it does not yet exist.

4. Enter for every premise of the rule an edge from this premise node to the conclusion node.

5.3.2 Shrinking of Strong Components

Here, we describe the first algorithm for abstracting the rule graph. Subgraphs of a directed graph are said to be strong components, if, for all pairs

[2] `max_of, count, sum_of, unknown.`

[3] Basic computations (`add, sub, prod, div`), comparisons (`eq,neq,gt,lt,ge,le`).

of nodes i and j, there exists a directed path from i to j and back. Strong components consists of at least one cycle and shrinking of all strong components leads to an acyclic graph [Lawler, 1976]. This is a handy abstraction, since normally the computations in such cycles are local, and local computations are not sufficient for understanding the structure of a knowledge base. Thus the first algorithm is the $O(n)$ algorithm of R. E. Tarjan [Sedgewick, 1988] to find the strong components and shrink each to one node. The nodes are visited in depth-first search (like in [Nilsson, 1982]). If a node can be visited twice in one path, a cycle is found. This cycle will be shrunk by backtracing the path to the first node of the cycle and merging all the nodes of the path together. Links inside the cycle will be lost by this operation, links from inside the cycle to a node outside and vice versa will be conserved.

5.3.3 Merging Nodes Depending on Neighborhoods

Shrinking of strong components alone is not a sufficient abstraction. The reduction of a graph is too small. Thus we need additional operations. We present in this section operations based on similarities of the predecessors and successors of a node. The predicate structuring tool contains two algorithms with these operations.

- Merging nodes with the same predecessors.
- Merging nodes with the same successors.

Figure 5.3 shows examples for these two cases and also, in part a, the case that both predecessors and successors must be equal. This was the first attempt to handle this kind of abstraction.

The first algorithm merges nodes with predicates that depend on similar premises. Thus, they describe similar conclusions, so their merging is an abstraction that does not destroy much information about the structure. Also, it is sensible to merge nodes whose predicates are used to infer the same conclusions. They are predicates describing a special class of "input"-premises.

The linked pairs of predicates grows monotonically by using these algorithms. And in only one very special case of a strong connected component with exactly two nodes and the same predecessors *and* successors, the growing is only monotonous and not strictly monotonic.

Additionally, the application of the algorithms will not lead to new cycles, because a new cycle has to visit a predecessor or a successor of the merged

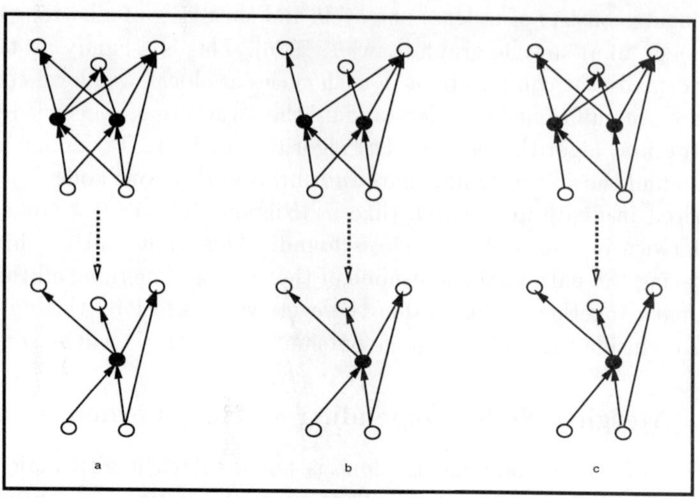

Figure 5.3: Merging of Nodes

node, and, because of the equality of the predecssors or the successors of the two original nodes, the same path must have existed before the merge.

First we had some trouble with the sequence of visiting the nodes because the merge of two nodes can imply new possibilities for merging other nodes. So we need an order which guarantees all possible merges. Regular breadth-first search order cannot do this because we can have multiple paths to a node. Figure 5.4(b) shows a situation where nodes 1 and 3 both have paths from node 0 of length one. So it is arbitrary whether a breadth-first search visits node 1 first or node 3. However, if node 1 is visited first, and nodes with same predecessors are merged, nodes 1 and 2 are first merged and then nodes 3 and 4, because now they have the same predecessor. Thus, we need an order, which guarantees to visit first nodes 1 and 2 and then 3 and 4. This is done by the topological order, that means, direct and indirect successors of a node in the graph are also successors relative to the order.

A topological order can be found by a modified depth-first search. Normally, in depth-first search, the visited node is handled first and then the successors of this node are visited. If we handle the node *after* visiting succeeding nodes, we have a reverse topological order. Thus we can control the

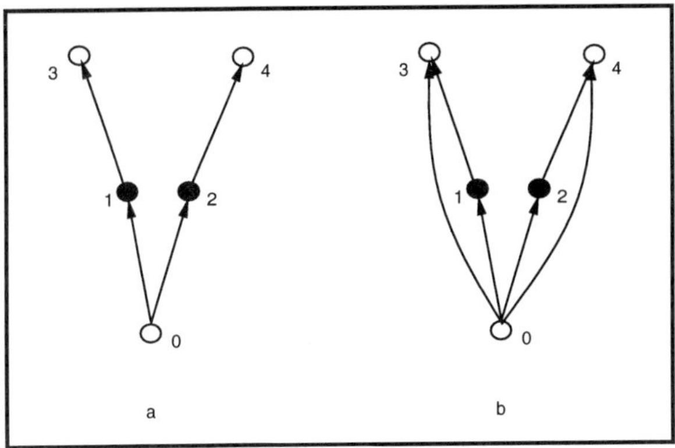

Figure 5.4: Problems with the Control Structure

merge as follows:

Same predecessors: We use the modified depth-first search to visit the graph contrary to the directions of the edges. So the order is topological, the search handles the predecessor-free nodes first.

Same successors: The modified depth-first search visits the graph normally, the resulting order is the reverse topological order. The search handles the successor-free nodes first.

Both algorithms lead to a merging of all mergeable pairs of nodes, running an algorithm twice will not imply new merges. They run in time $O(n^2)$ for n nodes, $O(n)$ to visit every node and $O(n)$ to search all mergeable partners for each node.

The abstractions described until now lead to graphs that can be easily inspected. However, we searched for more algorithms to handle special cases and greater domains.

Merging of Outsiders Sometimes there exist some nodes attached by only one predicate and linked to only one other node. These nodes we call outsiders. There is no loss of structure if we drag these nodes into the graph by merging them with the linked node. The time needed to find and merge all outsiders is $O(n)$. So this procedure was added to the mechanisms of abstraction.

Merging of Successor-free Nodes Sometimes, if the domain has a special target task, it can be useful to merge all top level nodes of the graph. That leads to a topology with only one target node. In our domains, the result of this operation was a loss of structure, so we do not use this operation for the abstraction.

Other Methods Although the results of the algorithms above are good, we investigated other methods based on graph theory to find incremental algorithms. We tried to use cut sets (like in the flow theory) but there are too many distinct cut sets and it is not possible to choose one of them. Therefore, we did not introduce any of these algorithms into our abstraction.

5.3.4 The Application of the Algorithms by the User

PST contains the parameter **pst_generating_algorithms**. This parameter consists of a list of names of algorithms, which will be applied to the rule base, if the user choose the MOBAL-menu entry **Generate Topology**. The possible items of the list are:

generate: PST will build the rule graph of the knowledge base and shrink the strong components to nodes with the name cycle_n.

top_down: The graph will be visited by reverse topological order to merge all nodes with the same successors.

bottom_up: The graph will be visited in topological order to merge all nodes with the same predecessors.

merge_top_level_nodes: The successor-free nodes will be merged.

merge_outsiders: The outsiders of the graph will be dragged into him.

All algorithms specified by **pst_generating_algorithms** are applied to the topology as is determined by the parameter **pst_topology_for_generating**. The order of the application of the algorithms is also determined by the parameter, and it is allowed, but possibly senseless, to use an algorithm more than once.

5.4 Topology-influenced Learning

MOBAL's learning tool RDT is a model-based algorithm. The hypothesis space is restricted by:

- rule models,
- the arity compatibility of the predicates and the predicate variables in the rule models,
- the sort compatibilities, based on user entered sorts or argument sort build by STT.

There are two main reasons to restrict the hypothesis space also by PST. First, if the user enters a topology, he gives the system a task structure. Learning by induction always contains the danger of learning senseless rules, if there is a basis for these rules in the knowledge base. Thus it is wise to use the given task structure to prevent the generation of senseless hypotheses by allowing only those that are compatible with the task structure. Second, the restriction of the hypothesis space reduces the time needed to test this space, so that learning becomes faster.

5.4.1 Restriction of the Hypothesis Space

PST enables a definition of rules that are admissible:

> A rule is *admissible* relative to a topology
> if the premises are attached only to nodes which are either
> predecessors of the conclusion node or this node itself.

Extended to pairs of predicates, the compatibility of predicates is defined as:

> A pair of predicates (i.e. a premise and a conclusion)
> is topology *compatible*
> if the premise is attached to a predecessor
> of the conclusion node, or to this node itself.

The relation of predecessors is not used transitively. The basic node of the used topology is an extraordinary node. The predicates of this node are compatible to all other predicates of the knowledge base.

5.4.2 Focusing of Learning

PST defines a special technique to focus on interesting hypotheses. The user is allowed to build different topologies for different tasks that are to be solved using the same basic set of knowledge. For instance, knowledge on drugs with their positive and negative effects can be used for recommending the best drug given a particular disease as well as for finding those drugs that should be put on a black-list. A third task to be solved using the same knowledge of drugs could be to find drugs for special types of people, e.g. those who are allergic to a certain substance or those who have a certain heart disease. Each topology can be used to focus the learning on those rules that are of interest for a special task. Depending on the selected topology, different rules will be learned.

A special case that can be used for further focusing learning is that a user-selected topology differs from the system-built topology. There are three kinds of a predicate pair, in principle:

1. The pair is not compatible relative to the user-selected topology. That means, the user does not want a rule with this combination.

2. The pair is compatible with both of the topologies. Then the combination of predicates is desired by the user, and the generated topology shows that such a combination really exists in the knowledge base.

3. The pair of predicates is compatible with respect to the user-selected topology, but it is not compatible with the one generated by PST. The user wants to have rules with this combination, but these do not yet exist. These pairs are very interesting for learning.

Corresponding to these three possible combinations, there are three possible uses of PST to restrict learning. The way PST restricts learning can be chosen using a parameter of RDT, called **rdt_topology_restriction**. This parameter can get one of three values:

no: The topology is not used to restrict the hypothesis space.

yes: The hypothesis space consists of rules which are compatible with the topology given by the parameter **pst_topology_for_learning**.

focus: The hypothesis space of the previous case is additionally restricted to hypotheses which are not compatible with the topology defined by the parameter **pst_topology_for_focusing**. That means, learning is

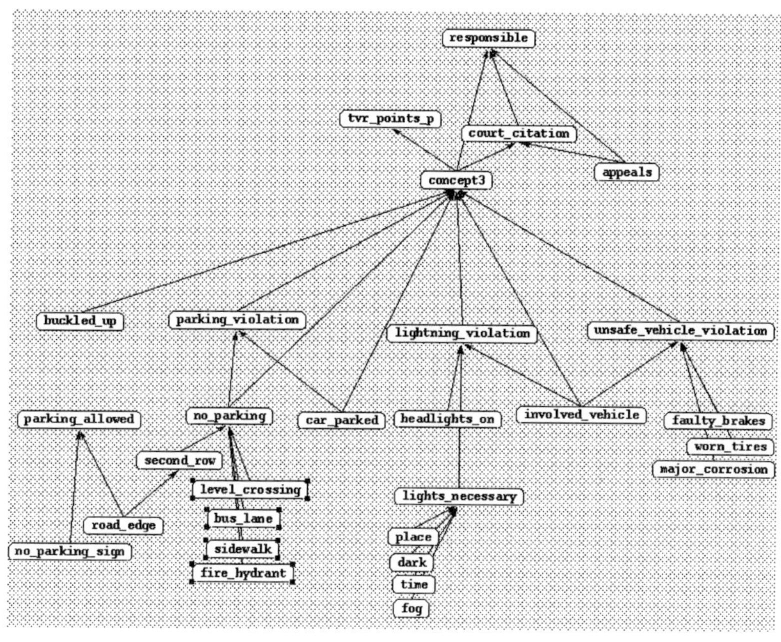

Figure 5.5: The Rule Graph of TRAFFIC-LAW

focused on rules which are compatible with the user-given topology but not (yet) with the system-built topology.

The user has to pay attention to the following aspects when using the parameters:

- If the user applies focused learning, the two topologies have to be different. Otherwise, the system restricts the hypothesis space only as usual, not focused.
- The selection of the topologies is unrestricted. The topologies need not be chosen as in the argument above, the first user-selected, the second system-generated.
- The topologies must exist. The user cannot choose other topologies by the human-computer interface.

5.5 Results

We have used PST to generate the topologies of two domains. The first is a small domain to test the several learning algorithms and to make understandable demonstrations of these algorithms. The domain handles the German traffic law. It consists of 22 rules and 42 predicates. The rule graph of the domain is shown in figure 5.5. We applied the algorithms **generate**, **top_down** and **bottom_up** to this knowledge base. The result is stated in figure 5.6[4].

The topology contains five larger groups of predicates:

sidewalk: the places of the domain.

no_parking: places and vehicles are related to the events.

parking_violation: the several violations of the knowledge base.

lights_necessary: some states of vehicles.

time: external conditions, influencing the classification of events.

Next we tested the generation of hypotheses with this topology. Five tests were made, none of which involved pruning the hypothesis space and restricting the space by the taxonomy of sorts, since these restrictions would have influenced the results. The five tests were:

[4] The nodes are named by an arbitrary representative of the attached set of predicates.

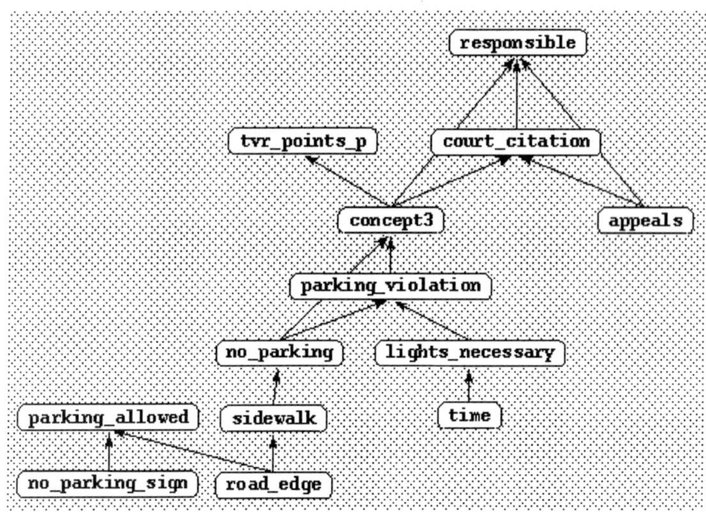

Figure 5.6: The Generated Topology of TRAFFIC LAW

1. No topology is used for learning.

2. The topology given by the user is applied.

3. The topology generated by PST is used.

4. Same as the previous, but without the unclassified predicates attached to the basic node.

5. Both topologies are used for focused learning.

We conducted the fourth experiment because the existence of unclassified predicates enlarges the hypothesis space enormously. Figure 5.7 shows the results of our experiment.

The second domain we used to test the algorithms of PST is a large medical domain, ICTERUS, containing 267 rules for 127 predicates. We applied all of our algorithms excluding only merging the top-level nodes to build a topology. The number of nodes which could be merged and the degree of reduction of nodes is presented in figure 5.8. Although the resulting graph is

	number of hypotheses	time to	test hypotheses
no topology	ca. 700 000	ca. 7-8	days
user topology	2 331	37	minutes
system topology	ca. 400 000	ca. 4	days
reduced system topology	2 042	31	minutes
focused learning	263	4	minutes

Figure 5.7: Results of the Restrictions of Learning

	#nodes	#edges	degree of reduction	#merged nodes
rule graph	125			
strong components	117	234	6 %	8
top-down	74	172	37 %	43
bottom-up	56	129	24 %	18
merge-outsiders	49	122	14 %	7
total	49	122	61 %	76

Figure 5.8: Results of the Generation of a Topology

not very small, users could indeed identify the several tasks of their medical application.

5.5.1 Discussion

Our approach to building the topology has several advantages. First, the user gets an easily understandable overview over the knowledge base. He is supported in understanding the structure of the knowledge base by the built topology. Since the algorithms are not based on heuristics, the user can keep track of the merging of nodes very easily. Thus he knows which information was lost during the abstraction.

Second, the built topology is consistent with the rule base. Because of the monotonic growth of the set of compatible predicate pairs, rules admissible at the beginning of the building are admissible at every stage of the process.

Third, the used algorithms are efficient. They all run in time $O(n^2)$. It is sufficient to apply an algorithms once in order to reduce the graph as much as it is possible by this algorithm. The merge-algorithms find all possible merges. Their choice of nodes to be merged guarantees that no new cycles arise.

The fourth advantage of our way of building an abstract rule structure is its generality. The flexibility in choosing the algorithms to be applied to the rule graph enables good abstractions for many different knowledge bases. For the future, it is easy to bind new, perhaps better algorithms into PST.

However, PST also shows some problems and directions for future work. The phase of building the rule graph causes a loss of context in the use of predicates within the rules. First, the information about the junctors is dropped. Possibly, it is better to hold such information incase there is a chance to make a better abstraction with them. The second idea for further research is the usage and analysis of the argument-sorts of the STT to identify similar predicates in different rules. This will push the purely syntactic operations towards more semantic ones. However, both extensions need a completely different representation and usage of the topology, which was not the scope of this work.

The only algorithm which can be applied incrementally is the shrinking of strong components. Thus we can use PST incrementally only if we want to restrict abstraction to that method.

PST offers a fixed criterion for the admissibility of rule-model instantiations. One way of reducing the hypothesis space even further is to attach a topology node to every predicate variable in a rule model. Whereas all premises are now treated equally, more specific admissibility conditions could be formulated if topology nodes were attached to predicate variables in a rule model. However, this approach contradicts the goal of presenting an abstracted overview of the rules to the user; hence, it would be an additional structuring for predicates, not an alternative one. In fact, for an application of MOBAL to a domain of failure messages of networks this additional structuring has been performed. Sets of predicates could be linked with predicate variables in rule models and the hypothesis space was thus further restricted.

PST does not influence the inference engine. Therefore, it cannot be used to define particular inference strategies for particular excerpts of a knowledge base as has been described by Clancey [Clancey, 1986].

Chapter 6

Model-driven Rule Discovery

6.1 Introduction

In a knowledge acquisition system built according to the *balanced cooperative modeling* paradigm, the learning modules play a very important role: they can be seen as *assistants* to the user that incrementally propose additions to the knowledge base based on the user's inputs. They thus constitute the automatic part of the iterative model building process of knowledge acquisition. As discussed in chapter 1, this role in a cyclic process has important consequences for the nature of the learning modules that are used. Most important of all, they must be able to incorporate their learning results into the existing knowledge base, and also use the existing knowledge base as the basis for further learning (*closed-loop learning*).

MOBAL contains three learning modules that cooperate to achieve the desired functionality in the balanced cooperative modeling context. RDT, the *rule discovery tool* to be described in this chapter, is responsible for inducing new rules based on facts that were input by the user, or derived from input or learned rules. Since RDT does not modify learned rules because of new input, a second module, KRT, the *knowledge revision tool* to be presented in chapter 7, is capable of incrementally refining rules that have been produced by RDT as soon as they have become incorrect with respect to newly entered information. Third and last, CLT, the *concept formation tool*, is responsible for learning concept definitions in the form of necessary and sufficient conditions for concept membership; it will be described in chapter 8.

In the rest of this chapter, we first introduce the learning problem faced by RDT (section 6.2). We then position our approach in comparison to other approaches to learning in logic (section 6.3), and introduce the general idea of model-driven learning (section 6.4). Section 6.5 contains a discussion of the exact forms of model knowledge used by RDT, and is followed by the description of the RDT algorithm proper (section 6.6). We conclude with a brief summary (section 6.7).

6.2 The Learning Task of RDT

The goal of RDT is to extend an evolving MOBAL knowledge base by inducing additional rules. More precisely then, in the classification given in section 1.3, the learning task of RDT is *concept learning from examples.* The examples are sets of facts which need not be given by the user as examples for the concept (i.e. the conclusion of the rule to be learned), but are gathered by the system. The learning task of RDT can be stated as follows. Given a background theory B, sets of positive examples E^+ and a set of negative examples E^- of the concept to learned (where B alone does not imply E^+ nor E^-), all expressed in MOBAL's knowledge representation, the task is to find an inductive hypothesis H (again expressed in MOBAL's knowledge representation) such that:

- background knowledge, hypothesis, and positive examples together are consistent ($B, H, E \not\models \bot$),
- background knowledge and hypothesis together imply the positive, but not the negative examples ($B, H \models E^+$, but $B, H \not\models E^-$).
- H is maximally general, i.e., RDT is a *most general discrimination* learner in the classification of section 1.3.

As described by Mitchell [Mitchell, 1982], this learning task can be understood as a process of search in a space of hypotheses that is ordered by the generality relationship between hypotheses. The size of this space and the properties of its generalization relation determine the difficulty of finding the desired target concept, i.e., a concept that covers all positive examples (completeness) and none of the negative examples (consistency). For attribute-based (propositional, feature-vector) formalisms, the space of hypotheses is finite, and there are only a few generalizations/specializations of any given hypothesis. As a result, it has been possible to construct very efficient learning programs for attribute-only languages, such as ID3 [Quinlan, 1983] and its successors.

As pointed out above, the representation for RDT is the representation of MOBAL, and thus not an attribute-based, but a first-order Horn clause formalism, albeit without function symbols. In the case of full first-order logic, the hypothesis space is of course infinite, and worse, the generalization relation has very bad properties. Since logical inference in the general case is undecidable, it is even undecidable whether a hypothesis covers an example, or whether one hypothesis is a generalization of another. In a language without function symbols as for RDT, logical inference is decidable; in particular, we even showed that inferences in MOBAL can be provided reasonably efficiently (cf. section 2.2).

Nonetheless, the size of the resulting hypothesis space is still enormous, so that additional measures are necessary to reduce the size of the space that is to be searched.

6.3 Other Approaches to Hypothesis Space Reduction

With the choice of a representation formalism, the designer of a learning system determines the maximal size of its hypothesis space. In the domain of learning in logical formalisms, such an implicit restriction on the size of the hypothesis space is used by nearly all learning methods. To our knowledge, full first-order logic is not used by any existing learning algorithm except Plotkin's relative least general generalization (RLLG) method [Plotkin, 1970], which uses definite clauses but was severely limited in its implementation[Muggleton, 1990]. Instead, most research concentrates on Horn clause logic (pure Prolog) and subclasses thereof, in particular the subclass of function-free Horn clause programs that is used in RDT (Datalog programs, [Ceri *et al.*, 1990]) in which the generalization relationship is decidable. This choice of representation was made in for example ARCH [Winston, 1975], INDUCE [Michalski, 1983], MARVIN [Sammut and Banerji, 1986], CLINT [De Raedt and Bruynooghe, 1989b], and FOIL [Quinlan, 1990]. MIS [Shapiro, 1983], even though operational in full Horn clause logic, suffered from complexity problems that prevented it from learning certain concepts even though they were in its hypothesis space [Muggleton, 1990]. Other programs that use full Horn clauses as their basic hypothesis space typically use other restrictions to reduce the size of the space (e.g. CIGOL, IRES, LFP2, or GOLEM, see below).

As the complexity of deciding inference is also directly related to the kind of background knowledge that is admitted (without background knowledge, the generalization relationship between two clauses is decidable, even though still NP-complete [Garey and Johnson, 1979]), many learning programs restrict the use of background knowledge to be only in the form of ground unit clauses (facts). In MARVIN [Sammut and Banerji, 1986], this is done by forward applying the available inference rules to generate additional facts about an example ("elaboration" of the example); in IRES [Rouveirol and Puget, 1989], a similar process is called *saturation*[1]. In GOLEM [Muggleton and Feng, 1990], a program based on an extension of Plotkin's relative least general generalization (RLLG) approach, the background knowledge is required to be "generative", which again means that all derived unit clauses will be ground. As we will see below, RDT uses the same technique, relying on MOBAL's inference engine to perform inferences with the available rules, thus converting background knowledge rules into facts.

Within the maximal hypothesis space defined by the representation, many learning programs in addition define subspaces to which they limit their search. This can be done either by restrictions on the language, or restrictions on the operators that search the hypothesis space. For example, DeRaedt's CLINT [De Raedt and Bruynooghe, 1989b] uses a series of languages that are defined by allowing increasingly more existential variables (variables not found in the head of the clause), and increasingly more relations between those variables. In GOLEM [Muggleton and Feng, 1990], the related notion of *ij-determinacy* is used that limits the indeterminate introduction of new variables in the body of a clause. It has recently been shown [Kietz, 1993], that no proper superset (i.e. indeterminate clauses and not depth-bounded determinate clauses) can be learned effiently.

The alternative way, i.e., using restricted operators, has been used in for example the CIGOL system [Muggleton and Buntine, 1988]. This system uses inverse resolution generalization operators (absorption and identification) that are in principle capable of producing any Horn clause expression, but are restricted to unit clauses to reduce their complexity. Rouveirol and Puget [Rouveirol and Puget, 1989] discuss the difficulties involved in removing

[1]Indeed, generalized subsumption with background knowledge is equivalent to θ-subsumption on saturated examples. This follows immediately from their properties as described in [Buntine, 1988] and [Rouveirol, 1991], cf. [Kietz, 1992; Jung, 1993].

this restriction for their IRES system. LFP2 [Wirth, 1989], also based on inverse resolution, is not restricted to unit-clauses, but uses restrictions on the inverse substitutions that may be assumed.

6.4 Model-driven Learning

Model-driven learning can basically be described as a consequential and explicit extension of the approaches discussed at the end of the preceding section. Instead of using fixed restrictions to define a hypothesis subspace to be searched, the learning program is given additional knowledge about the form of possible hypotheses, and uses this knowledge to restrict its search. Such explicit knowledge about the form of hypotheses is called a *model* of possible hypotheses, hence "model-driven learning".

Before explaining what kinds of model are used in RDT, let us briefly provide an overview of previous research on model-driven learning. There are only a few systems that directly belong to this category. One example is the META-DENDRAL system [Buchanan and Mitchell, 1978], which uses knowledge of molecular physics and chemistry (e.g. the knowledge of possible fissions or fusions of atoms) for learning purposes. This knowledge is used to generate hypotheses of rules that refer to particular classes of fusions of molecules.

Similarly, the system developed by Shrager [Shrager, 1987] uses already existing knowledge to learn or modify a theory about a domain. The existing knowledge consists of *abstract knowledge structures*, which are termed "views". For example, a view is an abstract model of a memory. This model can be used by the learner to devise a theory about parts of a digital watch, a microwave oven or a compact disc player.

SPARC/G [Dietterich and Michalski, 1985] uses three different basic models which describe the syntactic form of the rules to be learned. The rules to be learned are restricted to sequence-generating, predicting rules. The learning procedure was tested with a card game (Eleusis), where it was supposed to discover a pattern in a sequence of cards. One of these basic models is the "decompositon model", which stipulates that a set of implications be the form of a rule to be learned. The other two models consist of a periodic description of rules and the description in a disjoint normal form. Each model can be specialized by the determination of parameters. All models can be combined to produce more complex models. This enables the three models to be manipulated.

All the discovery systems in the BACON series [Langley *et al.*, 1987] are also model-driven. BACON is given a series of numerical measurements, e.g. of planetary motion, and is to discover laws that describe these measurements. Of all the possible mathematical functions, BACON is restricted to low-order polynomials by an appropriate model. This model, however, is implicit in the program, and not explicitly given as data.

TEIRESIAS [Davis, 1979] is a system that also uses rule models. It is not used to provide the basis of a learning procedure but to refine and interpret a domain model. The rule models describe *prototypes* of a rule set in a particular domain. They basically contain examples of rules and combinations of rules that provide more general or more specific rule models. The dialog with the expert results in the rule models being generated and revised.

For completeness, we should mention two other recent model-driven approaches that have incorporated the syntactic rule models of BLIP into their own programs, namely CIA [De Raedt and Bruynooghe, 1989b], where rule models are used to construct new concept definitions by analogy, and FOCL [Silverstein and Pazzani, 1991], where rule models are used in very much the same way as in RDT, but in a greedy top-down learner of the FOIL type.

6.5 Model Knowledge in RDT

RDT possesses two types of model knowledge, namely *rule models*, which are a model of the syntactic form of possible hypotheses, and the *predicate topology*, which is a task-oriented model of semantic relationships between the predicates of a hypothesis.

6.5.1 Rule Models

A *rule model*, or *rule schema*[2], is a syntactical device for specifying the form of possible rule hypotheses. Rule models were already introduced in chapter 2. They are rules in which predicate variables are used instead of actual domain predicates. We repeat the precise definition of their syntax from chapter 2, section 2.2.1:

[2] In this chapter, the terms rule model and rule schema are used interchangeably. The former emphasizes the functional aspect as a model of hypotheses, the latter the structural aspect of a rule with predicate variables.

> If R is a rule of type t, and RS is obtained by replacing in at least one literal of R the functor predicate with a variable of type t, then RS is a *rule schema.*

These rule schemata, as you will recall, are part of *metapredicates*, and used there to define how a metafact is translated into a domain level rule. Here, they are used to define the hypothesis space for learning, i.e., the rule schemata of all metapredicates known in a MOBAL knowledge base comprise the set of rule models available to RDT[3]. In the following, we use both the rule and the metapredicate form of learning hypotheses. Through metapredicate definitions, these are interchangeable anyway.

In chapter 2 (section 2.2), we have introduced the notion of a *substitution* that is applicable to variables of all types. In this chapter, we use lowercase Greek letters for substitutions of term variables (e.g. σ) and capital Greek letters (e.g. Σ) for substitutions of predicate variables. To facilitate some definitions in the description of RDT below, we introduce a specialized type of substitution called an *instantiation.* An instantiation Σ is a finite set of pairs P/p, where P is a predicate variable, and p is a predicate symbol, both of the same arity. The set of all p is called the *range* of Σ. The application of an instantiation Σ to a rule schema R (denoted $R\Sigma$) denotes the result of replacing each predicate variable mentioned in Σ by the corresponding predicate symbol. R is called *predicate ground* if all its predicate variables are instantiated, i.e., R is a rule.

Based on the set of rule models $\mathcal{R}$ provided to RDT, and the set of domain predicates $\mathcal{P}$ in the knowledge base, the hypothesis subspace that is searched is defined as the set

$$\mathcal{H} = \{R\Sigma | R \in \mathcal{R} \wedge range(\Sigma) \subseteq \mathcal{P} \wedge R\Sigma \text{ predicate ground}\}$$

i.e., as the set of all possible predicate ground instantiations of rule models with domain predicates.

This way of defining a hypothesis subspace can be contrasted with the use of specialization operators as in MIS [Shapiro, 1983], or FOIL [Quinlan, 1990]. Even though $\mathcal{R}$ is simply an unordered list of rule schemas, a generalization relation on $\mathcal{R}$ can be defined by suitably extending the standard clause subsumption relation. Before presenting our extension of subsumption for rule models (section 6.6.1), let us elaborate on how such a generalization relation can then be used. Given a hypothesis H and $R \in \mathcal{R}$ such that

[3]There is a system parameter that allows selecting only a subset of these for learning.

$H = R\Sigma$, we find all $R' \in \mathcal{R}$ that are specializations of R, and instantiate them in all possible ways (see section 6.6.1ff. for the details of this process). Thus, $\mathcal{R}$ constitutes an extensional definition of a specialization operator on hypotheses: it defines the operator by listing the form of hypotheses it produces, where normally the form of hypotheses is determined by the operator specification.

The advantage of this approach is that the hypothesis space is under very explicit user control. Based upon the elements of $\mathcal{R}$, it is easy for the user to see which form the learnable hypotheses will have[4]. Furthermore, the hypothesis space can be controlled in a very finely grained fashion, as individual hypothesis forms can be removed or added at will. By partially instantiating rule schemata, the user can even incorporate knowledge about individual domain predicates, as in eg.

P1(S1) & preceding_state(S1,S0) & P2(S0) → Q(S1)

where the name of the state successor predicate is explicitly given to avoid having to test other binary predicates in its place. All of this would be more difficult if a general operator specification had to be changed. The disadvantage of this form of learning model is the need to define the set $\mathcal{R}$ for an application, which is not always easy; often, a standard set of rule models is used. In section 6.7, we discuss ways of extending $\mathcal{R}$ automatically through the use of rule schema modification operators.

As explained in the preface to this book, the approach presented here originated in Emde's METAXA system [Emde *et al.*, 1983; Emde, 1987] and was also used in the BLIP system [Emde *et al.*, 1989; Wrobel, 1989]. De-Raedt and Bruynooghe [De Raedt and Bruynooghe, 1989a] have examined the use of rule schemata as defined here to propose new concept definitions by analogy (the CLINT/CIA technique).

6.5.2 Predicate Topology

Almost all learning approaches cope with the complexity of learning in logic by defining various syntactic restrictions on their hypothesis space or learning operators. This ignores an important source of control for learning: the use to which the learning results are to be put. Any learning program is used to achieve a specific goal, its output is to subserve a specific task. Thus,

[4]This can be compared to a requirement on "functional" knowledge representations that originated in the KL-ONE school [Brachman and Schmolze, 1985]: that the set of inferences provided be easily recognizable by a user.

task-oriented restrictions on the hypothesis space can tap into an important source of efficiency.

In RDT, we implemented such a task-oriented restriction in the form of a predicate *topology* ([Morik, 1990; Klingspor, 1991], see chapter 2, section 2.1.6, and chapter 5). For our purposes here, we regard a predicate topology as a grouping $\mathcal{T} = \{T_1, \ldots, T_m\}$ of the predicates $\mathcal{P}$ into possibly non-disjoint sets T_i, the topology *nodes*, each of which is labelled with a mnemonic name by the user. The topology nodes, in turn, can be connected to each other by directed links to form a hierarchy. This hierarchy is used further to restrict the hypothesis space of RDT by allowing only those hypotheses that use predicates within a topology node, or that use predicates within one topology node in the premises, and a predicate from one of its parents in the conclusion. More precisely, the hypothesis space $\mathcal{H}^{\mathcal{T}}$ can be defined as follows:

$$\begin{aligned}\mathcal{H}^{\mathcal{T}} = \{H \in \mathcal{H} | H = p_{prems} \rightarrow P_{concl} :\\ \exists T_i \in \mathcal{T} : p_{concl} \in T_i \wedge P_{prems} \subseteq T_i \cup children(T_i)\}\end{aligned}$$

where $children(T_i)$ denotes the union of the direct subnodes of T_i.

The topology nodes thus provide a means of subdividing a domain into regions with different purposes, and the links allow the user to restrict the hypotheses that will be examined by the system to those that are interesting in the specific task context. Furthermore, the direction of the links can be used to reflect the desired direction of inference in the domain. By providing a finely grained topology, a very effective reduction of the hypothesis space is possible. RDT can be used without a topology as well; in this case, $\mathcal{H}$ is the relevant hypothesis space.

Our topology approach is similar in spirit to approaches that allow the specification of irrelevance relationships, such as the one discussed by Subramanian and Genesereth [Subramanian and Genesereth, 1987]. Putting a predicate p in a different topology branch from predicate q in effect tells the system that p is irrelevant for constructing rules about q, or rather, that we are not interested in learning such rules.

6.5.3 Acquisition of Model Knowledge

The MOBAL system provides the opportunity for the user to enter and modify model knowledge, i.e., both rule models and topology. The manual entry of rule models occurs as part of metapredicates, and is described in chapter 2. The topology can be input manually, or is automatically acquired by the methods described in chapter 5. Here, we briefly discuss how the *model acquisition tool*, MAT, automatically abstracts metapredicates (rule schemes) from input rules.

The first step of such an abstraction process is very simple, and replaces the domain predicates used in the input rules with predicate variables, one per predicate used. Predicates symbols that name built-in predicates of the inference engine, however, are not replaced by predicate variables, and remain as are. In a second step, MAT reorders the premises of the input rule to ensure that the arguments of all computed predicates are properly bound before they are used. This is done by moving the premises in question to the end of the rule body. In a third step, the rule schema thus abstracted is checked against all existing metapredicates to prevent redundancies; this is done using the extended θ-subsumption relationship between rule models as it is described below (section 6.6.1). If the rule model is redundant, it is entered only on explicit user request. Finally, for accepted rule models, a metapredicate definition is generated for which the user can supply a mnemonic name if desired.

6.6 The RDT Algorithm

In this section we present an efficient algorithm to learn all valid nonredundant (i.e., maximally general) rules which are instances of rule models (see last section). It is not required to learn rules that cover all examples[5], nor that each example is covered only once.

The hypothesis space, defined by the sets of available rule models and predicates and the topology, is searched top-down from general to specific. The search is along the generality hierarchy with pruning of specializations of accepted and failed hypotheses. Acceptance and failure are decided with a user-specifiable acceptance criterion.

Further effectiveness comes from the use of a many sorted logic. The sort taxonomy tool STT (see chapter 4) automatically builds up a lattice of sorts. The sort taxonomy reduces the size of the hypothesis space very effectively (see section 4.4.4), since only well-sorted hypotheses are generated. This enhances the efficiency of learning.

In this section we first explore the generality structure between rule models to improve the search in the hypothesis space. Second, we define an order

[5] CLT, the concept learning tool of MOBAL described in chapter 8, has this global view and checks the quality of the rule set [Wrobel, 1988a].

of the premises within a single rule model to make the pruning mechanism applicable to partially instantiated rule models. Third, we show how these structures are used by the RDT algorithm to prune the search. The specializations of both unacceptable hypotheses and already accepted hypotheses are pruned: the former because they are surely wrong, and the latter because they are redundant. Acceptability of hypotheses is determined using an acceptance criterion which can be set by the user. Finally, we present a pseudocode summary of the algorithm.

6.6.1 Exploiting the Generality Structure of the Rule Models

Since RDT is a model-driven algorithm, the hypothesis space is defined by the set of rule models. This means we do not have a specialization operator as does, say, MIS [Shapiro, 1983] or FOIL [Quinlan, 1990] that incrementally builds the hypothesis space to be searched. Instead MOBAL's model knowledge can be partially ordered by an extended form of θ-subsumption [Plotkin, 1970] defined below. The proposed algorithm searches this partial ordering from the most general to the more specific hypotheses. A breadth-first search strategy is used to avoid testing hypotheses that are later subsumed by more general ones (this could happen if one were to use depth-first search). The hypotheses that have already been confirmed or pruned as too special (the leaves of the search, see below) are remembered and checked to avoid exploring their specializations.

Suppose for example one of MOBAL's standard rule model sets. This rule model set was constructed for learning in domains that consist largely of feature vectors with nominal attributes, together with a two-place connection predicate linking some feature vectors. This set consists of seventeen rule models (rule schemas) of increasing complexity, and is shown in table 6.1.

For an efficient search through the hypothesis space and to prevent redundant hypotheses, we have to arrange this unrelated set of rule models with respect to a generality relationship that allows us to prune the search (see figure 6.1).

This generality relation is computed without taking the available meta-level background knowledge (metarules) into account. If we take for a moment the P_i as predicates and not as predicate variables then we could use θ-subsumption from [Plotkin, 1970], i.e., a hypothesis H θ-subsumes a hypothesis H' (in clausal form), $H \geq_\theta H'$, iff there is a substitution σ such that $H\sigma \subseteq H'$.

However, because the P_i are predicate variables, the situation is a little

---

I1(P0,Q) : P0(Y) → Q(Y).

I2(P1,P0,Q) : P0(Y) & P1(Y) → Q(Y).

I3(Q) : conn(Y, N0) → Q(Y).

I4(P0,Q) : P0(Y) & conn(Y, N0) → Q(Y).

I5(P1,P0,Q) : P0(Y) & P1(Y) & conn(Y, N0) → Q(Y).

I6(Q) : conn(Y, N0) & conn(Y, N1) → Q(Y).

I7(P0,Q) : P0(Y) & conn(Y, N0) & conn(Y, N1) → Q(Y).

I8(P1,P0,Q) : P0(Y) & P1(Y) & conn(Y, N0) & conn(Y, N1) → Q(Y).

I9(P0,Q) : conn(Y, N0) & P0(N0) → Q(Y).

I10(P1,P0,Q) : P0(Y) & conn(Y, N0) & P1(N0) → Q(Y).

I11(P2,P1,P0,Q) : P0(Y) & P1(Y) & conn(Y, N0) & P2(N0) → Q(Y).

I12(P0,Q) : conn(Y, N0) & conn(Y, N1) & P0(N0) → Q(Y).

I13(P1,P0,Q) : P0(Y) & conn(Y, N0) & conn(Y, N1) & P1(N0) → Q(Y).

I14(P2,P1,P0,Q) : P0(Y) & P1(Y) & conn(Y, N0) & conn(Y, N1) & P2(N0) → Q(Y).

I15(P1,P0,Q) : conn(Y, N0) & conn(Y, N1) & P0(N0) & P1(N1) → Q(Y).

I16(P2,P1,P0,Q) : P0(Y) & conn(Y, N0) & conn(Y, N1) & P1(N0) & P2(N1) → Q(Y).

I17(P3,P2,P1,P0,Q) : P0(Y) & P1(Y) & conn(Y, N0) & conn(Y, N1) & P2(N0) & P3(N1) → Q(Y).

Table 6.1: Example Rule Model Set

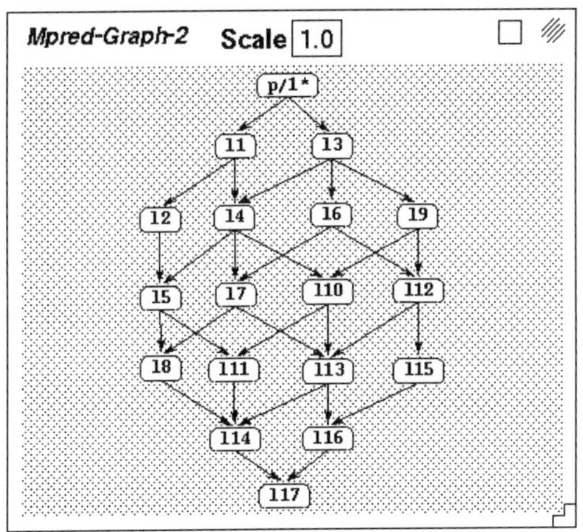

Figure 6.1: Generalization Relationships between Rule Models

more complicated. First of all we should clearly say what we mean by the generality relationship in the case of rule schemata with predicate variables. Clearly, we do not mean what θ-subsumption originally means, i.e. if H is true (in the intended interpretation) and $H \geq_\theta H'$ then H' must be true (in the intended interpretation) as well. This is because rule models can be neither true nor false, only predicate-ground instantiations of rule schemata, i.e., where all predicate variables are replaced with predicates, can be true or false. These considerations lead directly to a required property on the definition of our generality relationship $\geq_{RS}$ between rule models.

Corollary 6.1 *If there exists an instantiation $R\Sigma$ of a rule model R and R is more general than R' ($R \geq_{RS} R'$), then there exists an instantiation $R'\Sigma$ of R', and $R\Sigma \geq_\theta R'\Sigma$* [6].

This corollary explains how $\geq_{RS}$ is to be used to specialize hypotheses. But we still need a definition that allows us to compute $\geq_{RS}$ without looking at instantiations. Therefore, in addition to the substitution applied to term variables as used in the definition of $\geq_\theta$ we use a substitution Σ applied to predicate variables to rename or instantiate the predicate variables. Note

[6]This presupposes that R' can in principle be instantiated, i.e. for each predicate variable there exists at least one predicate of the same arity.

that a substitution σ applied to term variables always leads to a specialization (i.e. $\forall\sigma : R \geq_{RS} R\sigma$), whereas a substitution applied to predicate variables could lead to a generalization (i.e. $R\Sigma \geq_{RS} R$) if this substitution unifies some predicate variables. For instance,

$$\text{P(X,Y)}\sigma = \text{P(X,X)}, \text{ with } \sigma = Y/X \text{ and P(X,Y)} \geq_{RS} \text{P(X,X)}$$

On the other hand,

$$P1(X,Y), P2(X,Y)\Sigma = P1(X,Y), \text{ with } \Sigma = P2/P1 \text{ and}$$
$$P1(X,Y) \geq_{RS} P1(X,Y), P2(X,Y)$$

With these considerations in mind it is easy to see that the following is the correct and effectively computable definition of $\geq_{RS}$.

Definition 6.1 *Let R be a rule schema, σ a substitution applied to term variables, and Σ a substitution applied to predicate variables such that Σ does not unify different predicate variables.* R rule-schema-subsumes R' *if and only if*

$$R\sigma\Sigma \subseteq R'$$

If $R \geq_{RS} R'$, then at least one such predicate variable substitution Σ exists. For each substitution Σ there exists exactly one substitution σ such that $R\sigma\Sigma \subseteq R'$. However, possibly more than one substitution Σ exists. If more than one substitution Σ exists, we can distinguish two cases:

- Substitutions which lead to identical specializations except for variable names.
- Substitutions which lead to different specializations.

Suppose for example we have, in clausal form,

$$R = \{\neg \text{P(X)}, \neg \text{R(X,Y)}, \text{Q(Y)}\}, \text{ and}$$
$$R' = \{\neg\text{P11(X1)}, \neg\text{P12(X1)}, \neg\text{R1(X1,Y)}, \neg\text{P21(X2)}, \neg\text{R2(X2,Y)}, \text{Q(Y)}\}$$

then

$$\Sigma = \{\text{P/P11, R/R1}\} \text{ and}$$
$$\Sigma = \{\text{P/P12,R/R1}\}$$

lead to identical specializations with $\sigma = \{\text{X/X1}\}$, whereas

$$\Sigma = \{\mathrm{P/P21, R/R2}\}$$

leads to a different specialization with $\sigma = \{X/X2\}$.

This differentiation is not important as long as R does not contain any predicate symbols. But if R is partially or fully instantiated, i.e., R contains predicate symbols, the resulting specializations are different.

6.6.2 The Order of Premises Within a Rule Model

The $\geq_{RS}$ order on rule models builds a structure of the hypothesis space which is used for pruning the search. But this is only a kind of a macro structure. There are still many possible hypotheses for a single rule model, namely, all instantiations of the predicate variables of the rule model with predicate symbols. This section is concerned with a fine structuring of the space of hypotheses for a single rule model. This allows the search to be pruned of hypotheses also within a single rule model. Suppose we have a rule model with two premises, and we do not find a predicate for the first premise which fulfills our acceptance criterion. We then need not look for predicates for the other premises. This requires, however, an order on the premises which respects the variable bindings of the rule model. An example may illustrate this. Suppose the rule model is

$$P(X_2), R(X_1, X_2) \rightarrow C(X_1)$$

It does not make sense to look for a predicate for P before we have found one for R. Every predicate could be used for P without any effect on the acceptance criterion as long as we have not related the variable X_2 to the variable of the conclusion via the relation R. Similar problems occur in other FOL learning algorithms. In FOIL or MIS, this problem is solved by adding only those literals to the premises which share one variable with the other premises or the conclusion.

To solve this problem for RDT, we first define the *connection* of a variable to the conclusion. Based on the connection, we are able to define a measure for the distance of a variable from the conclusion. This measure is then used to determine the premise order.

Definition 6.2 *The* connection *of a variable X to the conclusion via the relation chain $rc(X)$ is defined as follows:*

- *A variable X occurring in the conclusion of a rule model is connected via the empty relation chain ($rc(X)=\emptyset$).*

- *A variable X_i ($1 \leq i \leq n$) occurring in a premise $R(X_1, X_2, \ldots, X_n)$ is connected via the relation chain $rc(X_i) = R \circ rc(X_j)$*[7]*, iff a variable X_j ($1 \leq j \leq n$), $i \neq j$ of $R(X_1, X_2, \ldots, X_n)$ is connected via the relation chain $rc(X_j)$.*

A variable can have more than one relation chain. But a rule model which contains an unconnected variable is not allowed.

Definition 6.3 *The* distance *of a variable X is then defined as the length of the minimal relation chain connecting it to the conclusion.*

$$\delta(X) = min(\{length(rc(X)) \mid rc(X) \text{ is a connection relation chain for X}\})$$

The order of premises *is then defined using the distances of the variables occurring in it.*

$$P \leq_P P', \text{iff} \quad min(\{\delta(X) \mid X \text{ occurring in } P\}) \leq min(\{\delta(X) \mid X \text{ occurring in } P'\}.$$

If we instantiate the premises of a rule schema with respect to this order, i.e. if $P \leq_P P'$ then P is instantiated before P', it makes sense to test all partial hypotheses (the partial instantiations of a rule model). This testing can be done by the same procedure as the test of the fully instantiated rule model, by simply dropping all uninstantiated premises. Incremental instantiation (with dropping of uninstantiated premises) produces a sequence of rules $r_1, r_2, \ldots, r_n$ that are in θ-subsumption order, i.e. $r_1 \geq_\theta r_2 \geq_\theta \cdots \geq_\theta r_n$. So the same kind of pruning that applies to rule models along the $\geq_{RS}$ order can also be applied incrementally to partially instantiated rule models.

6.6.3 Pruning the Search through Incremental Testing

The search in the hypothesis space is pruned in several ways. First, the predicate topology and sort lattice are used to avoid considering unrelated predicates for specializations. In addition, the RDT algorithm will not search for specializations of hypotheses that already have too few instances (because the specializations could never be confirmed), nor for specializations of those hypotheses that are confirmed (since their specializations are redundant).

[7] $\circ$ denotes list concatenation, and $R \circ \emptyset = R$.

The threshold for too few instances is computed from the user-specified acceptance criterion that is defined as follows. Let H be a possible hypothesis:

$$H = p(X_1, \ldots, X_m) \rightarrow q(X_1, \ldots, X_n)$$

where $m \geq n$, and $p(X_1, \ldots, X_m)$ represents the conjunction of the premises $p_1, \ldots, p_j$ over the variables $X_1, \ldots, X_m$. Then the primitives for the user-specifiable acceptance criterion are defined as the cardinalities of:

- pos(H) := $\{(c_1, \ldots, c_n) | p(c_1, \ldots, c_m) \& q(c_1, \ldots, c_n)\}$, the positive instances of H.
- neg(H) := $\{(c_1, \ldots, c_n) | p(c_1, \ldots, c_m) \& not(q(c_1, \ldots, c_n))\}$, the negative instances of H.
- pred(H) := $\{(c_1, \ldots, c_n) | p(c_1, \ldots, c_m) \& unknown(q(c_1, \ldots, c_n))\}$, the unknown, i.e. neither provable true nor provable false, instances of Q which will be predicted by H.
- total(H) := $\{(c_1, \ldots, c_n) | p(c_1, \ldots, c_m)\} = pos(H) \cup neg(H) \cup pred(H)$, the total instances of H.
- unc(H) := $\{(c_1, \ldots, c_n) | q(c_1, \ldots, c_n)\} \setminus \{(c_1, \ldots, c_n) | p(c_1, \ldots, c_m)\}$, the instances of Q which are uncovered by H.
- concl(H) := $\{(c_1, \ldots, c_n) | q(c_1, \ldots, c_n)\}$, all instances of the conclusion Q.

The acceptance criterion is a logical expression of conjunctions and disjunctions of arithmetical comparisons (i.e. $=$, $<$, $\leq$, $>$, $\geq$) involving arithmetical expressions (i.e. $+$, $-$, $*$, $/$) built from numbers and the above primitives. An example is:

pos $>$ 5, neg $<$ 2, pos/total $>$ 0.7, pred/pos $<$ 0.3, unc/concl $<$ 0.5

For the acceptance criterion primitives the following relations to θ-subsumption $\geq_\theta$ hold. Let H and H' be two hypotheses and $H \geq_\theta H'$ then

1. pos(H) $\supseteq$ pos(H')
2. neg(H) $\supseteq$ neg(H')

3. pred(H) $\supseteq$ pred(H')

4. total(H) $\supseteq$ total(H')

5. unc(H) $\subseteq$ unc(H')

6. concl(H) = concl(H')

Using these relations between the primitives and $\geq_\theta$ together with the semantics of the expression building operators, a pruning criterion is derived from the acceptance criterion. This derived pruning criterion only prunes hypotheses, which cannot fulfill the acceptance criterion, i.e. if a hypothesis h fulfills the pruning criterion, then no specialization of h will fulfill the acceptance criterion. For our example, the derived pruning criterion is:

pos $\leq$ 5, unc/concl $\geq$ 0.5

In "normal" expressions[8] the qualities 1, 4 and 5 can be used to prune the search. If a hypothesis H does not fulfill the acceptance criterion with respect to pos, total, or unc, then all specializations of H will not either. On the other hand, if a hypothesis H fulfills the acceptance criterion, then we need not look at the specializations of H. This step also prevents the addition of redundant conditions.

In summary, the use of a pruning criterion as described here guarantees that the algorithm will be complete with respect to the hypothesis space $\mathcal{H}^{\mathcal{T}}$, i.e. it will find all hypotheses in $\mathcal{H}^{\mathcal{T}}$ that are acceptable according to the chosen acceptance criterion, and that are not subsumed by other accepted hypotheses.

6.6.4 Learning Rules with Constants and Computed Predicates

In many domains with attributive or relational data, it is very important to have the facility to learn rules with constants and computed comparison predicates, such as:

place_description(X,bus_lane) → no_parking(X)
human(X) & body_temperature(X,T) & gt(T,37.5) → fever(X)

[8] In principle the user could build any expression, but it is very unlikely that he uses something like neg $>$ 2 (i.e. to accept the hypothesis it must have more than two negative examples).

In keeping with the model-based spirit of RDT, the user can supply rule schemata for rules such as the ones above, i.e., including computed predicates and specially marked arguments where the system is to search for constants. Since RDT already allows rule schemata whose predicate variables are partially pre-instantiated with domain predicates, computed predicates can be included simply by using their (reserved) names in the rule schema. The argument positions in which the system has to look for constants are identified within the metapredicate header. This is done by having not only the predicate variables of the rule schema in the metapredicate header but also the constant variables of the rule schema. The metapredicates for our example rules would then look like:

mp1(R,T,C):R(X,T) → C(X)
mp2(C,R,T,C2): C(X) & R(X,Y) & gt(Y,T) → C2(X)

In this example R, C, and C2 are predicate variables and T is a variable for a constant to learn.

To use such rule schemata for learning, RDT needs to recognize the names of computed predicates, and call their evaluation procedures instead of looking in the knowledge base. For constants, the appropriate procedure depends on the argument in which the constant is to be substituted. For the computed predicate **eq** (and for constants in non-computed predicates), all possible remaining instantiations of the variable must be tried; for comparison predicates on ordered values like **ge** (greater than or equal) etc., the semantics of the comparison predicate are used to avoid testing constants. If e.g. a constant **t** in **gt(X,t)** is searched for, RDT starts searching with the smallest term **t** from the instances of X for which the rule instantiation is a positive one, i.e. the most general hypothesis. If a hypotheses is accepted or rejected, all greater terms are pruned. Obviously, all values that are smaller than the above initial value will lead to worse results, so they need not be considered.

To make the process of looking for constants maximally efficient, it is properly integrated into RDT's incremental process of instantiating and testing partial rule schemata. Because there are in most cases many more constants than predicates, RDT looks first for the predicates, and then looks for the remaining constants, i.e. constants are incorporated in the premise order after all premises.

6.6.5 Summary of the Algorithm

```
rdt(Q)
  set RS to {}
  set LEAVES to {}
  for all known rule models R
    if the conclusion C of R is unifiable with Q
    then push RΣ, where Σ = {C/Q} onto RS
  while RS ≠{}
      pop a most general (with respect to ≥_RS) rule model R from RS
      instantiate-and-test(R,TOO-GENERAL)
      for all X element RS which are specializations of R
          pop X from RS
          for all Y element TOO-GENERAL
              for all really different Σ: Yσ ≥_RS XΣ)
                  push XΣ onto RS
          endfor
      endfor
  endwhile
```

Figure 6.2: RDT Top-level Loop

Figures 6.2 and 6.3 show a pseudocode summary of the algorithm that was described above. The algorithm is called using the command <rdt(Q)>, where Q is a literal with the target predicate for which the RDT algorithm is to learn all possible rules. If the literal is negative, the algorithm learns the negation of the target predicate based on the available members of $\mathcal{R}$ with negative conclusions.

The hypothesis queue <RS> and the list of leaves <LEAVES> together represent the state of the search. This makes it easy to suspend and resume the search and to learn rules for several concepts in parallel.

Note that the generalization hierarchy and the premise order are independent of the learning task. They depend only on the available rule models. This means that both can be precomputed, and the time for building them need not be spent again for each learning task. We thus use a format that supports quick access to the most general rule models, to all specializations of a rule model together with the possible matches (i.e.Σ), and to the ordered premises; this does not incur any extra cost for learning.

Further optimizations were made in the hypothesis test step by remem-

```
instantiate-and-test(HYPO,TOO-GENERAL)
  while HYPO ≠ {}
        pop a hypothesis H from HYPO
        if there are premises with uninstantiated predicates in H
        then let PREM be the smallest (with respect to ≤P) of these
                  premises and P its predicate
          for all predicates p which are
                  (arity-compatible with P) and
                  (topology-compatible with the conclusion of H) and
                  (sort-compatible with H)
              set H to HΣ with Σ = {P/p}
              test(H)
          endfor
        else select a constant T to learn with smallest δ(T)
          for all terms t suitable for T
              set H to Hσ with σ = {T/t}
              test(H)
          endfor
        fi
  endwhile

test(H)
  if the instantiated part of H is not a specialization (≥θ)
    of an element of LEAVES
  then test the instantiated part of H against the acceptance criterion
        if H is not to special (i.e. is acceptable with
                                  respect to pos, total and unc)
        then if all premises of H are instantiated
               then if H is acceptable with respect to all criteria
                     then push H onto LEAVES
                           assert H in the KB
                     else push H onto TOO-GENERAL
               else push H onto HYPO
        else push H onto LEAVES
  fi
```

Figure 6.3: RDT Instantiate-and-test Subroutine

bering the instances of the parent hypothesis (as in FOIL). This means that we only need to check the newly added premises against this instance set instead of checking the entire hypothesis against the entire knowledge base.

The test against the acceptance criterion is based on the user-specifiable parameter. The building blocks for this criterion are discussed in section 6.6.3, above.

6.7 Future Research and Summary

The version RDT described here is implemented and integrated into the MOBAL system. From our experiences with RDT, we have identified some issues that could still be addressed in future versions of RDT:

- The integration of heuristic search control criteria.
- Means of automatically extending the set of rule models $\mathcal{R}$.

Heuristic Search Control One of the simplest, but nevertheless powerful, improvements is the use of an information theoretic criterion like the one in FOIL combined with best-first selection of specializations of rule schemata. This seems to be a very promising direction, since our method of specialization based on rule schemata allows us to overcome the myopy problem of FOIL, and we can introduce more than one conjunct at a time in a controlled fashion.

Automatic Extension of $\mathcal{R}$ MOBAL contains a tool (MAT) for the abstraction of a rule schema from user given rules. This tool could be used automatically to acquire new rule schemata in cases where the current ones are not sufficient for learning by using a non-model-driven learning method to search the "gaps" left by the existing model. This could be done by any learning method capable of dealing with RDT representation (function-free Horn clauses), e.g. ARCH, INDUCE, FOIL, MIS. Any rules found by this more complete search would then be abstracted by MAT and added to the rule model. This approach has to be combined with a usefulness criterion and the deletion of useless rule schemata.

Most promising in this direnction seems to be the direct integration of RDT with a learning program that is not model-based and also searches top-down (e.g. FOIL). In such an approach, the efficiency of RDT is used for scanning the search space. This search is done much faster than is possible by any algorithm that does not employ models. However, if RDT fails to learn, the most promising hypothesis could be further refined by the other algorithm. Such an integrated approach combines two advantages: the efficiency of model-based learning and the flexibility of other algorithms. In addition, it overcomes the restriction of model-based learning, namely that well-suited models need to be given. If needed, new rule models can be found by the "backup" algorithm. In addition, this approach overcomes the restriction of non-model-based heuristic algorithms such as FOIL, namely the short-sightedness of heuristic search. These algorithms now only need to learn within a subarea of an already scanned hypothesis space. Therefore, they do not rely so much on their heuristics but can search this subspace more completely.

Chapter 7

Knowledge Revision

7.1 The Maintenance Problem

In the years since the construction of the first expert systems in the early seventies [Shortliffe, 1976], knowledge-based systems (KBS) have proven to be a powerful technology for addressing application problems the solution of which requires large amounts of specialized knowledge. To properly exploit the power of the KBS technology, it is necessary to construct application-specific knowledge bases that contain all the necessary knowledge, properly represented and properly structured. The field of AI was quick to realize that the construction of such knowledge bases is a major problem, and various methods were devised to cope with this *knowledge acquisition* problem (see chapter 1 for an overview of the different approaches).

As knowledge-based systems became of age, however, it turned out quite clearly that the initial focus on the construction of knowledge bases was too limited. First, no matter what methodology for knowledge acquisition is being followed, for complex problems it is not possible to construct a perfect knowledge base containing all the necessary information and no errors. Second, as knowledge based systems are used in an application, the requirements posed by the application environment are likely to change, so that previous knowledge is no longer correct, and new knowledge may need to be added. Therefore, in addition to the problem of constructing knowledge bases, the problem of *maintaining* knowledge bases has increasingly become recognized as an important issue. This parallels earlier and ongoing discussions in the field of software engineering, where a focus on the entire software lifecycle including maintenance is commonplace. The sloppy modeling paradigm according to which MOBAL was constructed has recognized this problem from very early on [Morik, 1987] (see chapter 1).

In addition to the general software engineering considerations towards maintenance detailed above, the use of an inductive learning method to acquire and extend knowledge bases especially requires facilities for maintaining knowledge bases and recovering from errors. In MOBAL, the inductive learning module RDT (see chapter 6) is used to learn rules that are statistically confirmed in the knowledge base. Since the knowledge base undergoes permanent changes during modeling, however, a rule that has been found to be valid at a certain point of time can become invalid later on: The user pursues a strategy of incrementally inputting data that are selected by the user himself or herself, so it is possible that these initial examples are intentionally or unintentionally non-representative of the domain (the so-called *example selection bias*). Any rules learned on the basis of such non-representative examples will cover only part of the desired target concept, and are therefore incomplete or even incorrect. If new examples are then input that cover other parts of the target concept, incorrect inferences will be produced. Moreover, facts that were entered earlier can turn out to be erroneous so they are retracted; as a result, an input that was confirmatory can now become contradictory.

As an example of the knowledge base maintenance problem, consider the telecommunications access control application that was developed in MOBAL in cooperation with Alcatel Alsthom Recherche (see section 9.3). In this application, the knowledge base contains facts that describe the configuration of a telecommunications network, including information about the employees of the various companies involved in the operation of the network. Based on these facts, a set of *access control rules* is used to derive which employees may perform which operations on which systems in the network. This application clearly illustrates the maintenance problem. Given an initial manually created list of access rights, RDT was used to induce a set of rules. Due to the sparseness of the examples, however, these rules were not perfect, which became apparent as soon as facts about new employees and systems were added to the knowledge base. At this point, the knowledge base deduced incorrect access permissions, and the rules needed to be modified.

This chapter presents KRT, the *knowledge revision tool* of the MOBAL system. KRT is designed to support a user in exactly the kind of situation described above. In more abstract terms, KRT supports the user whenever he or she detects one ore more incorrect inferences in the knowledge base, and wants the rules or facts in the knowledge base to be changed such that the incorrect inferences are not produced any more.

7.2 An Overview of KRT

KRT is an interactive knowledge revision tool, that is, its primary purpose is to act as an assistant to a user who wants to remove one or more incorrect inferences (KRT is capable of performing multiple simultaneous revisions). Roughly speaking, the services of KRT are the following. First, KRT identifies, from the information stored in the inference engine, exactly which entries in the knowledge base participated in the derivation of the incorrect inference. This information is graphically presented to the user as a *derivation*, which is a directed acyclic *or-and* graph (or-and DAG) containing all possible ways of proving the incorrect inference from the current knowledge base. Figure 7.1 shows the interaction window that KRT presents to the user whenever it is called to remove an incorrect inference. Shown in the figure is a knowledge revision interaction from the telecommunications domain mentioned above. In the top row, there are 4 text boxes showing information about the current revision problem. The leftmost one of these shows the incorrect inferences that the user has selected for removal. In this case, two incorrect facts about access permissions were selected. Below the four text boxes, the system graphically displays the derivation.

At the top of the graphical derivation display, the root nodes of the DAG represent the two incorrect inferences that are to be removed. Like all fact nodes, they have a white background. Each of the children of a fact node is a so-called *support* that contributes positive or negative evidence (marked + and –, respectively). The source of a support can be either a user input (a so-called *input support*, such as for all facts at the bottom of the diagram), or a rule application (a *derived support*, such as the supports for the two root nodes). Since there can be more than one support for a given inference, all support children of a fact node are implicitly connected disjunctively (an "or" level in the DAG). In this example, each fact node actually has only one support. Each rule application node (drawn with a grey background) displays the rule's identifier along with the variable bindings that were used in this rule application. Below each rule application node, the facts that were used as *antecedents* of the rule application are shown. Since all antecedents need to present conjunctively, the antecedents constitute the "and" levels of the derivation. Each antecedent in turn recursively possesses its own supports, until finally an input support is reached.

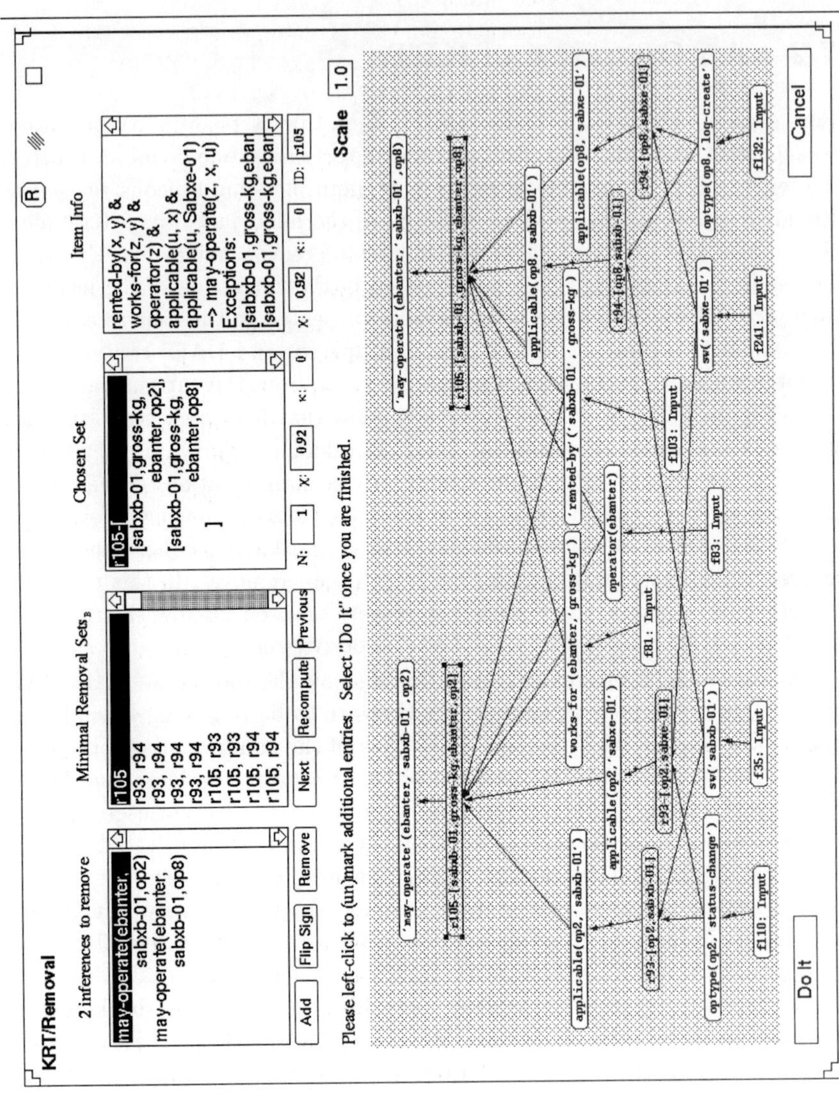

Figure 7.1: Knowledge revision example from telecommunications domain

The second service offered by KRT is the computation, from the derivation, of the set of all possible minimal knowledge base revisions that would be necessary and sufficient for removing the offending inferences. This step is based on the theoretical concept of a *minimal base revision* [Wrobel, 1993b], i.e., a revision that alters the existing knowledge base minimally. We will describe it in some more detail below (section 7.3). The possible revisions are shown to the user in the second text box from the left, labeled *minimal removal sets.* Each line in this text field shows one possible revision, and the currently chosen revision is shown in inverse video. The user can scroll through these revisions or freely select an element from the list. In any case, KRT marks the elements that would be removed if the chosen revision were performed by four little black boxes. The third and fourth text boxes show more detailed textual information about the chosen revision.

Since the set of possible revisions can be large, the third service offered by KRT is a heuristic proposal of which of the possible minimal revisions to choose. Since all of them are minimal according to the theoretical notion of a minimal base revision, the choice is based on a pragmatic criterion of *confidence* in the various elements of the knowledge base. To this end, the user can specify for individual statements or group of statements a confidence class and/or a continuous confidence value, and the system orders the possible minimal revisions so that revisions in less trusted classes are preferred to revisions in more trusted classes, and that the loss of confidence is minimized within the chosen class. This heuristic choice function enables KRT to also function in an off-line, non-interactive mode as a fully automatic knowledge base revision system. In section 7.4, we describe in more detail the two-tiered confidence model upon which the choice of preferred revisions is based. Of course, in interactive use, the user is free to ignore the system's proposal and choose another one.

As soon as a minimal revision has been selected, KRT performs the necessary changes to the knowledge base to implement the revision. After that, the fourth service offered by KRT is *rule reformulation.* To perform minimal revisions, KRT uses a technique that stores explicit exceptions to rules in a so-called *support set* (see below). Whenever the exception list of a rule has become implausibly long (according to a parametrized criterion), KRT offers to the user to search for better, more special rules that would render the explicit exception list unnecessary. This is done by looking in the knowledge base for existing predicates that could be added to the rule as additional premises, or even by calling the concept learning tool CLT (see chapter 8) to introduce a new concept for this purpose. The user can trigger the reformulation search manually if he or she wants to and can control the depth and direction of the search interactively if needed. At the end, the system presents all reformulations that were found and lets the user choose the preferred one. In section 7.7, we will present in some detail how the reformulation process is carried out.

In summary, KRT thus offers to the user a range of support services in knowledge base revision that can be used in interactive or non-interactive mode. It has proven especially useful in large knowledge bases, where the knowledge base parts that contributed to incorrect inferences are difficult to identify, and where the selection of minimal and sufficient revisions is difficult for users. Since KRT automatically determines these revisions, it allows users to check the correctness of knowledge bases on the factual level without having to understand the rules, and then let the system worry about how to make the rules produce only the desired facts. This is especially important if end users are to be involved in the process of correcting knowledge bases.

KRT has been applied successfully in a number of domains, including a medical domain developed in cooperation with ICS/FORTH, and the above-mentioned telecommunications domain developed in cooperation with Alcatel Alsthom Recherche, Paris, which is described in the applications chapter (section 9.3).

7.3 Minimal Base Revisions

7.3.1 The Notion of Minimality

As outlined above, the general goal of knowledge revision is clear and simple: to alter the knowledge base in a way such that the unwanted incorrect inferences are not produced any more. Unfortunately, this general goal severely underconstrains the problem, since it admits even solutions as trivial as deleting the entire knowledge base and replacing it by an empty knowledge base. Clearly, this removes the incorrect inference, but it is certainly not an ideal solution. Intuitively, what we want is a revision that follows a *conservative* strategy [Salzberg, 1985], that is, a strategy that modifies the knowledge base *minimally* and lets us keep most of our existing knowledge. This strategy can be motivated by the human response to information that contradicts one's own perception of the world: we always change only those beliefs that directly contradict the new evidence.

Given that we want minimal revisions, we are left with the problem of how to precisely define what a minimal revision is. In MOBAL, we rely on the definition of minimality that was developed in [Wrobel, 1993b; Wrobel, 1993a]; there, it is shown that minimal revision must not be interpreted as minimal specialization, but instead as minimal base revision. We cannot go into all the details of this discussion here, but we can illustrate the major points. Technically, in revising MOBAL knowledge bases, we are concerned with the revision problem for *first order theories*, that is, sets of first-order logical statements. A *minimal specialization* (as defined by [Muggleton and Bain, 1992]) of such a theory is a set of statements that absolutely minimizes the loss of inferences without any concern towards preserving the structure of the original theory.

As shown in [Wrobel, 1993b] based on previous work on the logic of theory change by Nebel [Nebel, 1989], the choice of such minimal specializations for revision means that the revised theory may not be a subset of the original theory and may not have a finite representation. Furthermore, inferential relationships are not preserved. Consider a simple example. From the (propositional) theory $\{p, p \rightarrow q\}$, q can be inferred. If we are now told that p is incorrect, and want to remove it, a minimal specialization would contain the statements $\{p \rightarrow q, q\}$, since there is no reason to "lose" the inference q. In other words, a minimal specialization in this case deletes the antecedent p and keeps the consequence q, even though the latter had originally been derived from the former.

We therefore need a notion of minimality that somehow preserves the structure of the original theory. In [Wrobel, 1993b], such a notion of minimality is defined and referred to as *minimal base revision*. The primary difference between minimal specialization and minimal base revision is that the result of a minimal base revision is required to contain only statements that were in the original knowledge base, plus perhaps new statements that are specializations of existing statements. As shown in [Wrobel, 1993a], this avoids the unwanted effects of minimal specializations while still allowing revision operations that keep most of the existing knowledge. The key to achieving this is the introduction of a particular kind of new, specialized statements, namely statements with explicit exception lists stored in a data structure called a *support set* [Habel and Rollinger, 1982].

7.3.2 Support Sets

Each MOBAL rule R (with variables $V(R) := \{X_1, \ldots, X_n\}$) has an attached *support set* $S(R)$, which is an expression of the form

$$(X_1, \ldots, X_n) \in D_1 \times \ldots \times D_n \setminus GE$$

where GE, the set of *global exceptions*, has the form

$$\{(c_{1,1}, \ldots c_{1,n}), \ldots, (c_{m,1}, \ldots c_{m,n})\}$$

The $c_{j,i}$ ($j \in \{1, \ldots, m\}$, $i \in \{1, \ldots, n\}$) are constants, and $m \geq 0$. Each of the *domains* D_i ($i \in \{1, \ldots, n\}$) in turn has the form

$$p_i \setminus LE_i$$

where each of the *local exception* sets LE_i has the form

$$\{d_{i,1}, \ldots, d_{i,k_i}\}$$

The $d_{i,k}$ ($i \in \{1, \ldots, n\}$, $k \in \{1, \ldots, k_i\}$) are constants, $k_i \geq 0$ for all i, and the p_i are unary predicates, or the special symbol all that stands for the set of all constants. Such a support set specifies the permitted substitutions on the variables of a rule and can easily be translated into a more standard notation using the following set of additional rule premises[1]:

$$p_1(X_1)\& \ldots \& \, p_n(X_n)\& \; X_1 \notin LE_1\& \; \ldots \& \; X_n \notin LE_n\& \; (X_1, \ldots, X_n) \notin GE$$

With respect to exceptions, a support set thus achieves the same effect as the *censored production rules* of [Michalski and Winston, 1986], and the *conditional rules* used in [Kodratoff, 1986, p. 65]. The exception list notation is also equivalent to the *exception predicate* notation used recently in [Muggleton and Bain, 1992], but in contrast to the latter, does not require the use of a non-monotonic semantics. Support sets achieve the same effect by relying on a simple membership predicate.

In the following, we will often omit the explicit list of variables in the support set description, and simply write

$$S(R) = D_1 \times \ldots \times D_n \setminus GE$$

when the variables of the rule are clear from the context. Indeed this is exactly the format in which support sets are printed in MOBAL's knowledge representation, where a rule with a support set is shown as for example:

```
involved_vehicle(X,Y) & owner(Y,Z)
        → responsible(X,Z) – (minor_violation × all × all)
```

[1] Indeed this is precisely the internal format used in the inference engine (see section 3.2.3).

which says that variables Y and Z may take on any values, whereas X is limited to instances of the predicate **minor_violation**. The maximal support set of a rule with n variables is of course the n-dimensional Cartesian product

$$(\mathsf{all} \times \ldots \times \mathsf{all})$$

Since metafacts can used to generate rules (see chapter 2), metafacts also have an attached support set. The inference engine makes special provisions in its representation of metapredicates and metafacts to ensure that support sets are correctly propagated when generating rules from metafacts (see section 3.2.3).

7.3.3 The MBR Operator

The key idea of the minimal base revision operation used in KRT is to exclude from the rules participating in an incorrect inference exactly those substitutions that were used in the derivation, and nothing else. [Hayes-Roth, 1983] refers to this manner of knowledge revision as *exclusion method.* Support sets facilitate the use of the exclusion method to resolve conflicts, since the offending substitutions can now simply be added to the exception list [Emde *et al.*, 1983]. In other words, the minimal base revision operation does not select entire statements for removal, but individual *applications* of statements with a particular substitution. For illustration, in figure 7.1, the rule nodes in the graphical display of the derivation show the identifier of the rule along with the bindings of variables that were used. When KRT computes the minimal removal sets, its collect all such applications of statements, and then selects from these the minimal subsets that need to be removed.

In [Wrobel, 1993b; Wrobel, 1993a], the above notions of derivations, applications and variable bindings are defined precisely and with great technical detail. Here, we will continue to rely on the intuitive notions given by the graphical representation of a derivation, and give a simple example to clarify how the minimal base revision operator works. So consider the knowledge base

$$\{\mathsf{p(a)}, \mathsf{p(X)} \rightarrow \mathsf{q(X)}\},$$

and let us assume that q(a) is to be removed from this knowledge base. There is only one way of proving q(a), so the derivation is the simple structure shown in figure 7.2.

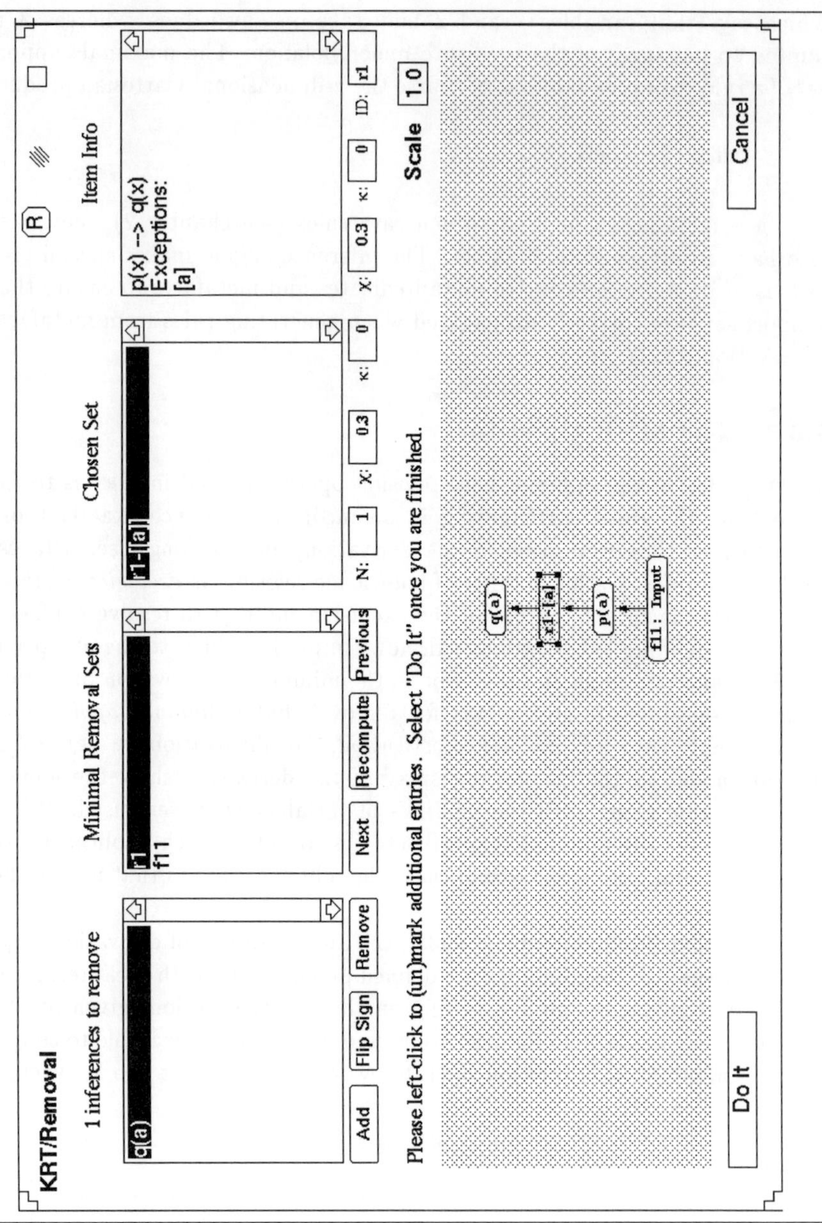

Figure 7.2: Knowledge revision interaction panel for simple example

From the graphical display, we can see that the statement applications with respect to q(a) in this derivation are:

$$\{(\mathsf{p(a)}, \emptyset), (\mathsf{p(X)} \rightarrow \mathsf{q(X)}, \{\mathsf{X/a}\})\}.$$

In this set, we have shown each application as a pair of a statement and a substitution on its variables. Note that for (ground) facts, the substitution is empty. For each statement mentioned in an application set, the minimal revision operation also needs the set of substitutions that were used, and the set of variable *instances*, i.e., variable bindings. In the example, the substitution set of p(a) is simply

$$\{\emptyset\},$$

whereas for p(X) → q(X), it is

$$\{\{\mathsf{X/a}\}\}.$$

Since p(a) has no variables, its instance set is undefined. The instance set for p(X) → q(X), on the other hand, is simply

$$\{(\mathsf{a})\}.$$

To perform a minimal revision, KRT first computes the application set of the derivation, and then determines the maximal correct subsets of the application set, or conversely, determines which minimal sets of clause applications need to be disallowed to prevent the incorrect inference. Due to the derivation information that is available from the inference engine, this computation fortunately does not need to look at all the different subsets of the application set. Instead, the minimal removal sets can be computed recursively from the derivation as follows. For each *or*-node in the derivation, pick a minimal removal set for each of its children and form the union of these sets. For each *and*-node (rule node) in the derivation, either remove the application mentioned in the node, or take the minimal removal set of one of its antecedents. This recursion terminates whenever a leaf of the derivation is reached. A tricky case arises whenever the derivation is a DAG and not a tree. In this case, clause applications are shared between the different branches, so care must be taken when combining removal sets at an or-node. When incompatible choices are made in the different branches, the union of the minimal removal sets will not be minimal. It can be shown, however, that the set of all removal sets created at an or-node always contains, for any non-minimal set, a subset of this set that is minimal [Wrobel, 1993a]. This means that non-minimal elements can be filtered out.

In our example, the set of minimal removal sets is

$$\{\{(\mathsf{p(a)}, \emptyset)\}, \{(\mathsf{p(X)\rightarrow\ q(X)}, \{\mathsf{X/a}\})\}\}.$$

Once the user (or the system based on its heuristics) has chosen one of the minimal removal sets, KRT performs the revision by replacing each statement mentioned in the chosen minimal removal set with a set of more specialized statements. This is where the support set comes in, since it easily allows the required specialization to be performed. If we let $I(R, M)$ denote the instance set of rule R in the minimal removal set M, then this specialization is done as follows:

Exclusion operator on R with respect to M: If $S(R) = D_1 \times \ldots \times D_m \setminus GE$, then set $S(R) := D_1 \times \ldots \times D_m \setminus (GE \cup I(R, M))$.

In addition, KRT adds a set of statements that ensure *recovery* [Gärdenfors, 1988]. The recovery postulate deals with the case that a knowledge base is first revised to exclude an incorrect inference, and that this inference later turns out to be correct and is re-added to the knowledge base. The recovery postulate requires that all inferences that were possible with original knowledge base be possible with the revised knowledge base plus the re-added statement. In KRT, this is achieved by adding the incorrect statement as an additional premise to specialized versions of all statements that are removed [Wrobel, 1993b; Wrobel, 1993a].

For illustration, consider our example from above where we had two possible minimal removal sets. If the first of these is chosen ($\{(\mathsf{p(a)}, \emptyset)\}$), we need to remove p(a) from our theory, and replace it by

$$\{\mathsf{q(a)\rightarrow\ p(a)}\},$$

so the resulting modified knowledge base is

$$\{\mathsf{q(a)\rightarrow\ p(a)}, \mathsf{p(X)\rightarrow\ q(X)}\}.$$

If the second minimal removal set is chosen ($\{(\mathsf{p(X)\rightarrow\ q(X)}, \{\mathsf{X/a}\})\}$), we need to remove p(X)→ q(X), and replace it by

$$\begin{aligned} & \{\mathsf{p(X)\rightarrow\ q(X)-\ all} \setminus \{(\mathsf{a})\}, \mathsf{q(a)\&\ p(a)\rightarrow\ q(a)}\}; \\ = \ & \{\mathsf{p(X)\rightarrow\ q(X)-\ all} \setminus \{(\mathsf{a})\}\}, \end{aligned}$$

so the resulting revised knowledge base is:

$$\{\mathsf{p(a)}, \mathsf{p(X)} \rightarrow \mathsf{q(X)} - \mathsf{all} \setminus \{(\mathsf{a})\}\}.$$

Note that in the first case, when removing q(a), we had to remove and thus lose p(a). Since we also add q(a) → p(a), however, this lost inference will be recovered should q(a) ever be added back in again. Clearly, this kind of recovery behavior is not always desirable, so KRT has a parameter that allows recovery to be turned off.

To see why the revision operator must consider individual clause applications in deciding about minimal removal sets, consider the example of

$$\left\{\begin{array}{l} \mathsf{q(a)} \\ \mathsf{q(b)} \\ \mathsf{q(X)} \rightarrow \mathsf{p(X)} \\ \mathsf{p(a)} \& \ \mathsf{p(b)} \rightarrow \mathsf{r(a)} \end{array}\right\}$$

from which we want to remove r(a). If we choose to modify q(X)→ p(X) (or rather, one or more of its applications), the MBRoperator will correctly produce either one of

$$\left\{\begin{array}{l} \mathsf{q(a)} \\ \mathsf{q(b)} \\ \mathsf{q(X)} \rightarrow \mathsf{p(X)} - \mathsf{all} \setminus \{(\mathsf{a})\} \\ \mathsf{r(a)} \& \ \mathsf{q(a)} \rightarrow \mathsf{p(a)} \\ \mathsf{p(a)} \& \ \mathsf{p(b)} \rightarrow \mathsf{r(a)} \end{array}\right\} \text{ or } \left\{\begin{array}{l} \mathsf{q(a)} \\ \mathsf{q(b)} \\ \mathsf{q(X)} \rightarrow \mathsf{p(X)} - \mathsf{all} \setminus \{(\mathsf{b})\} \\ \mathsf{r(a)} \& \ \mathsf{q(b)} \rightarrow \mathsf{p(b)} \\ \mathsf{p(a)} \& \ \mathsf{p(b)} \rightarrow \mathsf{r(a)} \end{array}\right\}$$

whereas a revision operation not based on individual clause applications would have to produce the overly specific

$$\left\{\begin{array}{l} \mathsf{q(a)} \\ \mathsf{q(b)} \\ \mathsf{q(X)} \rightarrow \mathsf{p(X)} - \mathsf{all} \setminus \{(\mathsf{a}), (\mathsf{b})\} \\ \mathsf{r(a)} \& \ \mathsf{q(a)} \rightarrow \mathsf{p(a)} \\ \mathsf{r(a)} \& \ \mathsf{q(b)} \rightarrow \mathsf{p(b)} \\ \mathsf{p(a)} \& \ \mathsf{p(b)} \rightarrow \mathsf{r(a)} \end{array}\right\}$$

This concludes our brief overview of the minimal revision operator in KRT. For more details, the reader is referred to [Wrobel, 1993b; Wrobel, 1993a].

7.4 Choosing Preferred Revisions

In the above simple example, there already were two possible minimal removal sets that could be used to remove the incorrect inference. In most applications of revision operations, the number of knowledge base elements involved in the derivation of an incorrect fact is much larger, resulting in a large number of revision possibilities. Even though ultimately, the choice of a preferred element in the set of possible minimal revisions can only be made on pragmatic grounds by the user, it is highly desirable for a revision support system such as KRT to at least order the possible revisions according to some user-specified preference measure. If this is done, the user can look at the "best" revisions first, and may not need to look at the entire list that is offered to him or her. Furthermore, a built-in preference criterion allows fully automatic revision without user interaction, which may be important in certain applications.

In essence, the question we need to answer is which statements of our theory, i.e., which entries in our knowledge base we are most willing to modify or delete, and which entries we are most interested in keeping. We are thus interested in some measure of *confidence* in the statements in our knowledge base such that we are more likely to change or delete statements in which we are less confident. The notion of confidence can be implemented in basically two ways, as discrete classes or continuous values. In the first view, each statement in the knowledge base is assigned a confidence class, and a statement of a higher confidence class is modified or deleted only if revisions of statements in lower confidence classes are insufficient [Nebel, 1989, ch. 6]. The system would thus rather delete any number of statements from lower classes than a single statement from a higher class. In the second view, each statement is assigned a real-valued confidence, and we prefer revisions that minimize the sum (or some other combination) of the confidence values of the statements that are to be modified or removed. In this case, it is thus possible that the system will prefer to delete one statement with high confidence in order to keep a large number of statements with lower confidence.

Both approaches can be justified pragmatically in a learning knowledge acquisition system such as MOBAL. The first interpretation, confidence classes, is very appropriate to distinguish between statements of different origin, for example between user inputs and learning results. Indeed in many situations we would probably rather modify a large number of learning results than a single user input. Due to their discrete nature, confidence classes are also easier to handle for users. The second view, on the other hand, seems more appropriate to deal with revisions in sets of statements from the same source, e.g. to select which among a set of learned rules to modify. Each such rule has been verified during learning with a certain confidence, and it would not be appropriate to delete many rules that were confirmed at 60 percent to keep one that was confirmed at 70 percent.

In MOBAL, we have therefore decided to provide to the user both possibilities of specifiying confidence. Each input statement can be assigned a continuous confidence value between 0 and 1 (the χ-value), and an integer-valued confidence class (the κ-value). The user thus defines two functions for all input facts and all rules:

$$\chi : \Gamma \rightarrow [0,1] \subseteq \mathbb{R}$$

and

$$\kappa : \Gamma \rightarrow \{0, \ldots, \kappa_{max}\} \subseteq \mathbb{N}$$

where Γ denotes the set of all statements in the knowledge base.

Given these two values, KRT orders all minimal removal sets by first considering classes and then considering the continuous values. If a minimal removal set contains modifications in a higher class than another one or if the former's modification in its highest class are a subset of the latter's modifications in the same class, then the former is preferred over the latter. If two minimal removal sets require incomparable modifications in the same highest class (neither one is a subset of the other), KRT computes the sum of the continuous confidence values for both sets and prefers the set with the smaller sum. This preference ordering is defined more precisely in [Wrobel, 1993a], where we also give a bounded algorithm for computing preferred minimal removal sets and discuss the effect of the two confidence measures on the algorithm's computational complexity.

7.5 Confidence Propagation

An interesting case arises in MOBAL whenever the user asks for the revision of a contradictory statement. Recall that in MOBAL, the knowledge base in not required to be consistent all the time, so that a user may choose to ignore a contradiction and decide to revise it later on. To support this, the system provides the *agenda*, where all consistency and integrity violations are recorded so they can be worked on at a convenient time. When the user calls knowledge revision on one of these contradictory statements, the goal is to remove "one side" of the contradiction, i.e., either the positive or the negative evidence, so that the statement is no longer contradictory. This of course requires the choice of which side of the contradiction to remove with the revision operations described above.

While KRT allows the user to make this choice, the system also uses the confidence functions χ and κ to provide a heuristic proposal which can also be used in automatic, non-interactive mode. The idea simply is to remove the side of the contradiction in which the system has less confidence. Since only input statements have user-assigned confidence values, this requires the definition of propagation rules that assign confidence values to derived statements as well. The intuitive idea that underlies this extension is that derived facts somehow inherit confidence from the statements from which they were derived. More precisely, if f is a statement derived from a knowledge base, and its immediate supports in the derivation are $s_1, \ldots, s_k$, we can define

$$\chi(f) := f_{or}(\{s_1, \ldots, s_k\}),$$

where f_{or} is a function that combines the confidence of the different supports of the derivation into a confidence level for the resulting fact. One reasonable choice for f_{or} is

$$f_{or}(S) := max(S),$$

i.e., simply taking the maximum confidence of all proofs that support f.

We can now define the confidence of a support s as follows. If s is an input support from input fact g, we simply define:

$$\chi(s) := \chi(g)$$

If, on the other hand, the support is a derived support from the application of a rule r with antecedents $g_1, \ldots, g_m$, we define

$$\chi(s) := f_{and}(\chi(r), \{g_1, \ldots, g_m\})$$

Here, f_{and} is a function that computes the confidence level of the rule conclusion based on the confidence level of the antecedents and the confidence in the rule itself. One reasonable choice for f_{and} is

$$f_{and}(\chi(r), S) := \chi(r) \cdot min(S)$$

which uses the confidence value of the rule as a discounting factor on the minimum premise confidence. Using these definitions, KRT can recursively determine the confidence in each side of a contradiction, and propose to modify the side with smaller confidence.

Readers of chapter 3 may have noticed that the confidence computation described above is similar to the evidence point computations performed by the inference engine. There also, an evidence transfer function is used to compute the conclusion evidence of a rule, and a multiple-derivation combination function is used to compute the evidence point for a fact. Given this similarity, it seems an attractive possibility simply to identify χ with the evidence functions. This, however, would not accurately reflect the meaning of the two: it is possible for a derivation to contribute a lot of evidence with little confidence, as well as little evidence with perfect confidence, so the two must be kept separate.

7.6 Plausibility and Non-minimal Revisions

As pointed out above, the rationale behind the minimal base revision operation used in KRT is to remove unwanted inferences with minimal changes to the knowledge bases and a minimal loss of inferences. By introducing exceptions into the support set of a rule, the minimal base revision operation avoids having to delete successful rules just because there are a few exceptions. On the other hand, even though minimal revisions are a safe starting point, there are situations where further specializations of revised rules, and thus non-minimal revisions, are desirable. This is the case whenever the exception list of a rule has grown very long in relation to the list of its correct applications. In such a case, the entire rule must be regarded as *implausible*.

Whenever a rule has been modified by the exclusion operator of a minimal base revision, KRT therefore verifies that the number of instances and exceptions to the rule still meet a user-specifiable *plausibility criterion*. This plausibility criterion is a conditional expression in which pos denotes the number of instances of the rule, and neg denotes the number of exceptions as recorded in the global exceptions list (GE) of the rule's support set. An example of a plausibility criterion from the traffic law domain is

pos > 0 & (neg < 4 ; neg < 0.3*pos)

If this criterion is not met, KRT proposes to the user to try to *reformulate* the support set by performing further specializations beyond the minimal one produced by the exclusion operator. The user is of course free to cancel the proposed reformulation attempt, perhaps to have it performed at a more convenient later point in time.

7.7 Support Set Reformulation

The task of the process that reformulates the support set is to provide a support set that did not meet the plausibility criterion with a "more plausible" form. The plausibility concept in this context is primarily based on the extent to which a rule is universal: only rules that are universal, i.e. that do not have an explicit list of the valid and invalid applications, can be regarded as plausible. Consequently, the aim of the reformulation process must be to replace a very large *extensional* description of exceptions by an *intensional* description on the basis of a domain concept [Emde *et al.*, 1983]. To perform such reformulations, KRT possesses a number of reformulation operators that are summarized in table 7.1. In this table, $\pi_{i_1,\ldots,i_m}(S)$ of a set S of n-tuples ($m \leq n$) denotes the projection of S on positions $i_1, \ldots, i_m$, i.e.,

$$\pi_{i_1,\ldots,i_m}(S) := \{(c_1, \ldots, c_m) \mid \exists t \in S : c_1 = t[i_1], \ldots, c_m = t[i_m]\}$$

For projections on a single dimension, we regard the result as a simple set, i.e., $\{(c_1), \ldots, (c_n)\}$ is regarded as $\{c_1, \ldots, c_n\}$. Where no confusion can arise, we have simply written $p(t)$ instead of $p(c_1, \ldots, c_n)$ where $t = (c_1, \ldots, c_n)$. Also, throughout the table we denote the current knowledge base by the greek letter Γ and use the abbreviation $I(R, \Gamma)$ to denote the set of instances of R in Γ (tuples of variable bindings used in all current applications of R in Γ). Finally, vars(R) denotes the ordered set of variables of R.

7.8 Example

In this section, we illustrate the effect of KRT's reformulation operators with a few examples from our "traffic law" test domain (see section 9.1). As a starting point, assume that in our traffic law knowledge base Γ, the system has learned the rule r37

involved_vehicle(X,Y) & owner(Z,Y) → responsible(Z,X)

with the initial support set S(r37)

(1) *localize*(X_i) : Localize exceptions to individual variable domains.
$X_i \in \text{vars}(R)$. Let $Int := \pi_i(I(R,\Gamma)) \cap \pi_i(GE)$. In $S(R)$, replace GE by $\{t \in GE \mid \pi_i(t) \in Int\}$, and replace LE_i by $LE_i \cup (\pi_i(GE) \setminus Int)$.

(2) *add_ei*(V',p): Add an existing predicate (instances).
$V' = [X_{i_1}, \ldots, X_{i_k}]$ is a sequence of elements of vars(R), and p must be an existing predicate of arity $|V'|$ such that $\forall t \in \pi_{i_1,\ldots,i_k}(I(R,\Gamma)) : p(t) \in \Gamma$. Add the additional premise $p(X_{i_1}, \ldots, X_{i_k})$ to R, and in $S(R)$, replace GE by $\{t \in GE \mid p(\pi_{i_1,\ldots,i_k}(t)) \in \Gamma\}$. If $V' = \{X_j\}$, replace LE_j by $\{s \in LE_j \mid p(s) \in \Gamma\}$.

(3) *add_ee*(V',p): Add an existing predicate (exceptions).
$V' = [X_{i_1}, \ldots, X_{i_k}]$ is a sequence of elements of vars(R), and p must be an existing predicate of arity $|V'|$ such that $\forall t \in \pi_{i_1,\ldots,i_k}(I(R,\Gamma)) : \mathsf{not}(p(t)) \in \Gamma$. Add the additional premise $\mathsf{not}(p(X_{i_1}, \ldots, X_{i_k}))$ to R, and in $S(R)$, replace GE by $\{t \in GE \mid \mathsf{not}(p(\pi_{i_1,\ldots,i_k}(t))) \in \Gamma\}$. If $V' = \{X_j\}$, replace LE_j by $\{s \in LE_j \mid \mathsf{not}(p(s)) \in \Gamma\}$.

(4) *add_ni*(V'): Add newly formed predicate (instances).
$V' = [X_{i_1}, \ldots, X_{i_k}]$ is a sequence of elements of vars(R). Call CLT to form a new concept c of arity k, specifying $\pi_{i_1,\ldots,i_k}(I(R,\Gamma))$ as instances and $\pi_{i_1,\ldots,i_k}(GE)$ as non-instances. If CLT successfully forms a concept c (producing a knowledge base Γ') such that $\forall t \in \pi_{i_1,\ldots,i_k}(I(R,\Gamma)) : c(t) \in \Gamma'$, add the additional premise $c(X_{i_1}, \ldots, X_{i_k})$ to R, and in $S(R)$, replace GE by $\{t \in GE \mid c(\pi_{i_1,\ldots,i_k}(t)) \in \Gamma'\}$. If $V' = \{X_j\}$, replace LE_j by $\{s \in LE_j \mid c(s) \in \Gamma\}$.

(5) *add_ne*(V'): Add newly formed predicate (exceptions).
$V' = [X_{i_1}, \ldots, X_{i_k}]$ is a sequence of elements of vars(R). Call CLT to form a new concept c of arity k, specifying $\pi_{i_1,\ldots,i_k}(GE)$ as instances and $\pi_{i_1,\ldots,i_k}(I(R,\Gamma))$ as non-instances. If CLT successfully forms a concept c (producing a knowledge base Γ') such that $\forall t \in \pi_{i_1,\ldots,i_k}(I(R,\Gamma)) : \mathsf{not}(c(t)) \in \Gamma'$, add the additional premise $\mathsf{not}(c(X_{i_1}, \ldots, X_{i_k}))$ to R, and in $S(R)$, replace GE by $\{t \in GE \mid \mathsf{not}(c(\pi_{i_1,\ldots,i_k}(t))) \in \Gamma'\}$. If $V' = \{X_j\}$, replace LE_j by $\{s \in LE_j \mid \mathsf{not}(c(s)) \in \Gamma\}$.

Table 7.1: KRT's Reformulation Operators

(X, Y, Z) ∈ all × all × all

i.e., the unrestricted default support set where $GE = \emptyset$. The above rule is actually incorrect, since in reality, it holds for minor traffic violations like false parking only. For all other violations, the driver is responsible. So suppose that at this point, we enter three additional cases that are not minor violations. Using the incorrect rule above, the system will derive conclusions about responsibilities that directly contradict the stated information in the three cases:

responsible(john,stolen_event) - [1000,1000]
responsible(sw,loan_event) - [1000,1000]
responsible(ace_cab_co,cab_event) - [1000,1000]

These contradictions are stored on the system *agenda* from which the user can select them for handling at any time. Once this happens, a knowledge revision interaction is started (figure 7.3).

As described above, KRT has selected a preferred revision according to the confidence functions χ and κ, and has marked this revision in the graphical display with four little black squares around the nodes to be removed. Assuming that the user goes along with this suggestion, the chosen minimal removal set for minimal base revision, as shown in figure 7.3, is

M ={ (r37, (cab_event,cab1,ace_cab_co)),
(r37, (loan_event,b_xs_400,sw)),
(r37, (stolen_event,b_dx_986,dx)) }

KRT then applies the exclusion operator, and the new support set is[2]:

all × all × all \ {(cab_event,cab1,ace_cab_co),
(loan_event,b_xs_400,sw), (stolen_event,b_dx_986,dx)}

This support set is the basis for the application of the reformulation operators, and we will assume it is judged implausible by the system or the user so that reformulation is attempted.

To demonstrate the reformulation operators, assume that r37 has the following instances in Γ:

[2] In the following, we omit the variable list of the support set.

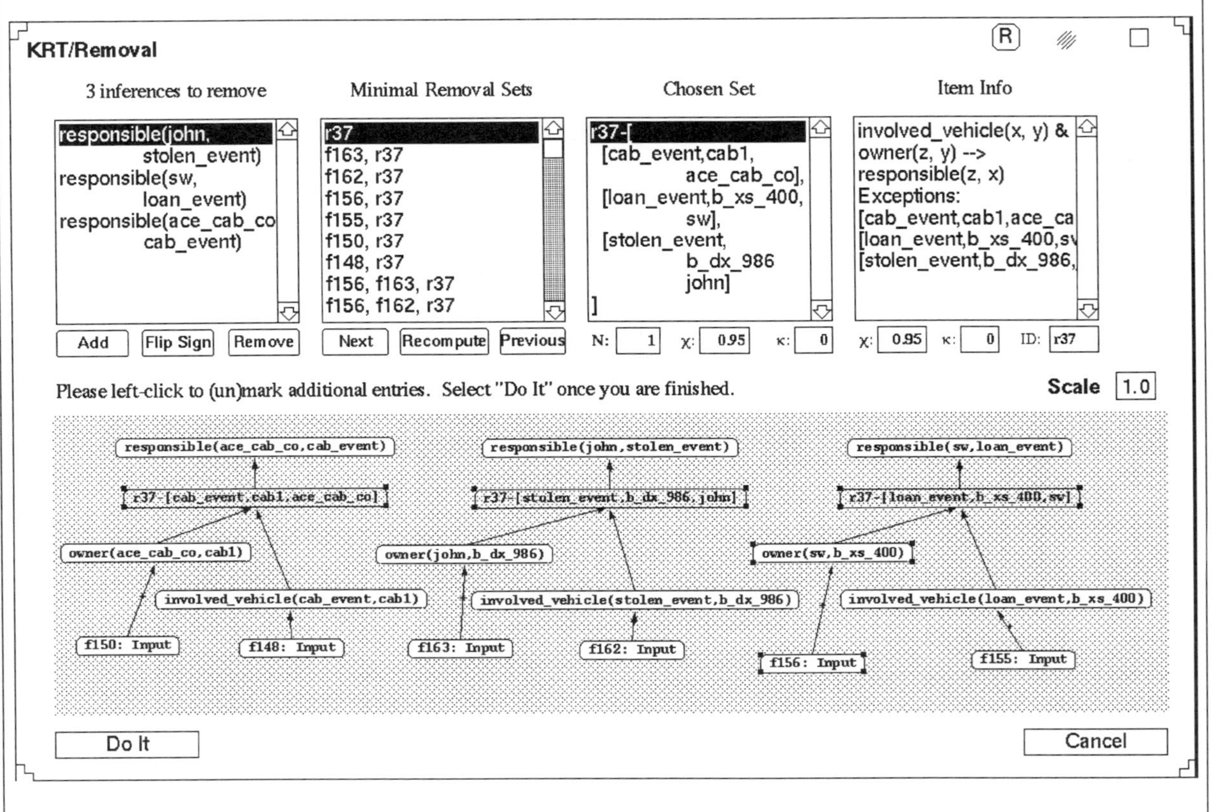

Figure 7.3: Knowledge revision example from the "traffic law" domain

$I(\text{r37}, \Gamma) = \{$ (event1,b_au_6773,sw), (event2,b_dx_1385,dj),
(event3,hh_mo_195,mo), (event4,b_md_4321,md),
(event5,b_st_888,st), (event6,b_ab_89,ab),
(event7,b_bc_90,bc), (event8,b_cd_01,cd),
(event9,b_de_12,de), (event10,b_ef_23,ef),
(event11,b_fg_34,fg), (event12,b_gh_45,ef) $\}$

The effects of the different operators, if applied during the reformulation search (see section 7.10), are the following. The *localize* operator moves exceptions from GE to one of the local exception lists. *localize*(X) ($i = 1$) would produce:

$$(\text{all} \setminus \{\text{cab\_event, loan\_event, stolen\_event}\}) \times \text{all} \times \text{all}$$

leaving no global exceptions, whereas *localize*(Z) ($i = 3$) would produce:

$$(\text{all} \times \text{all} \times (\text{all} \setminus \{\text{ace\_cab\_co, dx}\})) \setminus \{(\text{loan\_event,b\_xs\_400,sw})\}$$

since $Int := \pi_3(I(\text{r37}, \Gamma)) \cap \pi_3(GE) = \{sw\}$. The reformulation operators *add_ei* and *add_ni* both add an extra, positive premise to the rule: *add_ei* uses an existing predicate that can be specified, whereas *add_ni* calls the concept formation tool CLT (see chapter 8) to form a new concept for a specified set of variables. Assuming that Γ contained a predicate sedan defined by the following facts:

sedan(b_au_6773).	sedan(b_dx_1385).	sedan(hh_mo_195).
sedan(b_md_4321).	sedan(b_st_888).	sedan(b_ab_89,ab).
sedan(b_bc_90).	sedan(b_cd_01).	sedan(b_de_12).
sedan(b_ef_23).	sedan(b_fg_34).	sedan(b_gh_45).
sedan(b_dx_986).	not(sedan(b_xs_400).)	

the operator *add_ei*({Y}, sedan) would produce the rule:

involved_vehicle(X,Y) & owner(Z,Y)
& sedan(Y) → responsible(Z,X)

with the new support set:

$$\text{all} \times \text{all} \times \text{all} \setminus \{(\text{stolen\_event,b\_dx\_986,dx})\}$$

since b_dx_986 is also a sedan, but an exception to the rule. In the actual run that these examples are taken from, KRT used the operator *add_ni*({X}), and CLT indeed found a new concept minor_violation[3] which was used to construct

[3]This name was provided by the user after the concept had been found. CLT just uses "gensym" names like concept1.

the correct rule:

involved_vehicle(X,Y) & owner(Z,Y) &
minor_violation(X) → responsible(Z,X) — all × all × all

The reader is referred to chapter 8 for a detailed explanation of how CLT is used to form new concepts for use by the *add_ni* and *add_ne* operators.

Similarly, the reformulation operators *add_ee* and *add_ne* both add an extra, negative premise to the rule: *add_ee* uses an existing predicate that can be specified, whereas *add_ne* calls the concept formation tool to form a new predicate. Assuming that Γ contained a predicate motorcycle defined by the facts:

motorcycle(b_xs_400). not(motorcycle(cab1)).

then the application of the operator *add_ee*({Y}, motorcycle) would result in the new rule:

involved_vehicle(X,Y) & owner(Z,Y)
& not(motorcycle(Y)) → responsible(Z,X)

with the new support set:

all × all × all \ {(cab_event,cab1,ace_cab_co)}

since cab1 is not a motorcycle, and still an exception to the rule.

7.9 Properties of the Reformulation Operators

We omit the example for *add_ne*, and instead point out some properties of the reformulation operators. The operators are defined in such a way that the specialization they produce remains complete, i.e., the rules they produce are guaranteed still to cover $I(R, \Gamma)$. For the *localize* operator, this is ensured by allowing only non-members of the set *Int* to be added to the local exception list; for the other operators, this is ensured by requiring that all instances (or rather, their appropriate projections) must match the new premise that is added. This means that extensionally, a reformulated rule is no more special than the original rule with the exception list (it still covers the same instances and excludes the same exceptions). The situation changes, however, when new objects are introduced into the knowledge base (in a "growing" language). The original rule with an exception list will always be applicable to such new objects since these are not mentioned in the exception list. A reformulated rule with an additional premise, however, will be applicable to a new object only if the object is known to be an instance of the new premise predicate. This may not be the case, so intensionally, the reformulated rule is indeed a non-minimal specialization.

Even though the reformulation operators used by KRT cover an important and hopefully natural set of specializations of a rule, they are not complete, that is, there are specializations that cannot be produced by any of these operators. As an example, consider specializations that require the substitution of constants for variables in a rule or specializations that require new variables. An interesting possibility would thus be to extend KRT's reformulation operators towards a complete specialization operator such as Shapiro's ρ operator for first-order clauses [Shapiro, 1983].

As a final point, note that KRT uses the support set representation only to list explicit exceptions, i.e., the GE and LE_i parts of a support set; the domains themselves are not modified by KRT, and usually remain all. The reasons for choosing to add an extra premise instead of including a concept in the support set were uniformity and understandability: since the support set representation only allows unary positive concepts to specify domains, additional premises would have been necessary anyway in all cases where exception concepts or relational concepts are used. Furthermore, users generally have an easier time understanding additional premises than complex support sets.

The disadvantage of this strategy is that new metapredicates are often needed to represent the rules that are the result of knowledge revision reformulations. If the new rule does not match any existing metapredicate, a new one will automatically be generated, but this new metapredicate is not integrated into the system's meta-metaknowledge, so the user would ultimately have to add metarules to express the properties of the new metapredicate or its connections to other metapredicates. Supports sets were originally introduced to circumvent this problem by attaching support sets to metafacts as well, thus allowing the original metapredicate to be used. In practice, it has turned out that metarules are used much less frequently than we had envisioned, so uniformity and understandability of KRT results took precedence. In any case, the results of the *localize* operator can still be expressed using the support set only; furthermore, the full support set format can be used for manual input.

Level	*Operators*	*Arguments*
1	$localize(i)$	$\forall i : \pi_i(I(R,\Gamma)) \cap \pi_i(GE) = \emptyset$
2	$add\_ei(\{V_i\}, p)$	$\forall i : \pi_i(I(R,\Gamma)) \cap \pi_i(GE) = \emptyset$, all unary p in Γ
	$add\_ee(\{V_i\}, p)$	$\forall i : \pi_i(I(R,\Gamma)) \cap \pi_i(GE) = \emptyset$, all unary p in Γ
3	$add\_ne(\{V_i\})$	$\forall i : \pi_i(I(R,\Gamma)) \cap \pi_i(GE) = \emptyset$
4	$add\_ni(\{V_i\})$	$\forall i : \pi_i(I(R,\Gamma)) \cap \pi_i(GE) = \emptyset$
5	$add\_ni(\{V_i, V_j\})$	$\forall (V_i, V_j) \in \text{vars}(R) \times \text{vars}(R), V_i \neq V_j$

Table 7.2: Cost Levels of Reformulation Operators

7.10 Search Strategy

The operators defined in table 7.1 only define the search space of possible KRT reformulations. They do not yet prescribe a particular search strategy. Since it would be much too expensive in practice to try all these reformulations, KRT employs a greedy, heuristic strategy that searches the space partially according to a fixed ordering of operators that reflects the costs of executing the operator. This ordering assigns each of the operators a search depth level as summarized in table 7.2[4].

As can be seen in this table, KRT's efforts are kept low on levels (1) through (4) by limiting the search to unary reformulations, and including only those variables for which a "perfect" reformulation can be found, i.e., where the lists of instances and exceptions do not overlap so that in principle, a predicate can be found that includes all instances, and excludes all exceptions.

The progression from one to the next higher search level is governed by a user-specifiable parameter that specifies a default search depth up to which KRT will search. Within the specified search levels, the plausibility criterion introduced in section 7.6 is used as a filter, i.e., only those reformulations that pass the plausibility criterion are collected. In this context, the plausibility criterion is applied not to the global instance and exceptions sets, but to their projections on the variable X_i that was chosen as the argument for the reformulation operator. If no satisfactory reformulation was found within the allocated effort, the user is queried about whether to proceed. In addition, the user can request to be queried before each individual application of the *add_ni* or *add_ne* operators, i.e., before each call to CLT. This is especially necessary for search on level 5 where all combinations of variables would

[4]As a future extension of KRT, more flexible user-specified search strategies are planned.

otherwise be searched.

At the end of the search, KRT applies a heuristic evaluation metric to select one of the reformulations that were found. This evaluation metric orders all reformulations according to the number of explictly remaining exceptions, and prefers those with fewer exceptions. Among reformulations with equal numbers of exceptions, those that use existing concepts are preferred over reformulations with newly formed concepts, and concepts that cover the instances are preferred over those that cover the exceptions to a rule. In any case, the user is given a chance to modify the system's choice, or to specify a reformulation on his or her own.

When the above steps in the reformulation process have led to a plausible support set description, the knowledge revision process can be terminated successfully. Otherwise, the system will ask the user for a reformulation, and if none is supplied, delete the rule entirely.

7.11 Related Work

In section 7.3, we already discussed the problems of the minimal specialization hypothesis that was proposed in [Muggleton and Bain, 1992]. In the same paper, the authors also present a specialization algorithm based on the introduction of non-monotonically interpreted premises with new predicates. Thus, for example, if the substitutions $\{\{X/a\}, \{X/b\}\}$ were to be excluded from $p(X) \rightarrow q(X)$, the algorithm of Muggleton and Bain would produce the theory

$$p(X) \wedge not(c1(X)) \rightarrow q(X); c1(a); c1(b),$$

where $c1$ is a new predicate, and *not* is interpreted as negation by failure. As can easily be seen, this is a notational variant of the exception set method used to specialize clauses used in BLIP and KRT/MOBAL. Thus, the introduction of non-monotonically interpreted predicates just adds unnecessary complexity, as it is not necessary for correct minimal specialization of clauses. The algorithm of [Muggleton and Bain, 1992] always selects to modify those clauses that have directly resolved with the fact that is to be removed. Nonetheless, contrary to what is implied in [Muggleton and Bain, 1992], this is insufficient to guarantee minimal specialization (see [Wrobel, 1993b; Wrobel, 1993a] for the details).

Our method of using exception lists to specialize individual clauses has also been adopted in the algorithm proposed in [Ling, 1991]. This paper also introduces the important notion of learning in a growing language: specialization operations should be such that when a new constant is added to the language anything provable about the new constant with the original theory should also be provable from the specialization. As Ling points out, the exception methods ensures that this is the case. He also points to an important problem that was also recognized in [Wrobel, 1988a; Wrobel, 1989]: if exclusion is used as the only specialization operator on individual clauses, we may build up long (possibly infinite) exception lists. As we saw in sections 7.6 and 7.7, this problem is addressed in KRT through a user specified *plausibility criterion* and the subsequent application of reformulation operators. Ling instead uses a *complete* set of refinement operators, i.e., capable of producing all specializations of a clause, and simply replaces a clause by all of its specializations. This guarantees minimal specialization and thus identification in the limit, but brings with it the undesirable properties of minimal specializations as spelled out in section 7.3.

MIS [Shapiro, 1983] was one of the first first-order learning systems to include theory revision. In MIS, however, minimality of revision was not a concern, since subsequent generalization steps were relied upon to fix up a theory that had become overspecialized. Nonetheless, the MIS approach is highly relevant to the work presented here, since its backtracing algorithm offers a way of determining with a minimum number of user queries which possible revision to choose, i.e., it offers one particular way of implementing the choice function among minimal revisions. As described above, KRT uses a different method that relies on a two-tiered model of confidence in statements, and proposes to the user the revision that would entail a minimal loss of confidence. Evidently, this could easily combined with a backtracing strategy. The backtracing strategy of MIS is also used in the interactive learning programs MARVIN [Sammut and Banerji, 1986] and CLINT [De Raedt, 1991] to recover from overgeneralizations that lead to incorrectly covered negative examples.

7.12 Summary

KRT is a knowledge revision tool that can be used both as part of a non-interactive learning system, and as an interactive tool for modifying knowledge bases under user control. In the latter case, the system's built-in heuristics for selecting preferred revisions, and for selecting among the possible reformulations, are used to generate proposals for the user that can easily be modified. In the former case, they are relied upon exclusively to permit non-interactive operation.

Besides this kind of built-in support, the particular strengths of KRT are first its use of a minimal base revision method that avoids the disadvantages of minimal specialization. The method guarantees a minimal modification of the existing knowledge base with the maximum preservation of existing inferences.Second, KRT is capable of automatically triggering further reformulations on such minimally modified rules to find shorter and more plausible forms. Third, through its close integration with CLT, KRT is capable of triggering the introduction of new concepts into the representation, and to find reformulations that would have been impossible with the existing vocabulary.

Chapter 8

Concept Formation

8.1 Representation Bias in Learning

The knowledge representation available to a learning system has a decisive influence on whether a given learning goal can be reached, and if so, how quickly it can be reached: anything that is to be *learnable* must first of all be *representable*, so anything that cannot be represented, cannot be learned. Consequently, the knowledge representation used by a learning system defines the maximal *hypothesis space* of the learner: it is simply the set of all expressions of the representation. By choosing an appropriately limited representation, the time taken to search the so-defined hypothesis space can be kept low. If the space is too small, however, the target concept may no longer be contained in it. Within a given hypothesis space, many learning systems use some form of *syntactic bias* to decide which part of the space to search, or which hypothesis among a set of possible hypotheses to accept. Often, the shortest or simplest hypotheses are preferred, so again, the representation has an important influence. These various influences of the representation on the learning process are collectively known as *representation bias* [Utgoff, 1986].

Representation bias can be identified at two different levels of a representation: namely at the level of representation *formalism*, i.e., the syntax and semantics of the representation, and at the level of representation *vocabulary*, i.e., the set of symbols, attributes, or predicates available in a given formalism. The problem of introducing new elements into the vocabulary is also referred to as the *new term* problem. In MOBAL, the representation formalism is a variant of Horn clause logic as defined in chapter 2, which makes search in the hypothesis space defined by this representation more tractable. In addition, RDT uses its rule models as an explicit bias.

Whereas the representation formalism used by MOBAL is fixed, the system is capable of extending its representation *vocabulary*: in this chapter, we present CLT, the *concept learning tool* of the MOBAL system, which addresses the problem of representation vocabulary bias, and is capable of automatically introducing new concepts (predicates) into the system's representation[1]. CLT takes a *concept formation* approach to the problem of representation change, and exploits the problem solving context in MOBAL's knowledge revision process to trigger its concept formation activities. The system then tries inductively to characterize the aggregate supplied by KRT with a generalized Horn clause concept description, using MOBAL's rule discovery tool RDT. If the new concept is then judged useful according to structural constraints, it is introduced into the representation and used to reformulate existing inference rules of the problem solver. CLT is based on the original idea of exploiting exceptions in METAXA [Emde *et al.*, 1983], and our previous work on concept formation in BLIP respectively the MODELER [Wrobel, 1988a; Wrobel, 1989], but uses a much improved concept characterization step, is capable of forming relational (n-ary) concepts, employs a theoretically more sound restructuring step based on resolution and θ-subsumption, and includes a concept garbage collector.

In the rest of this chapter, we first explain what we mean by a concept formation approach to representation change, and how it differs from the complementary *constructive induction* approach. We identify possible types of constraints on concept formation, and discuss where CLT fits into the spectrum of previous approaches to the problem (section 8.2). We then discuss the representation of concepts in MOBAL (section 8.3). Section 8.4 is the central part of the chapter, as it explains how CLT uses RDT to form an intensional description of the aggregates that are supplied by KRT, how it evaluates new concepts, and how it uses them to restructure the rule base. Section 8.5 contains an evaluation of the quality of CLT concepts, followed by a discussion of related work (section 8.6) and our conclusions (section 8.7).

---

[1]All new concepts introduced by CLT are constructed from existing components. The problem of truly new concepts is discussed in detail in [Wrobel, 1991b] and [Wrobel, 1993a].

8.2 Constructive Induction vs. Concept Formation

The problems involved in selecting an appropriate vocabulary for a learning problem has long been known in machine learning. In 1983, Quinlan [Quinlan, 1983] discussed how much effort was necessary to hand-craft a set of attributes so that ID3 could learn a chess endgame concept. The same is of course true for RDT, with its strong limit on the forms of possible hypotheses: an additional predicate may make a rule learnable that would not otherwise have fit the existing rule models. Consequently, it would be very desirable for a learning system automatically to extend its vocabulary when necessary. To this end, two capabilities are needed:

- the capability to *recognize* inadequacies of the representation,
- the capability to *remedy* such shortcomings.

In existing learning systems, two complementary approaches have been chosen to tackle the problem of introducing a new attribute or predicate (in short: a new descriptor) into a representation. The first, often referred to as *constructive induction* [Michalski, 1983], is to use a set of descriptor construction operators. Each such operator can be understood as a mapping from the existing set of descriptors to an augmented new set of descriptors. An example of such an operator is Michalski's *maximum* operator [Michalski, 1983]. It is applied to a binary descriptor that describes an ordering relation, and produces a descriptor that designates the maximum element of the ordering. For the "above" relation, this construction operator would thus add the descriptor "top".

Construction operators can be general and domain independent, such as the intraconstruction operator in inverse-resolution learners [Muggleton and Buntine, 1988; Wirth, 1989; Rouveirol and Puget, 1990], Rendell and Seshu's FC operator [Rendell and Seshu, 1990], or the operators used for adding conjunctions or disjunctions of existing descriptors in STAGGER [Schlimmer, 1987] or the FRINGE systems [Pagallo, 1989]. Alternatively, they can be used to capture knowledge about features that could potentially be useful in a domain. For example, BACON's [Langley *et al.*, 1986] operator for introducing new terms relied on built-in knowledge about the form of physical laws ("small exponents"); AM [Lenat, 1982] had mathematics-specific heuristics that suggested interesting concepts to form; De Raedt proposed the CIA technique for the acquisition of such domain-specific operators [De Raedt and Bruynooghe, 1989b]. Independent of the type of operator provided, the central problem is to control their application, i.e., the search in the descriptor space that they define, and to evaluate the quality of descriptors they have produced; different solutions have been found in the above-cited systems.

CLT, the concept formation tool of MOBAL that is described in this chapter, is an instance of the second, complementary way of introducing a new descriptor into a representation. This approach does not take the set of known descriptors as its point of departure, but instead looks at the set of known *objects* (instances, individuals, cases, events), and tries to find subsets of such objects that could usefully be aggregated into a group, and labeled with a common descriptor. This descriptor is then defined by inducing a description of the set of objects that it covers. We will refer to this approach as the *concept formation* approach. Where a constructive induction approach starts out by introducing a new descriptor definition (intension), thus defining a new set of objects (extension), a concept formation approach first identifies a set of objects to be aggregated (extension), and then induces a definition (intension).

More precisely, by concept formation we refer to the following task (borrowing terminology from [Easterlin and Langley, 1985]):

- *Given* a set of object (instance, event, case) descriptions (usually presented incrementally),
- *find* sets of objects that can usefully be grouped together (*aggregation*), and
- *find* intensional definitions for these sets of objects (*characterization*)[2].

The non-incremental variant of this task is usually referred to as *conceptual clustering.* In the context of representation change, an additional requirement is:

- *Define* a new name (predicate) for the new concept, and introduce it into the representation, so that it can be used in, say, the definition of further concepts, or for the description of future input objects.

[2]Our use of the term concept formation is thus more general than the definition used by Gennari *et. al.* [Gennari *et al.*, 1989] who included the additional requirement of forming a hierarchical organization, and also restricted the term to divisive, hill-climbing methods.

In hierarchical concept formation systems [Michalski and Stepp, 1983; Lebowitz, 1987; Fisher, 1987; Gennari *et al.*, 1989], this latter step is usually not included, i.e., these systems aggregate objects and characterize them, but do not give them names that are available elsewhere.

Corresponding to the problem of search control in constructive induction approaches, the central problem in a concept formation approach is how to find useful sets of objects to group together. Since the search space to be considered is the powerset of the set of known objects, the number of candidate sets grows exponentially in the number of objects, requiring strong constraint on aggregation. Existing concept formation systems have mainly used three types of constraints on aggregation: similarity-based, correlation-based, and structure-based.

Similarity-based constraints rely on a context-free numerical measure of similarity between two objects such as Euclidean distance. Such measures are most heavily used in numerical taxonomy systems [Everitt, 1980], but have also been used in, for example, UNIMEM [Lebowitz, 1987] to decide when to combine two instances into a more general concept. Similarity-based constraints are simple, but the quality of the concepts that are formed depends very much on a proper definition of the similarity measure. For example, it has been noted that the effect of UNIMEM's parameters on its results remains unclear [Gennari *et al.*, 1989].

Feature correlation constraints are based on the assumption that the best conceptual systems are those that maximize intra-concept correlations, and minimize inter-concept correlations. Correlation measures, therefore, are not used to rate the distance between individual objects, but apply to proposed sets of concepts. They have been used in many existing concept formation approaches. The CLUSTER system [Michalski and Stepp, 1983] uses cluster distance, discrimination index, and dimensionality reduction as indirect measures of feature correlation in its lexicographic evaluation function (LEF); UNIMEM [Lebowitz, 1987] uses integer counters of predictability and predictiveness to decide when to fix a feature as part of a concept definition; COBWEB [Fisher, 1987] and its successor CLASSIT [Gennari *et al.*, 1989] both use probabilistical correlation measures based on feature correlations ("category utility") to compare proposed clusterings; WITT [Hanson and Bauer, 1989] uses another correlation-based measure ("cohesion") for bottom-up clustering.

Structural constraints refer to the syntactical structure of individual concept descriptions, or to the structure of the entire conceptual system. In CLUSTER [Michalski and Stepp, 1983], only aggregates that could be characterized by conjunctive expressions were considered, and those with shorter definitions (total number of "selector" conjuncts used in entire clustering) were preferred. In CLUSTER/G [Stepp and Michalski, 1986], the available descriptors had associated weights derived from a goal dependency network, and the system preferred clusterings that used descriptors with high weights. In KLUSTER [Kietz and Morik, 1991b], aggregation is restricted to subsets of the set of instances of a common superconcept, which are required to be disjoint.

Finally, there is fourth type of constraint that has not received as much attention, but is nonetheless strongly suggested by psychological literature on the goal-oriented nature of human concept formation [Nelson, 1983; Barsalou, 1983]: constraints derived from an embedding of a concept formation system into a *problem solving context.* The basic assumption of such constraints is that a concept formation system should usefully aggregate those objects that occur in the same context, or play a similar role, in a problem solving activity.

It is this fourth type of constraint that is exploited by CLT: the problem solving context consists of the knowledge revision activities of KRT, which are used to supply the aggregates upon which concept formation is then based. In this way, CLT's concept formation activities are well-focused. In section 8.4, we explain precisely how the concept formation process in CLT works; first, however, a few words about a seemingly obvious question: just what do we mean by a concept when we speak about concept formation?

8.3 The Representation of Concepts in Mobal

Generally speaking, a *concept* is a universal, summary description of a set of abstract or concrete objects which can be used to make propositions and inferences. Thus, a newly created term is only the name of a concept. It only becomes useful through the importance granted to it by a concept description.

Three basic types of concept description based on psychological models can be distinguished [Smith and Medin, 1981]:

- *The classical approach:* A concept is a brief description of the entire class and consists of individually necessary and collectively sufficient features.
- *The probabilistic approach:* A concept is a brief description of the

entire class; the instances, however, are more or less likely to have the features.

- *The exemplar approach:* A concept consists of a set of more or less abstract descriptions of exemplar or subsets of the instances.

Machine learning techniques are mostly based on the classical approach: very often, features are represented by one-place attributes. The probabilistic and the exemplar approaches have only recently been used for learning programs (see, for example, [Bareiss and Porter, 1987], [Fisher, 1987]). In [Wrobel, 1991a; Wrobel, 1993a], we discuss the problem of concept representation in more detail.

In order to be able to benefit from the available inference procedures and the rule learning techniques in RDT, MOBAL represents concepts with the existing representations, i.e., without any specific new constructs, by simply using unary or n-ary predicates: concept membership can be expressed by simple facts (the concept's *extension*, and the concept description (the concept's *intension*) consists of necessary and sufficient conditions which are represented by rules. Sufficient conditions are rules that contain the concept predicate in the conclusion; necessary conditions are rules that contain the concept as the only premise. Table 8.1 shows an example of a knowledge base that contains a concept parking_violation; the rules defining its intension are marked $I(C)$.

Though this quasi-classic approach does not meet all the requirements established in psychological studies, it does have a few advantages over the commonly used attribute-based classic approach:

- Concept descriptions are not limited to attribute information, but they can also represent relational components.

- Disjoint concepts can be represented, as not all sufficient features also need to be necessary. Such concepts are also called *polymorphic* [Hanson and Bauer, 1989].

The concept hierarchy that is typical of human conceptual systems is simply represented by corresponding metafacts/rules (Figure 8.1). Thus, it is possible for the inference engine to handle hierarchical inferences and concept membership, and the hierarchy can be acquired by the learning procedure.

For a more detailed discussion of this concept representation and the different psychological requirements, we refer the reader to [Wrobel, 1993a].

```
bus_lane(Place) → no_parking(Place)
fire_hydrant(Place) → no_parking(Place)
car_parked(Event,Place) & metered(Place) & unpaid(Event)
                                   → parking_violation(Event)      ⎫
car_parked(Event,Place) & no_parking(Place)                         ⎪
                                   → parking_violation(Event)      ⎪
parking_violation(Event) → fine(Event,20)                          ⎬ I(C)
parking_violation(Event) → minor_violation(Event)                  ⎪
parking_violation(Event) & appeals(Person,Event)                   ⎪
                                   → court_citation(Event)         ⎭
parking_violation(event2)
bus_lane(place1)
fire_hydrant(place2)
metered(place3)
involved_vehicle(event1,b_au_6773)
owner(b_au_6773,sw)
car_parked(event1,place1)
```

Table 8.1: A Theory with the Concept *parking_violation*

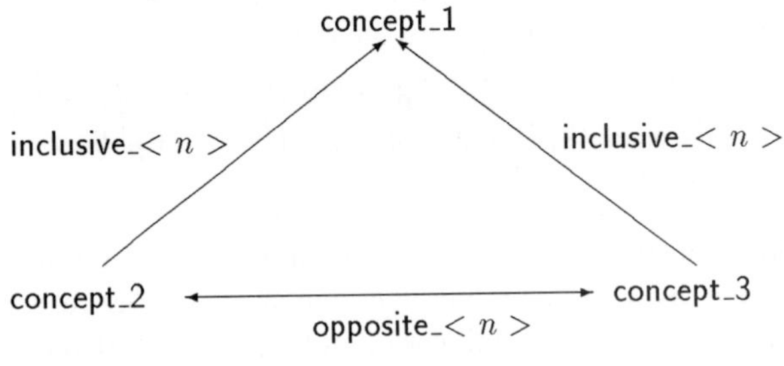

Figure 8.1: A Concept Hierarchy Represented with Metafacts/Rules

8.4 Demand-driven Concept Formation

In MOBAL the process of concept formation that leads to a representation extension is triggered whenever the reformulation phase of the knowledge revision process reaches an impasse, i.e. when none of the existing concepts is suitable to characterize the available instances and exceptions of the rule support set. In terms of the operators defined in table 7.1, this is the case whenever the search for reformulations on level 2, i.e., with the *add_ei* and *add_ee* operators, is not successful. In this case, CLT is called as a subroutine of KRT to search for a new concept that covers the instances and excludes the exceptions of the rule that is being modified by KRT (operator *add_ni*) or one that covers the exceptions, and excludes the instances (operator *add_ne*).

Thus, the knowledge revision process has already predetermined the extension of the concept to be examined, i.e. the *aggregation step* [Easterlin and Langley, 1985] of the concept formation process has already been taken, and all that remains to be done is to provide the new concept with an intensional description.

8.4.1 Inducing an Intensional Characterization

Given instances and non-instances of the proposed concept, the characterization step of CLT merely involves the invention of a new name c for the concept, the introduction of positive and negative facts about c into the knowledge base, and then reduces to a learning from examples problem in a function-free Horn clause representation. Since we are interested not only in sufficient condition rules about c, however, the learning algorithm that is used must also be capable of searching for rules with c in the body.

In MOBAL, we are using the learning module RDT [Kietz and Wrobel, 1991] for the purpose of characterizing a new concept. RDT is a model-driven most-general learner, and can easily be adapted to finding rules with c in the body by partially instantiating its rule model with c, thus ensuring that c will occur in the body. RDT is then called on each predicate of the knowledge base, which is feasible only since the pre-instantiation of its rule models reduces its search space down to manageable proportions. For a data-driven learner such as FOIL [Quinlan, 1990], a similar reduction of the search space would not be possible, since whether c appears in a clause body can be determined only after the clause is complete. We cannot go into the details of how RDT is used for characterization here, and instead refer the reader to [Wrobel, 1993a].

8.4.2 Evaluating the New Concept

Since KRT and CLT are designed for interactive use, any new concept introduced by CLT is presented to the user for approval. The user can decide whether entirely to remove the new concept, keep only its extensional definition (the membership facts), or keep facts and learned rules. Keeping the facts only can be useful if the concept itself is meaningful in the domain, but the found characterization is incorrect, for example, because the knowledge base is still incomplete. In any case, the user can replace the system-chosen "gensym" name with a more appropriate domain-specific term. To help the user make these choices, the system presents the current list of members and non-members of the concept.

Furthermore, CLT uses its own set of internal evaluation criteria. In interactive use, this criterion is used to provide an initial recommendation that the user can override; in non-interactive use, this criterion is relied upon completely. The evaluation criterion used by CLT can be modified by the user, so what we describe here is the standard default criterion. This default criterion is motivated by generally desirable properties of useful concepts, namely that they be *recognizable*, and that they be *predictive*. Since our concept representation does not rely on probabilistic correlations, these requirements are implemented as lower bounds on the number of sufficient conditions and uses of the concept:

Default evaluation criterion. Accept a new concept c if:

1. at least two sufficient conditions were found about c (the concept must be *recognizable*), and if
2. at least two necessary conditions, or one rule in which c is used, were found (the concept must have *predictive power*).

As we show in section 8.5.1, this criterion ensures that any concept introduced by CLT will improve the structure of the knowledge base. Note that whereas the aggregation constraint used by CLT is derived from a problem-solving context, the above evaluation criterion is actually a structural constraint in the classification given at the beginning of the chapter. We should also point out that while other evaluation criteria are possible, the default criterion listed above has turned out superior to two other criteria in an empirical test reported in [Wrobel, 1993a] and [Wrobel, 1994]. We give some details of this empirical study in section 8.5.2.

Since the knowledge base may change after the introduction of a concept, it is not guaranteed that the above evaluation criteria will continue to hold if, say, a rule in which a concept was used is deleted. To ensure that concepts that have turned out useless are removed from the knowledge base, CLT verifies after each rule modification or deletion whether the evaluation criteria for a CLT-introduced concept are negatively affected, and removes the concept if this is the case. This process is also referred to as *concept garbage collection.*

8.4.3 Using the New Concept to Restructure the Rule Base

Whenever a new concept has been introduced and is approved by the internal evaluation criterion or the user, CLT examines whether the knowledge base can be simplified by using the new concept in existing rules. This restructuring task is performed by a set of routines in the ruleset restructuring tool RRT. It consists of deriving via resolution all rules implied by the concept rules found during characterization, and then removing all existing rules that are θ-subsumed by any of those resolvents.

More precisely, let $H(c,\Gamma)$ be the set of all rules in Γ where c occurs in the head, and $B(c,\Gamma)$ the set of all rules in Γ where c occurs in the body. If

$$R(c,\Gamma) := \{R|\exists R_1 \in H(c,\Gamma), R_2 \in B(c,\Gamma) : R = \text{resolvent}(R_1, R_2)\}$$

then the redundancy removal step of RRT can be defined as follows. Given a concept c in a knowledge base Γ, this step produces the knowledge base:

$$\Gamma' := \Gamma \setminus \{R|\exists\theta, R' \in R(c,\Gamma) \wedge R'\theta \subseteq R\}$$

In [Wrobel, 1993a], the restructuring step is described in more detail along with other possible restructuring operators.

8.4.4 Two Examples

To illustrate the above description of CLT's operation, we now give two examples of concepts that were introduced in two different domains. First, let us return to the example from section 7.8, where we used the TRAFFIC-LAW domain to explain the reformulation steps of the knowledge revision tool KRT. As promised there, we now show how the new concept used by KRT was formed by CLT. For this, we need provide a little more detail.

Recall that the TRAFFIC-LAW domain represents the kind of knowledge you might in your driving test, e.g., where and where not to park, speed limits, traffic safety, traffic violations, fines. In the TRAFFIC-LAW knowledge base, we initially included descriptions of various traffic violation cases committed by members of the KIT group[3] and a number of background knowledge rules. From this knowledge base, the system was able to learn the following set Γ_0 of additional rules:

involved_vehicle(X,Y) & not(buckled_up(Z,Y)) → not(tvr_points_p(X))
involved_vehicle(X,Y) & lights_necessary(X) & not(headlights_on(X,Y)) → not(tvr_points_p(X))
parking_violation(X) → not(tvr_points_p(X))

parking_violation(X) & appeals(Y,X) → court_citation(Y)
unsafe_vehicle_violation(X) & appeals(Y,X) → court_citation(Y)

involved_vehicle(X,Y) & owner(Z,Y) → responsible(Z,X)

The above rules (shown graphically in figure 8.2), except the last one, are correct in our example domain but overly special. The last one (numbered r37), as already pointed out in section 7.8, is too general and thus incorrect. It actually only holds for minor violations (like parking offenses). For major traffic violations, the driver of a car is responsible, and not the owner.

Indeed the initial knowledge contained only examples of minor violations, so there were no negative examples that could have prevented this overgeneralization. In response to the subsequent input of three major violation cases, KRT, as shown in section 7.8, reduces the support set of the rule. The support set is now:

$$(X, Y, Z) \in \text{all} \times \text{all} \times \text{all} \setminus \{(\text{cab\_event},\text{cab1},\text{ace\_cab\_co}), (\text{loan\_event},\text{b\_xs\_400},\text{sw}),(\text{stolen\_event}, \text{b\_dx\_986}, \text{john})\}$$

Here, we are not concerned with the results produced by reformulation operators (1), (2) and (3) (see section 7.8), but instead focus on a successful application of operator (4) which introduces a new concept for the instances of a rule. Recall from section 7.8 that the instances of the rule r37 in this knowledge base were:

[3]The KIT group is the AI group at Technical University of Berlin where MOBAL's predecessor BLIP was developed.

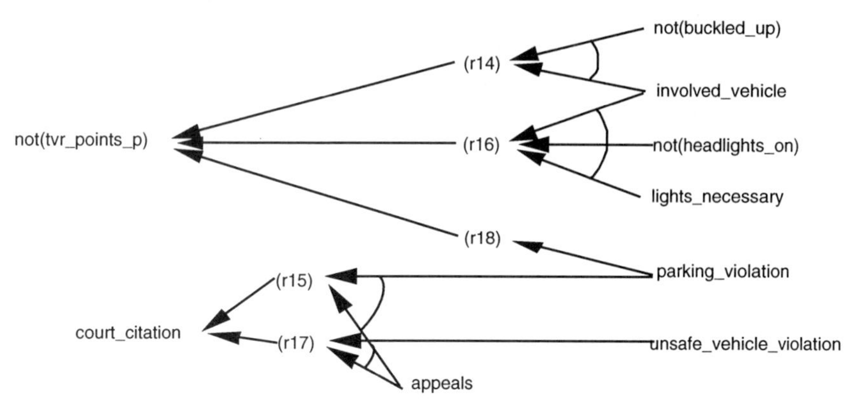

Figure 8.2: Rule Set before Introduction of minor_violation

I(r37, Γ) = { (event1,b_au_6773,sw), (event2,b_dx_1385,dj),
(event3,hh_mo_195,mo), (event4,b_md_4321,md),
(event5,b_st_888,st), (event6,b_ab_89,ab),
(event7,b_bc_90,bc), (event8,b_cd_01,cd),
(event9,b_de_12,de), (event10,b_ef_23,ef),
(event11,b_fg_34,fg), (event12,b_gh_45,ef) }

The global exception list of the support set is

{(cab_event,cab1,ace_cab_co),
(loan_event,b_xs_400,sw),
(stolen_event, b_dx_986, john)}

According to the search strategy defined in table 7.2 (page 217), this means that variable Z will not be considered any more, since $\pi_3(I(R,\Gamma)) \cap \pi_3(GE) \neq \emptyset$. Concept formation is thus attempted only on variables X and Y. We take the former as an example, that is, the operator application *add_ni*(X). As part of this operator, KRT passes to CLT the list of instances and exceptions of the proposed new concept. CLT invents a new name $c1$ and enters the facts corresponding to the instances and exceptions into the knowledge base:

```
c1(event1).      c1(event2). c1(event3).
c1(event4).      c1(event5). c1(event6).
c1(event7).      c1(event8). c1(event9).
c1(event10).     c1(event11). c1(event12).
not(c1(cab_event))
not(c1(loan_event))
not(c1(stolen_event))
```

RDT, when called for characterization as described in section 8.4.1, finds the following characterization for $c1$:

```
parking_violation(X) → c1(X)                                        ⎫
involved_vehicle(X,Y) & not(buckled_up(Z,Y)) → c1(X)                ⎪
involved_vehicle(X,Y) & lights_necessary(X)                         ⎬ H(c1,Γ)
                  & not(headlights_on(X,Y)) → c1(X)                 ⎪
unsafe_vehicle_violation(X) → c1(X)                                 ⎭
```

```
c1(X) → not(tvr_points_p(X))                     ⎫
c1(X) & appeals(Y,X) → court_citation(Y)         ⎭ B(c1,Γ)
```

Since $|H(c1,\Gamma)| \geq 2$ and $|B(c1,\Gamma)| \geq 2$, the evaluation criterion is met, and the concept is renamed by the user to minor_violation, and used to reformulate r37 which now becomes

```
involved_vehicle(X,Y)    & owner(Z,Y)    & minor_violation(X)
→ responsible(Z,X)
```

After that, the new concept is used for rule set restructuring by checking whether any existing rules are now redundant. As it turns out, all rules in Γ_0 are now θ-subsumed by rules derivable from $H(c1,\Gamma)$ and $B(c1,\Gamma)$, so they are removed. Figure 8.3 shows the resulting improvement in rule set structure obtained by introducing the concept minor_violation. Note that it of course depends on KRT's search strategy and parameter settings (see chapter 7) whether concept formation will actually be attempted.

Our second example shows the formation of a new relation. It is taken from the ICTERUS domain that was realized in the LERNER project at TU Berlin in cooperation with our partners (see section 9.2 for details). In this clinical medicine domain, the system had learned the following rule r8:

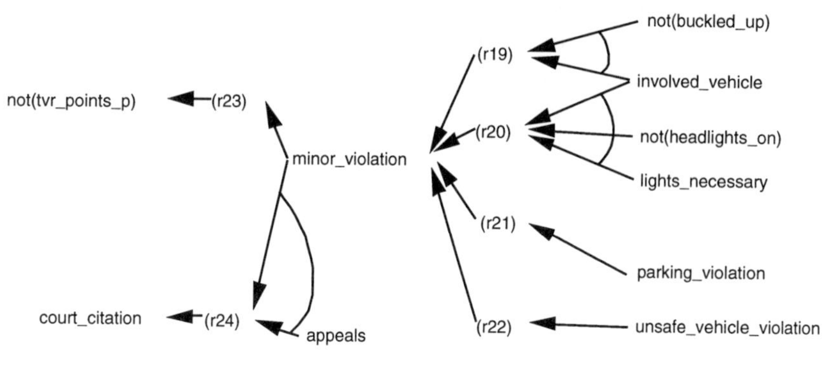

Figure 8.3: Rule Set after Introduction of minor_violation

indication(X,Y) & pathological(X,Z) → interesting(Y,Z)
 – all × all × all \ {(mucoviscidosis_in_family, mucoviscidosis, case4),
 (galactosis_in_serum, galactosaemia, case3),
 (galactosis_in_serum, galactosaemia, case4)}

which says that a diagnosis Y is interesting in a case Z if there is a clinical parameter X that is an indication for the diagnosis Y, and that parameter is pathological, i.e., abnormal, in case Z. Since there had been exceptions with this rule, KRT has already produced a restricted support set as shown above. As it turns out, these exceptions refer to cases where the parameter values that were compiled for the case were no longer valid, i.e., where too much time had passed since their measurement and their use for diagnosis. In this example, all variables domains intersect, so KRT begins to search on search level 5 (see table 7.2) for relations between the variables. In the course of this search process, CLT was called to try to form a new concept between variables X and Y, that is, between parameters and cases. As usual, CLT invented a new predicate name concept1 for the proposed relation. The characterization that was found turned out to be quite interesting:

concept1(X,Y) → pathological(X,Y)
compiled_earlier(X,Y) & constant(X) → concept1(X,Y)
recompiled(X,Y) → concept1(X,Y)

The above set of rules defines the concept of an "up-to-date" parameter X for a case Y. A parameter X is up to date for a case Y if it was compiled earlier and is constant, or if it was just recompiled. The first rule expresses that all parameters are pathological parameters. This reflects a bias in the construction of the domain, where only pathological parameters were included. Using the new concept, the original rule about interestingness can be modified and reads:

indication(X,Y) & pathological(X,Z)
& concept1(X,Z) → interesting(Y,Z) – all × all × all

8.5 Evaluating CLT

As pointed out above, the design of MOBAL and its learning components is based on Morik's paradigm of *balanced cooperative modeling* (see chapter 1), which views knowledge base construction as a cyclic process of continuing revisions in the interaction between user and system. A case in point is CLT with its use of a problem solving context to focus concept formation that is expressly designed for interactive use during knowledge revision.

Consequently, in the above presentation of CLT, we have assumed that each of the heuristically introduced new concepts is tested against an oracle in addition to the system's internal evaluation criteria. By querying the user, we can assume that independent of the system's own evaluation, each new concept is valid and useful to the user. In practice, users find it relatively easy to judge a new concept since the system shows the user the existing examples of the concept. Muggleton [Muggleton, 1987] has reported similarly about his DUCE system. In the interactive process of revising an incorrect knowledge base, CLT proposes new concepts that are *qua definitionem* likely to be relevant to the problem at hand.

An empirical evalution of this conjecture would require comparative studies of the structure and results of knowledge acquisition processes with and without CLT, which we have been unable to perform so far. In this section, we therefore want to focus on the quality and range of concepts that CLT introduces in a non-interactive setting, i.e., if only the system-internal default evaluation criteria are used. In the next section, we evaluate the quality of CLT concepts, and show that each concept that is introduced and kept in the knowledge base actually improves the quality of the knowledge base. We then briefly discuss how the use of a problem solving context to focus concept formation parallels related psychological results about the nature of human concept formation.

8.5.1 Quality of Concepts Introduced by CLT

A newly introduced concept influences the learning result along several dimensions: the learnability of the desired target concept(s), the classification accuracy of the rules that are learned, the speed of inference of the problem solver, and the structure and understandability of the resulting knowledge base, which is our focus here[4].

As Fu and Buchanan [Fu and Buchanan, 1985] have pointed out, a knowledge base consisting of compiled, single-step rules is not optimal in terms of understandability and robustness. The use of intermediate concepts captures knowledge in smaller chunks, summarizes intermediate states of the problem solving process, and provides a partial interpretation of the data even if the final target concept cannot be derived due to incomplete data. The indiscriminate introduction of intermediate concepts, on the other hand, can increase the size of the knowledge base, thus reducing understandability. We therefore need a measure that balances knowledge base size against the advantages of small chunk size.

Previous research (e.g. [Muggleton, 1987; Muggleton and Buntine, 1988]) has used as a quality measure the total size of the knowledge base as approximated by the number of premise and conclusion literals (call it TS). This, however, has counterintuitive effects, as the following simple knowledge bases Γ_1 and Γ_2 show:

$$\Gamma_1 := \left\{ \begin{array}{c} p(X)\&\ c(X) \rightarrow r(X) \\ a(X) \rightarrow c(X) \\ b(X) \rightarrow c(X) \end{array} \right\} \quad \Gamma_2 := \left\{ \begin{array}{c} p(X)\&\ a(X) \rightarrow r(X) \\ p(X)\&\ b(X) \rightarrow r(X) \end{array} \right\}$$

According to TS, Γ_2 is the preferred knowledge base, since $TS(\Gamma_2) = 6$, whereas $TS(\Gamma_1) = 7$. We therefore use a measure S that counts only premise literals, thus removing the penalty for extra clauses that TS imposes, while still incorporating a global measure of knowledge base size. According to S,

[4]In [Wrobel, 1989], we give an example of how a newly introduced concept may make a target rule learnable for RDT that was not learnable before. We have not evaluated changes in accuracy or speed of the resulting knowledge base, but suspect that the general utility problem of explanation-based learning or other compilation approaches would appear here as well.

the two theories are equally good, since $S(\Gamma_1) = S(\Gamma_2) = 4$. We then define a quality ordering $>_q$ on knowledge bases such that

$$\Gamma_1 >_q \Gamma_2 \text{ iff } S(\Gamma_1) < S(\Gamma_2) \text{ or } (S(\Gamma_1) = S(\Gamma_2) \text{ and } C(\Gamma_1) > C(\Gamma_2)),$$

where $C(\Gamma)$ denotes the number of predicates in Γ. In our example, we thus find $\Gamma_1 >_q \Gamma_2$.

Equipped with the quality measure $>_q$, we can now show that CLT's evaluation criteria, which were motivated on general grounds of recognizability and predictive power above, actually guarantee that a newly introduced concept wili improve the quality of the knowledge base.

Let Γ_1 be a knowledge base into which CLT has introduced (perhaps at an earlier time) a new concept c, let $\Gamma_1^H = H(c, \Gamma_1)$ the set of all rules with head c, similarly $\Gamma_1^B = B(c, \Gamma_1)$ the set of all rules with c in the body, and $\Gamma_1' := \Gamma_1^B \cup \Gamma_1^H$. Then define

$$\Gamma_2' := R(c, \Gamma_1) = \{R | \exists R_1 \in \Gamma_1^H, R_2 \in \Gamma_1^B : R = \text{resolvent}(R_1, R_2)\}$$

and $\Gamma_2 := (\Gamma_1 \backslash \Gamma_1') \cup \Gamma_2'$, i.e. Γ_2 is the knowledge base that would result if C were removed. The following holds:

> For any Γ_1 and Γ_2 as defined above, if C meets the evaluation criteria of section 8.4.2 at the time of its introduction, and the concept garbage collector is used, then $\Gamma_1 >_q \Gamma_2$.

The above can easily be verified by computing S for the new knowledge base with and without the new concept. In producing Γ_2 from Γ_1, all rules in Γ_1^H are simply removed, and in each rule in Γ_1^B, C is replaced by its definitions, resulting in $|\Gamma_1^H|$ new rules each. It is thus:

$$S(\Gamma_2') = |\Gamma_1^H| \cdot (S(\Gamma_1^B) - |\Gamma_1^B|) + |\Gamma_1^B| \cdot S(\Gamma_1^H)$$

and consequently the S-difference between the two knowledge bases is:

$$\begin{aligned}
&S(\Gamma_2) - S(\Gamma_1) \\
&= S(\Gamma_2') - S(\Gamma_1') \\
&= |\Gamma_1^H| \cdot (S(\Gamma_1^B) - |\Gamma_1^B|) + |\Gamma_1^B| \cdot S(\Gamma_1^H) - S(\Gamma_1^B) - S(\Gamma_1^H) \\
&= |\Gamma_1^H| \cdot (S(\Gamma_1^B) - |\Gamma_1^B|) + |\Gamma_1^B| \cdot S(\Gamma_1^H) - (S(\Gamma_1^B) - |\Gamma_1^B|) - |\Gamma_1^B| - S(\Gamma_1^H) \\
&= (|\Gamma_1^H| - 1) \cdot (S(\Gamma_1^B) - |\Gamma_1^B|) + (|\Gamma_1^B| - 1) \cdot S(\Gamma_1^H) - (|\Gamma_1^B| - 1) - 1 \\
&= (|\Gamma_1^H| - 1) \cdot (S(\Gamma_1^B) - |\Gamma_1^B|) + (|\Gamma_1^B| - 1) \cdot (S(\Gamma_1^H) - 1) - 1
\end{aligned}$$

From the evaluation conditions imposed by CLT, we know that C has at least two sufficient conditions, and thus $|\Gamma_1^H| \geq 2$ and $S(\Gamma_1^H) \geq 2$. Also, since it is required that either the concept have at least two necessary conditions, or is used in another rule (with other premises, e.g. in the rule that triggered the knowledge revision in the first place), we know that either (case a) $|\Gamma_1^B| \geq 2$ and $S(\Gamma_1^B) \geq |\Gamma_1^B|$ (if there are at least two necessary conditions for C), or (case b) $|\Gamma_1^B| \geq 1$ and $S(\Gamma_1^B) - |\Gamma_1^B| \geq 1$ (if C is used in another, longer rule). In case (a), we find that the difference in size between Γ_1 (including C) and Γ_2 (excluding C) is larger or equal to:

$$\geq (2-1)\cdot 0 + (2-1)\cdot(2-1) - 1 \;=\; 0$$

Similarly, in case (b), we find that the difference is larger or equal to:

$$\geq (2-1)\cdot 1 + (1-1)\cdot(2-1) - 1 \;=\; 0$$

The knowledge base including the new concept is thus guaranteed to be smaller or of the same size as the equivalent knowledge base without the concept, and since in any case, $C(\Gamma_1) > C(\Gamma_2)$, it is guaranteed that $\Gamma_1 >_q \Gamma_2$. Since the concept garbage collector maintains the evaluation criteria over time, any intermediate concept found in a knowledge base is guaranteed to be an improvement □.

8.5.2 An Empirical Test

To substantiate the theoretical argument above, we have also performed an empirical study of the effect of CLT concepts on learning accuracy. The goal of this study was to determine whether the default evaluation criterion was indeed appropriate to exclude uninteresting or harmful concepts while accepting the beneficial ones. For this study, which is reported in more detail in [Wrobel, 1993a] and [Wrobel, 1994], we used the "kinship" domain of Hinton (1986) in which the goal was to learn the definition of the predicate "aunt". To exclude any misleading effect due to inappropriate rule models in RDT, we used the data-driven learner FOIL for the characterization step of CLT. Two other concept evaluation criteria were used for comparison with our default criterion. The first one was a stricter version of the default criterion, and the second one was the the "null" criterion of [Muggleton and Bain, 1992] (no restriction on the introduction of new concepts). The empirical results show that, at least in this domain, the criterion used in CLT is superior to the other two, and that the new concepts introduced by CLT were beneficial (figure 8.4).

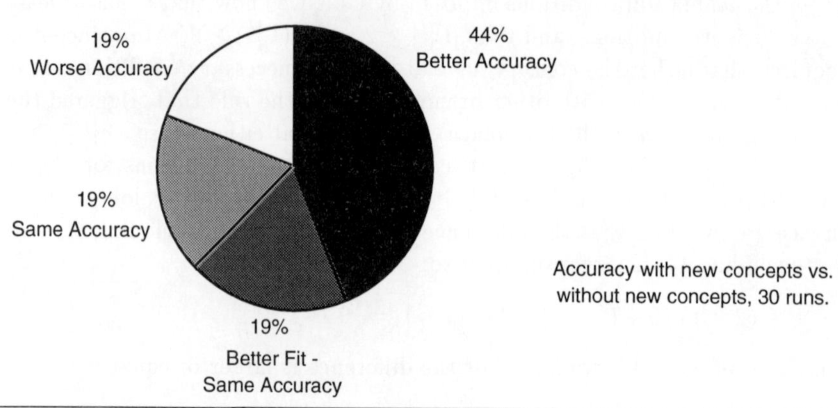

Figure 8.4: Results of Empirical Study in Kinship Domain

8.5.3 Relation to Psychological Findings

The use of a problem-solving context parallels psychological findings about the nature of human concept formation. As Wygotski observed, "a concept can arise and develop only if there is a *specific need*, the need for a concept, within a specific, conscious, *purposeful activity* that is directed towards reaching a *specific goal* or towards the solution of a specific task" [Wygotski, 1964, p. 112][5]. Wygotski himself did not investigate the role of a problem solving context much further, concentrating instead on the role of "internal thought", but there is more recent evidence in the work of Nelson on concept formation from event contexts [Nelson, 1983], and in Barsalou's research on *ad hoc* concepts arising during problem solving [Barsalou, 1983].

According to Nelson, *events* are the relevant context for the formation of concepts, and concept formation can be understood as separating out the different objects that occur in the same context of an activity, and aggregating them into a new concept. The key point is the shift from a "syntagmatic" to a "paradigmatic" organization, i.e., from a set of objects that play a certain role in an activity, to a concept that is primarily characterized without reference to the initial temporal event context.

The same point is emphasized by Barsalou's work on *ad hoc* categories. An *ad hoc* category is a category that is created for and during the solution of one particular task, and generally has the form "things instrumental to

[5]Translated from the German edition and italics added by the author.

achieving goal X". To explain experimental findings about such categories, Barsalou again assumes that the appearance of a set of objects in a problem solving context is the initial principle of aggregation for the category, but that an additional process of characterization must occur before this category is present in memory as a concept. In this way, frequently used *ad hoc* categories (like "things to sell at a garage sale", which may be useful every Saturday) may become fully accessible concepts.

The aggregation principle used in CLT focuses exactly on the key point raised by Nelson's and Barsalou's research, namely the aggregation of objects that play a similar role in the problem solving activities of the system: the objects that are aggregated are exactly those that permit (or prevent) a successful problem solving inference chain. This also offers a possible explanation for why users in an interactive setting find the concepts proposed by CLT easy to judge: perhaps because they correspond well to concepts that a human might have formed in a similar situation.

8.6 Related Work

The usefulness of exploiting a problem solving context to focus learning activities has also been demonstrated in Utgoff's STABB system [Utgoff, 1986], an extension of symbolic integration program LEX [Mitchell, 1982] capable of introducing new disjunctive descriptors into the representation language. Where, in our method, the problem solving context consists of general inference rules, STABB is more specialized, and uses the positive and negative instances of LEX's operator applications as the basis for the introduction of new terms. This eliminates the need to perform blame assignment. As LEX uses an attribute-based representation, STABB's method for characterizing the positive instances is not as powerful as our Horn-clause method, and is limited to the introduction of attribute disjuncts on single variables. STABB does not attempt a characterization of the exception set, does not perform a quality check on the proposed new term, and does not have methods of removing useless concepts.

Another way of looking at the aggregation constraint used by CLT is that it responds to the need to *refer* to a certain set of objects for which no name is yet available in order to complete a particular task[6]. This aggregation constraint has been used in the concept formation system KLUSTER [Kietz

[6]This is why we are referring to this as *demand-driven* concept formation [Wrobel, 1988a; Wrobel, 1989].

and Morik, 1991b], which forms concepts in a term subsumption representation language similar to KL-ONE. In KLUSTER, objects are first aggregated based on their common occurrence in the same argument place of a predicate; a similar but simpler aggregation rule had also been used in GLAUBER [Langley *et al.*, 1986]. The system then tries to differentiate and characterize these extensional aggregates, and if it needs to refer to a particular set of role fillers for which no existing concept is adequate, a new concept is introduced. KLUSTER, therefore, does not use an external problem solving activity as a constraint for concept formation, but uses its own concept formation activity for that purpose.

In the more general context of learning in a problem solving context, there is a large amount of work on approaches that try to improve the performance of the problem solver by analyzing solved problems, and creating generalized compiled rules from them that replace a number of problem solving steps by one single step. Examples of such approaches are the various *explanation-based learning* methods [Mitchell *et al.*, 1986; De Jong and Mooney, 1986], macro-operator learning (e.g. the early STRIPS approach [Fikes *et al.*, 1972]), or chunking in SOAR [Laird *et al.*, 1986]. While all of these approaches exploit the problem solving context to decide where to learn and what to learn, they do not address the representation or concept formation problem, as the discovered sets of preconditions are local to an individual compiled rule.

More relevant to the work described here are approaches generally referred to as *problem reformulation*, that are exemplified by the work of Amarel (1968), Korf (1980), Subramanian (1990), and others[7]. While also motivated by the goal of improving problem solver efficiency, these methods generally attempt to reach this goal not by the introduction of compiled rules, but by a change in problem representation that fundamentally changes the search space of the problem solver. This can involve the removal of irrelevant predicates from a theory, as in [Subramanian, 1990], or the creation of abstract states that aggregate states that can be treated identically in planning [Knoblock, 1990]. They are thus much closer in spirit to the work discussed here than compilation methods.

[7][Benjamin, 1990] contains a number of relevant papers.

8.7 Conclusion

A central point of this chapter is that concept formation, in contrast to constructive induction, can be understood as a process of forming extensional aggregates of objects, and then characterizing them with an intensional definition. If, as in MOBAL, the so-formed concept is given a name, and made available in the representation, then concept formation is an answer to the new-term problem of machine learning. Our work has put the focus on the constraints that can be used to control the aggregation process, and we have identified four possible types of constraints. The goal of the research on CLT presented in this chapter was to examine how problem solving derived constraints can be used in concept formation.

The contribution of CLT is to have identified one particular way of using such constraints, namely by taking them from the knowledge revision process of an inferential problem solver, thus illustrating the general power of such constraints. We were also able to show that any concept introduced by CLT actually improves the structure of the knowledge base, and that the range of concepts introduced by CLT corresponds to general inversion resolution operators. Based on practical experience, and related psychological work, we have argued that problem-solving derived constraints are especially adequate in an interactive context like in MOBAL.

Nonetheless, the work as described here is incomplete in several respects that identify areas for future research. For the interactive use of CLT in a knowledge acquisition context, it would be desirable to perform empirical studies that define the usefulness of CLT's new concepts in terms of the time taken to build up a domain model, or the resulting quality of that model. Our own experience indicates that our approach to concept formation helps, but is insufficient for a safe confirmation. Second, for the non-interactive use of CLT, a theoretical evaluation of the kinds of knowledge base or the kinds of concept it can learn in the limit would be desirable. This would require a characterization of the properties of example presentations required for triggering knowledge revision, and the definition of what is to be considered as a target knowledge base. In theoretical learning models, completeness and consistency are used, but it is not clear what an optimally structured knowledge base or an optimal set of intermediate concepts for a domain would be.

Chapter 9

Practical Experiences

The MOBAL system has been successfully applied to model more than seven complex domains. Of particular interest are the applications of MOBAL in the framework of the *Machine Learning Toolbox* (MLT) ESPRIT project. In this project MOBAL was used to model real-world industrial domains:

- In the SATELLITE POWER SYSTEM domain MOBAL has been used to build a qualitative model which allows to evaluate possible fault states and their diagnosis in satellite power subsystems (see [Uszynski and Niquil, 1992]).

- In the DESGN FOR ASSEMBLY domain, the re-design of an aircraft fuselage panel has been modelled using MOBAL (see [Parsons and Puzey, 1992]).

- In the MESSAGE BURST ANALYSIS domain the MOBAL system has been used to build a model which allows to determine faults in a power distribution network (see [Hecht and Leufke, 1992]).

- In the medical MALDESCENSUS TESTIS domain MOBAL has been used to derive therapeutic rules (see [Potamias *et al.*, 1992]) and to filter medical cases using medical knowledge [Morik *et al.*, 1993].

- The application of MOBAL to elaborate a security policy for telecommincation networks (the SPEED domain) is described in more detail below (section 9.3).

In a new project[1] MOBAL is used for a navigation task of a mobile robot [Morik and Rieger, 1993]. Sensor measurements from several pathes of the robot in one known room form the examples of operational concepts, such as moving diagonally through a door. The learned concept descriptions can then be used to recognize objects in a previously unseen room. Learning was applied at several levels of abstraction: first, basic features for one sensor were learned; then, these features were used to learn more abstract features for sensor groups; finally, the abstract features were used to learn operational concepts. RDT learned from 28 traces, each with 27 time points where 24 sonar sensors measured the distance to the next object. From overall 18144 measurements, RDT learned more than 120 rules. MOBAL is applicable to such an application because it learns several rules - instead of just one most discriminating rule - and is able to combine the learning results of the several levels into one knowledge base. The time aspects that are required could be easily handled by MOBAL. The following rules for parallelly and diagonally moving through a doorway illustrate the approach.

```
sg_jump(Trace, right_side, T1, T2, Move) &
sg_jump(Trace, left_side, T1, T2, Move) &
parallel(Move) & le(Start, T1) & le(T2, End)
   → move_through_door(Trace, Start, End, Move)
sg_jump(Trace, right_side, T1, T2, Move) &
sg_jump(Trace, left_side, T3, T4, Move) &
diagonal(Move) & succ3(T1, T3) & le(Start, T1) & le(T4, End)
   → move_through_door(Trace, Start, End, Move)
```

The first rule states that the sensors at the right side as well as those at the left side recognize at the same time the abstract feature sg_jump. This feature describes the sensing of two parallel edges, one close to the robot than the other. It is itself defined by several learned rules of MOBAL. The second rule states that the sensors at the right side of the robot recognize the sg_jump pattern three points of time before the sensors of the left side perceive the same pattern (succ3). This time difference is the typical feature of a diagonal path through a doorway.

The prototypical applications of MOBAL were both very different with respect to the kind of knowledge which was represented as well as with

[1]BLearn II (P7274) is funded by the CEC within the ESPRIT program. BLearn II has started in September 1992.

respect to the features of the system which were used. Some of the applications have used MOBAL as knowledge acquisition system taking only little or no advantage of its inductive learning and knowledge revision components. Other applications focused on the inductive learning capabilities of the system. These differences follow from the goals of the applications and the differences of the domains. In some domains simply no learning data was available which could be used to support the development of a model and some applications were driven by the goal to find particular rules to uncover regularities in a data set without any need to develop a well elaborated model of the domain.

This chapter describes three representative applications of MOBAL in order to give an insight into the capablities and limitations of the system as a whole and its individual components as far as this issue has not been already met in the previuos chapters. Before explaining the three domains named TRAFFIC-LAW, ICTERUS, and SPEED in more detail in the following sections, we provide a brief overview of their structure and purpose.

TRAFFIC-LAW models background knowledge of some basic traffic regulations using a few sample cases of traffic violations. The purpose of the TRAFFIC-LAW modeling was to provide a domain which is suitable for experiments with the representation and above all the learning components. This required a sufficiently diverse and complex model with a medium-sized knowledge base (section 9.1).

ICTERUS models the branch of the post-natal intensive care medicine concerned with the diagnosis of jaundice symptoms. The aim of ICTERUS consisted of testing the expressive power and adequacy of the MOBAL knowledge representation. To this end, the modeling of the domain had to be rather detailed and comprehensive, thus creating a very complex and large model (section 9.2).

The telecommunications security domain, SPEED[2], finally, is a prototypical application of MOBAL to a telecommunications security problem developed in cooperation with Alcatel Alsthom Recherche, Paris, in the (MLT) ESPRIT project. This application is of particular interest for demonstrating the learning and knowledge revision capabilities of MOBAL in an interactive setting, and for illustrating a usage scenario of the system (section 9.3).

[2]SPEED was the name of the project at Alcatel Alsthom Recherche which gave rise to this MOBAL prototype.

9.1 The Traffic-law Domain

9.1.1 Introduction

The TRAFFIC-LAW domain is concerned with some basic knowledge about traffic regulations in Germany. Based on individual cases of traffic violations, the problem solving goal of the model is to derive a classification of the case along several dimensions, i.e., determining who will be held responsible for the violation, how high the fine will be, and whether the responsible person will have to go to court. The intention behind the creation of this domain model was to construct a model which could be used for experiments with MOBAL's knowledge representation and learning modules. We therefore did not try to cover the intricacies of German traffic regulations comprehensively, but instead concentrated on basic knowledge about parking regulations, speed limits, vehicle safety, and fines. The resulting domain, which consists of 15 represented cases plus background knowledge and induced rules, contains 40 predicates, 162 facts, and 26 rules. It is included in the standard distribution of the MOBAL system, and is used throughout this book for illustration.

9.1.2 Representation of Cases and Background Knowledge

The basis for the traffic law domain model consists of a representation of various cases of traffic violations. Each of these cases is represented by a number of MOBAL *facts* (see sections 2.1, 3.2.1), which provide featural and relational information. Table 9.1 shows such a case.

The facts in event1 state that the vehicle with the licence number b_au_6773 was involved in the above traffic violation, that a person with the initials sw is the owner of this vehicle, and that the vehicle is a sedan. The traffic violation consisted in the fact that the vehicle was parked in a bus lane and consequently towed away. The fine was DM 20, which was paid by the person responsible for the violation (sw). As the person did not appeal against the decision, he/she did not receive any points on his/her traffic violation record, and did not have to go to court.

As pointed out in section 2.1, and explained in detail in chapter 4, the system automatically constructs a sort lattice based on the actual arguments used as predicate arguments in a domain model. In addition, the user can provide explicit symbolic sort definitions for the predicates that are used; these names are then also incorporated and maintained in the automatically constructed sort lattice (see section 4.2.2). Table 9.2 shows the manually

```
involved_vehicle(event1,b_au_6773)
owner(sw,b_au_6773)
sedan(b_au_6773)
car_parked(event1,place1)
bus_lane(place1)
car_towed(event1,b_au_6773)
responsible(sw,event1)
fine(event1,20)
pays_fine(event1,sw)
not(appeals(sw,event1))
not(court_citation(sw,event1))
not(tvr_points_p(event1))
```

Table 9.1: A Case of Traffic Violation (event1)

input predicate definitions for the predicates used in table 9.1. The entries show the predicate name followed by its arity and the so-called *user sort names*, which together with the comment in the second line reveal the meaning of the predicate.

Topology As pointed out in section 2.1, MOBAL provides the predicate topology as an additional source of background knowledge that can be used to structure the domain, and provide guidance to the learning module RDT (see section 6.5.2). Such a topology can be acquired automatically by the system based on the current set of rules in the domain (see chapter 5), or is input manually. In the TRAFFIC-LAW model, we have used a manually constructed topology which is shown in figure 9.1.

The topology in figure 9.1 reflects the intended problem solving structure of the TRAFFIC-LAW domain: from a set of predicates representing basic information about a violation case, the involved vehicles and persons, and traffic regulations, the system infers a primary classification of the case (responsibility), and then decides what the fine will be, and who will have go to court.

Inferential Background Knowledge In addition to cases and topological background knowledge, the TRAFFIC-LAW model also contains back-

involved_vehicle/2: <event>, <vehicle>:
    <Vehicle> was involved in <event>.

owner/2: <person>, <vehicle>:
    <person> is the owner of <vehicle>

sedan/1: <vehicle>:
    <vehicle> is a sedan (a limousine).

car_parked/2: <event>, <place>:
    The vehicle involved in <event> was parked in <place>.

bus_lane/1: <place>:
    <place> is in a bus lane.

car_towed/2: <event>, <vehicle>:
    In <event>, <vehicle> was towed.

responsible/2: <person>, <event>:
    <person> is responsible for <event>.

fine/2: <event>, <amount>:
    <event> results in a fine of <fine>.

pays_fine/2: <event>, <person>:
    <person> paid the fine resulting from <event>.

appeals/2: <person>, <event>:
    <person> appeals against the decision made in <event>.

court_citation/2: <person>, <event>:
    <person> has to go to court for <event>.

tvr_points_p/1: <event>:
    <event> costs points on the traffic violation record (tvr).

Table 9.2: User Sort Definitions for Predicates used in event1

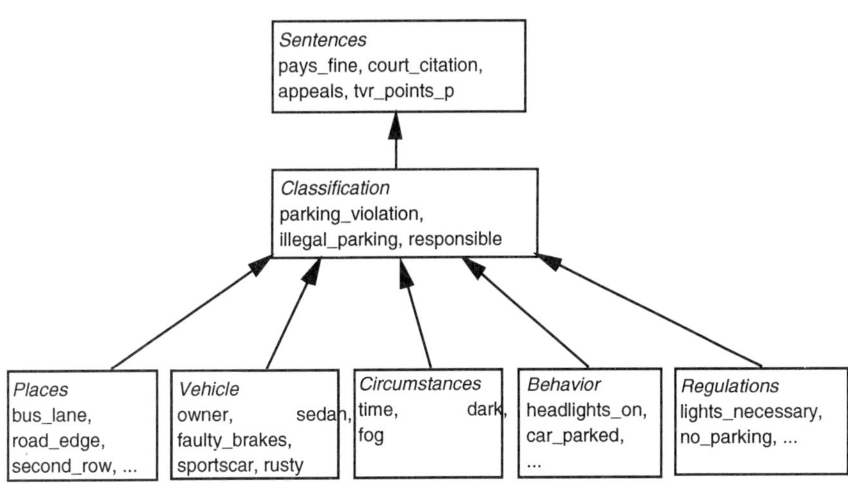

Figure 9.1: TRAFFIC-LAW Topology

ground knowledge of inferential relations in the domain. They are represented by rules (see sections 2.1 and 3.2.2). Table 9.3 shows the TRAFFIC-LAW rules which were provided as background knowledge.

Each of these rules should be interpreted as implicitly all-quantified; "&" refers to the conjunctive linking of the premises, "$\rightarrow$ " approximately corresponds to implication (see section 2.2.2 for an exact definition of the semantics, and section 3.3 for an operational description of the derivation process). The first rule thus represents the knowledge that it is forbidden to park on the sidewalk. In addition to other rules about unlawful parking we find some basic information about traffic safety, etc. Such rules can be entered by the user, but they can also be learned by the rule discovery tool RDT from an adequate fact basis (see chapter 6). In either case, they are immediately used as background knowledge for inferences and thus, in turn, for the learning process; this is often referred to as closed-loop learning.

As soon as fact has been entered, the system tries to use the available inference rules in a forward fashion to see if any additional facts can be derived. For `event1` the system will conclude that the event was a parking violation since the vehicle involved was parked in a bus lane. Table 9.4 demonstrates the *derivation tree* of the respective fact as it is presented

```
sidewalk(X) → no_parking(X)
second_row(X) → no_parking(X)
bus_lane(X) → no_parking(X)
fire_hydrant(X) → no_parking(X)
level_crossing(X) → no_parking(X)
road_edge(X) → not(second_row(X))
road_edge(X) & not(no_parking_sign(X))
        → parking_allowed(X)
car_parked(X, Y) & no_parking(Y) → parking_violation(X)
time(X, Y) & dark(Y) → lights_necessary(X)
time(O, X) & place(O, Y) & fog(X, Y)
        → lights_necessary(O)
involved_vehicle(X, Y) & major_corrosion(Y)
        → unsafe_vehicle_violation(X)
involved_vehicle(X, Y) & faulty_brakes(Y)
        → unsafe_vehicle_violation(X)
involved_vehicle(X, Y) & worn_tires(Y)
        → unsafe_vehicle_violation(X)
```

Table 9.3: Background Knowledge of TRAFFIC-LAW

to the user by the interface in textual format (a graphical display is also available).

```
fact F44: parking_violation(event1)
    because:
    R45: car_parked(x,y) & no_parking(Y) → parking_violation(X)
        premises:
        fact F41: car_parked(event1, place1), entry.
        fact F43: no_parking(place1)
            because:
            R40: bus_lane(X) → no_parking(X)
                premises:
                fact F42: bus_lane(place1), entry.
```

Table 9.4: A Derivation Tree using Facts from event1

9.1.3 Metaknowledge

The rules mentioned in the previous section (table 9.3) cover only one side of inferential knowledge representation. Equally important, is the alternative representation of inferential knowledge in the form of metafact (see sections 2.1 and 3.2.1), which are translated into rules based on their metapredicate definitions. Each metapredicate serves to express one particular inferential relation between predicates, which is defined by a rule model (see sections 2.1 and 6.5.1). We will demonstrate this by showing a simple and frequently used metapredicate:

inclusive_1(P,Q): P(X) → Q(X)

In such a definition the arguments occurring in the metapredicate head are to be interpreted as variables, i.e., P and Q are predicate variables. A metafact such as

inclusive_1(bus_lane,no_parking)

is then transformed into a domain level rule by replacing the variables in the rule scheme:

bus_lane(X) → no_parking(X)

The system automatically ensures the integrity of this rule-metafact relation[3], because it expresses and adds to the rule base each rule with the help of an adequate metapredicate. If necessary, it will generate new metapredicates through an abstraction process (see section 6.5.3). Hence, when modeling the domain, the user can concentrate exclusively on the domain level and is not necessarily obliged to deal with metaknowledge at all.

9.1.4 Learning Results

In order to test the learning component using the TRAFFIC-LAW domain, we proceeded as follows. In addition to the background knowledge described above, we first entered data consisting of a group of twelve sample cases (starting with event1) so as to provide a basis for the learning process. We then called RDT on a number of interesting predicates, and checked the rules that were discovered. In a typical sloppy modeling process, we found that some of the rules were not what we had intended, and augmented the knowledge base with additional facts and predicates. The system finally arrived at the set of rules shown in table 9.5.

Of all these rules,

involved_vehicle(X, Y) & owner(Z, Y) → responsible(Z, X)

is of particular interest. It states that the owner of a vehicle is responsible for all traffic violations in which this vehicle is involved. This indeed was true for all cases we had initially entered, since we had started out with lesser violations like parking or unsafe vehicle violations, for which in Germany the owner is responsible regardless of who was the driver. For all other violations, however, the driver is held responsible. The above rule is thus incorrect. To force the system to specialize this rule, we then added a number of cases where the driver, and not the owner, would be responsible. This led the knowledge revision tool, KRT, to add exceptions to the above rule, and ultimately to reformulate it. In the process, a new concept was discovered that corresponds very closely to the concept of a minor violation. Section 8.4.4 shows the details of this knowledge revision and concept formation process. There, we also show how the new concept was used to restructure the rule base.

---

[3]This can be avoided by using a system parameter.

R51: responsible(X, Y) & unsafe_vehicle_violation(Y) → appeals(X, Y)
R52: responsible(X, Y) & unsafe_vehicle_violation(Y) → court_citation(X, Y)
R53: court_citation(X, Y) & parking_violation(Y) → appeals(X, Y)
R54: involved_vehicle(X, Y) & owner(Z, Y) → responsible(Z, X)
R55: court_citation(X, Y) & unsafe_vehicle_violation(Y) → appeals(X, Y)
R56: appeals(X, Y) & parking_violation(Y) → court_citation(X, Y)
R57: appeals(X, Y) & unsafe_vehicle_violation(Y) → court_citation(X, Y)
R58: involved_vehicle(X, Y) & not(buckled_up(X, Y)) → not(tvr_points_p(X))
R59: involved_vehicle(X, Y) & lights_necessary(X) & not(headlights_on(y, X)) & → not(tvr_points_p(X))
R60: parking_violation(X) → not(tvr_points_p(X))
R61: lights_necessary(X) → not(tvr_points_p(X))

Table 9.5: Rules Discovered in TRAFFIC-LAW

9.1.5 An Assessment

The TRAFFIC-LAW domain as a medium-sized, relatively diverse model has proved the learning capabilities of the MOBAL system. Interestingly, even in such a small domain, we implicitly followed a "sloppy modeling" course of development as described in section 1.2.4: there was constant feedback between the learning modules routine and the system developer, with the result that the knowledge base was gradually enlarged. TRAFFIC-LAW thus served as a testbed both for the individual modules and the overall philosophy of MOBAL.

9.2 The Icterus Domain

Our joint project partner Stollmann Ltd in the LERNER project developed the ICTERUS system - an expert system prototype for the medical diagnosis of jaundice in infants. This expert system was built using the expert system shell TWAICE from Nixdorf Computers. The knowledge acquisition was performed by the Stollmann company in cooperation with a doctor [Biedermann and Müller-Wickop, 1988].

This section describes the ICTERUS model developed with the BLIP system by Ingo Keller[4] at the Technical University of Berlin. As the knowldege representation formalism has only been extended since BLIP ICTERUS is also available as a MOBAL domain model. The assessment of BLIP/MOBAL as a knowledge acquisition tool for the creation of a realistic and complex domain comprises the adequacy of MOBAL's knowledge representation, the use of MOBAL for running a consultation, and the support MOBAL provides in the modeling process.

9.2.1 The Diagnostic System Icterus

In contrast to other domains, some of which could be modeled pretty successfully with the help of expert systems, the discipline of medical diagnosis confronts the developer with all the difficulties that contributed to the term "expert systems" being coined. The domain is very complex, a lot of relationships are still unknown and can be formulated only vaguely using rules of thumb. The knowledge is incomplete and subject to alterations.

[4]Dr. Jürgen Müller-Wickop kindly provided the medical knowledge necessary to build this model. Angela Biedermann from the Stollmann company has supported the work with her experience as knowledge engineer in this domain.

The availability of input data (the information about the patient) is another source of problems, which was not taken into account in the case of the first and best-known approach called MYCIN. The necessary compilation of data is expensive and time-consuming (laboratory tests). Thoroughly compiling all the data is not possible. Hence, it is necessary to select the finacially justifiable parameters and to ensure in advance that they are compiled at intervals. To this end, the system needs to take account of the intervals between the various compilation stages, thus coping with the dynamic nature of a disease. Symptoms are variable, new diseases can develop, while others can heal: facts which must be incorporated into the model.

The ICTERUS system developed by Stollmann Ltd is geared to this type of problem. The concept of visits on which it is based provides a functionality that comes close to the requirements of a real application: it meets the user's point of view and reflects the doctor's decisions.

A session with the diagnostic expert system is divided into visits. At the beginning of each visit the system asks questions about the patient. These questions and the data compiled previously are used by the system to make a diagnosis. If the input data do not enable it to come to a satisfactory diagnosis, it considers the next steps that have to be taken, i.e. compiling the data needed to come to a diagnosis, to verify or reject assumptions. These data will be retrieved during the next visit.

The search for a diagnosis must be based on the available patient information. In the ICTERUS system the diagnosis will ensue either directly, as soon as the conditions of a particular diagnosis are satisfied, or indirectly, when all symptoms pointing to a diagnosis are evaluated.

The planning of the data compilation process constitutes the most important system component, as a diagnosis can only be made if the necessary data are available. The system should not arrange for too many laboratory tests to be made, since this entails unjustifiably high costs and is extremely time-consuming. On the other hand, if the system does not request enough data, it takes unnecessarily many visits to come to a diagnosis. Apart from the costs incurred, it is important to establish a diagnosis very quickly in order not to put the patient's life at risk. If the patient's condition is very serious, it is crucial to speed up the diagnosis-making process. Diseases that impose a high risk on the patient have to be taken into particular consideration.

A consultation consisting of several visits, which take place at intervals, also needs to take into account the dynamic and variable nature of the disease:

- Symptoms (parameters) can change, thus providing a basis for the reassessment of the diagnosis. Hence, one should be careful not to consider and evaluate variable symptom parameters if too much time has elapsed since they were compiled. If necessary, the data have to be recompiled.
- The patient's condition can deteriorate, i.e. the case can become more urgent, so the search for a diagnosis needs speeding up (more laboratory tests to be made or more parameters to be compiled).
- New diseases or complications can develop; for example, the patient can contract an infection, hence the search for a diagnosis should not be based on the visits being the only guideline.
- On the other hand, the patient's condition can improve. This also has to be considered by the system in order to avoid wasting of time and money.

The patient's condition is assessed with respect to the standard temporal development of a diagnosed disease or its typical parameters, respectively. When planning laboratory tests, the ICTERUS system solves the above problems as follows:

- Modifiability of parameters: the compiled data are divided into constant and variable parameters. The invariable data such as the blood group are valid for all visits. The validity of the variable parameters such as the temperature is limited, with the validation period of the individual parameters being separately specified. If a parameter no longer applies in a visit, it will not be included in the overall data evaluation. Invalid parameters are, if necessary, automatically recompiled.
- The patient's health condition: in each visit new parameters to determine the patient's condition are requested.
- New diseases: in each visit the situation is reassessed. The system takes several diagnoses into consideration, thus regarding symptoms that have not been accounted for by one diagnosis.

A detailed description of these concepts and their use in TWAICE is available in the reports published by Stollmann Ltd [Biedermann and Müller-Wickop, 1988; Biedermann, 1988]. The following sections describe the representation of the ICTERUS domain in MOBAL.

9.2.2 The Icterus Model in MOBAL

The objects in the ICTERUS domain are *patients*, *parameters*, *symptoms* (describing the condition of a patient), *diagnoses*, *visits*, and qualitative and quantitative attributes. The corresponding terms appear as arguments of facts.

The Topological Structure

An overview of the various model components and their interrelations is provided by the topology shown in figure 9.2. It has the modularization that is needed to represent the development of a complex system. The leaves of this graph contain the predicates that provide the (basic) knowledge of the domain, i.e. the (factual) knowledge of:

- the diagnosis hierarchy and disorders (Diagnosis tree),
- the risk levels (Diagnosis risks),
- the patient data (Input/Measurement),
- the knowledge of symptom parameters (parameter type, constant or variable, what type of representational model, the compilation costs etc.) (Parameter), and
- the probability of the parameters pointing to diagnoses (Indication Strength).

Linked by rules, these data are arranged in the graph in a hierarchical order. The nodes below the top-most node mirror the functionality of the overall system: compiling laboratory queries (Lab-Inputdata), compiling the set of parameters to be asked during the next visit (Inputdata), and establishing diagnoses (Diagnosis).

Basic Factual Knowledge

The major domain concepts and the concept membership of instances are represented in MOBAL by facts. The central medical concepts are:

- parameters,
- diagnoses,

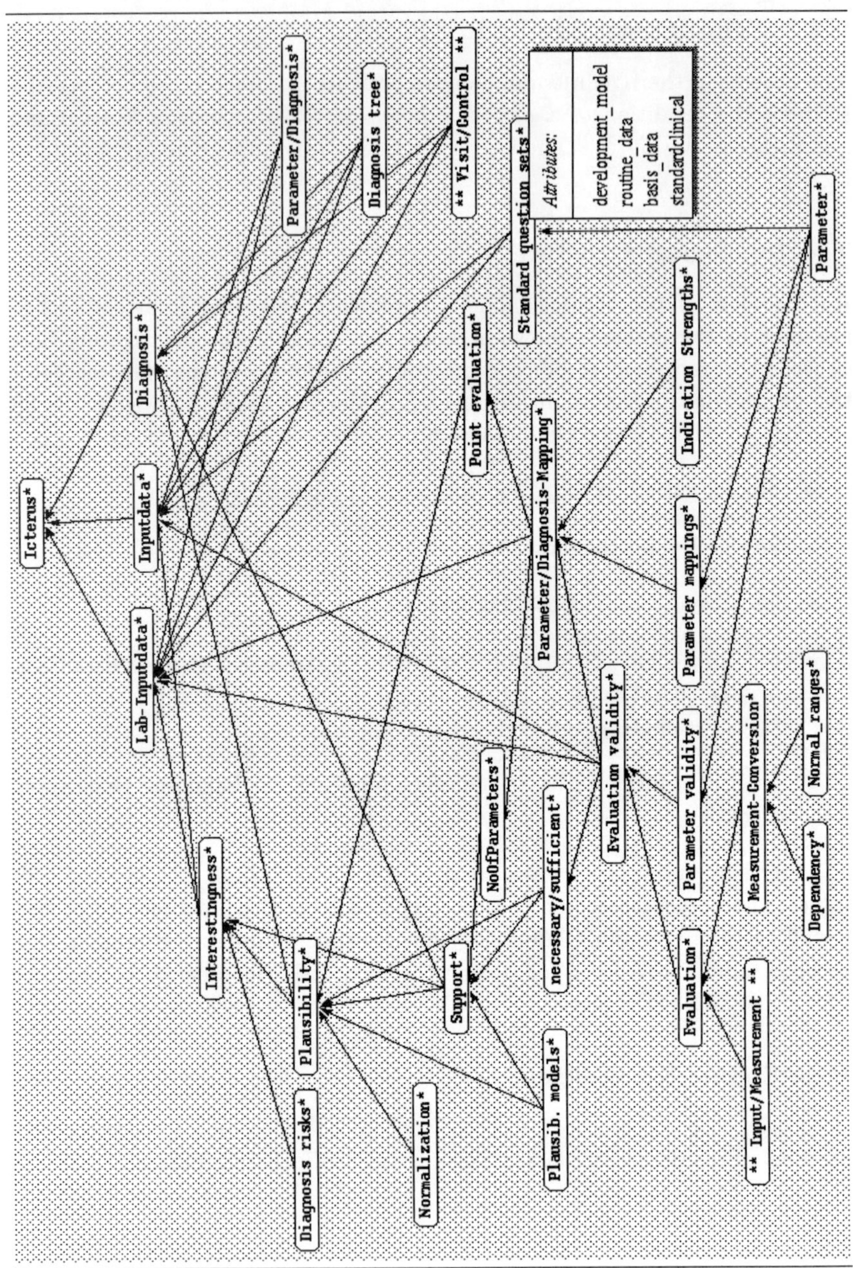

Figure 9.2: ICTERUS topology

- probability,
- interest of parameter compilation, and
- parameter evaluation.

Parameter The model displays different types of information about the parameters (symptoms): the distinction between constant and variable parameters, the validation period of variable parameters, the division into laboratory, clinical and anamnesis parameters, the parameters that are to be established during the first visit, the queries for models of a parameter's temporal development, and the standard clinical queries. Some of the corresponding predicates are:

```
constant_parameter(blood group)
variable_parameter(temperature)
parameter_validity_min_max(temperature,6,12)
is_clinical_parameter(temperature)
standard_clinical_question(temperature)
```

Diagnosis A diagnosis is evaluated with respect to several criteria:

- refinement of the diagnosis,
- importance of the diagnosis, and
- plausibility of the diagnosis.

The diagnoses are arranged in hierarchical order, with the more refined diagnosis being the possible cause of the less refined one.

```
cause(infection,bacterial)
cause(bacterial,sepsis)
cause(infection,viral)
cause(viral,hepatitis)
```

Here, hepatitis and sepsis are the more refined diagnoses. Hepatitis may cause a viral infection, sepsis may cause a bacterial infection. Infection is the least refined diagnosis. Of course, it is aimed at finding the most refined diagnosis.

Each diagnosis must state the risk posed by the disease, for example: risk_type(hepatitis,high). The importance of a diagnosis is given by this risk evaluation.

The link from parameters to diagnoses is given by the *probability* that a particular parameter indicates a particular diagnosis. The other way around, from diagnoses to parameters, is given by the *interest* in parameters regarding a diagnosis.

Probability. The probability factors constitute the central diagnosis evaluation. It uses points to describe the relevance of the (pathological) values of a parameter for the diagnosis:

```
probability(trypsin_in_serum,remarkable,mucoviscidosis,5)
probability(osmotic_resistant,questionable,rh_incompatibility,-1)
```

The first fact gives a weight of 5 to the relevance of a remarkable portion of trypsin for diagnosing mucoviscidosis (a disease which can occur in organs).

Interest of Parameter-compilation. According to the interest in justifying a particular diagnosis - which in turn is given by the risk as well as the plausibility of a diagnosis - three types of interest in a parameter are distinguished:

for_initial_assessment,
on_suspicion, and
for_verification.

As the predicate names say, the first predicate states the link between a parameter and a diagnosis for the initial assessment, where the interest in one of the possible diagnoses is not yet high. The second predicate links parameters to a diagnosis already under consideration, i.e. has a medium rating of interest. The third predicate identifies parameters for verifying a diagnosis, i.e. where a diagnosis already has a high rating. The relations between parameters and diagnoses reflect evaluations that take into account the costs and the usefulness of the compilation in order to come to a diagnosis. They are encoded using the three-place predicate for the interest as is shown in the following example fact:

```
interest_of_parameter_compilation(mucoviscidosis,trypsin_in_serum,
                                   on_suspicion)
```

Whether there is trypsin in the serum is only of interest if there is already the assumption - due to other parameters - that the child could suffer from mucoviscidosis.

The parameters relevant for the assessment of the diagnosis result from the above facts: they are divided into laboratory, clinical and anamnesis parameters. In our example, the parameter trypsin is classified by the following fact as a laboratory one:

```
lab_parameter(mucoviscidosis,trypsin_in_serum).
```

Parameter-evaluation The parameter evaluations are the system's basic knowledge of the patient. Each of these evaluations is a qualitative proposition about the current parameter value, such as moderately (pathological) or extremely (pathological).

Describing Inferential Relationships

This section provides rule examples to describe the major relationships. These rules are based on the above concept of visits, which states that the diagnosis-making process consists of the following steps:

- inputting data about the patient,
- search for a diagnosis,
- presenting a diagnosis,
- planning how to continue, and
- displaying laboratory queries.

Inputting Data A new visit begins with queries. The system uses forward-chaining inferences to determine the queries to be asked after a fact visit(<newborn-name>,<visit-number>) has been entered.

In the first visit the system requests all parameters that are registered as basic-data. The second visit brings up the queries according to the model of temporal development. In all visits the system presents the standard clinical queries as well as those queries that in the last visit were regarded as being of some interest and that are no longer valid in this visit. The corresponding rule is as follows[5]:

```
visit(Newborn,Visit) &
previous_visit(Newborn,Visit,PreviousVisit) &
disorder(Diagnosis) &
interest(Newborn,PreviousVisit,Diagnosis,Interest) &
interest_of_parameter_compilation(Diagnosis,Parameter,Costs) &
interest_justifies_costs(Interest,Costs)
    → parameter_is_necessary(Newborn,Parameter)
```

[5] Arguments beginning with a capital letter are variables.

The patient's data for a visit are entered as facts, for example:

```
input(anne,1,bili_total_increase,indecisive)
measured_value(anne,1,temperature,41)
```

Here, the patient anne has an indecisive increase in bili (which is the central blood parameter of icterus or anemia). She also has a body temperature of 41° C.

Parameter Evaluation. If a parameter is entered using quantitative measurements, conversion rules change the measured value into the qualitative evaluation: evaluation(anne,1,temperature,extreme).

The evaluation of some parameters requires other parameters to be considered. For instance, we can compute the rhesus factor of the child's blood if we know about the blood factors of the mother.

```
evaluation(Newborn,Visit,mother_subgroup,dd) &
evaluation(Newborn,Visit,subgroup,dd)
    → evaluation(Newborn,Visit,constellation_rh,yes)
```

In this process some queries may turn out to be redundant and system will withdraw its parameter request. This is achieved by the following rule:

```
parameter_is_needed(Newborn,Visit,Parameter) &
unknown(evaluation(Newborn,Visit,Parameter,U)) &
unknown(valid_evaluation(Newborn,Visit,Parameter,W)) &
unknown(input_terminated(Newborn,Visit) )
    → parameter_still_to_be_entered(Newborn,Visit,Parameter)
```

This rule derives all parameter values which still need to be entered. If a parameter value is inputted or can be inferred from other inputs, the corresponding inference becomes invalid, because the second and the third premise are no longer confirmed. Then, the conclusion is deleted from the knowledge base (see section 3.4). Here, we see how control knowledge is encoded in MOBAL. This example clearly shows that the task structure as displayed by the topology has no corresponding representational construct within the inference engine. Therefore, the tasks to be fulfilled, e.g. asking for data, coming to a diagnosis, etc., are compiled into rules such as the one above.

Valid Evaluations. The predicate valid_evaluation must be computed for variable parameters in each visit, as they may change. For instance, temperature is not a constant parameter. The variable parameters previously compiled are valid if the time elapsed between the compilation and the visit is less than the specified validation period. The parameters declared to be constant are valid for all subsequent visits. In this case, the evaluations are also automatically valid. The rules for evaluating parameters are the following:

```
parameter_is_variable(Parameter) &
last_valid_evaluation(Newborn,Visit,
                      VisitOfEvaluation,Parameter,Value) &
parameter_maximum_valid_time_period(Parameter,Zg) &
age_of_newborn(Newborn,Visit,Age) &
age_of_newborn(Newborn,VisitOfEvaluation,Time) &
sub(Age,Time,TimeDiff) &
ge(Zg,TimeDiff)
   → valid_for_visit_b(Newborn,Visit,VisitOfEvaluation,Parameter,Value)

valid_for_visit_b(Newborn,Visit,VisitOfEvaluation,Parameter,Value)
   → valid_evaluation(Newborn,Visit,Parameter,Value)
```

Valid Probability. The probability factors as well as the necessary and sufficient conditions constitute the central diagnostic knowledge. They are divided into laboratory, clinical, and anamnesis probability factors. The valid evaluation of a parameter and the probability factor of this parameter pointing to a diagnosis provide the valid probability:

```
clinical_parameter(Diagnosis_parameter) &
valid_evaluation(Newborn,Visit,Parameter,Value) &
probability(Parameter,Value,Diagnosis,Points)
   → valid_clinical_probability(Newborn,Visit,Diagnosis,Parameter,Points)
```

Some diagnoses can directly be exluded or established, provided that there is a particular and simple parameter constellation. These relationships of necessary and sufficient conditions are specified by rules. The following two rules encode such constellations:

```
positive(Newborn,Visit,coombs) &
constellation_rh(Newborn,Visit)
   → satisfies_sufficient_condition(Newborn,Visit,rh_incompatibility)

not(mother_antibodies(Newborn,Visit))
   → not(satisfies_necessary_condition(Newborn,Visit,rh_incompatibility)
```

To simplify the representation of these rules, a few evaluations have been reformulated using rules like the following which re-states facts about antibodies of the mother using the predicate mother_antibodies.

```
valid_evaluation(Newborn,Visit,mother_antibodies,no)
   → not(mother_antibodies(Newborn,Visit))
```

Coming to a diagnosis The evaluation of a disorder depends on the computed plausibility and the soundness of the various diagnoses. The central rule - again one, which encodes control knowledge for the overall diagnosis process - is the following:

```
input_terminated(Newborn,Visit) &
disorder(Diagnosis) &
overall_plausibility(Newborn,Visit,Diagnosis,Plausi) &
soundness(Newborn,Visit,Diagnosis,Soundness)
   → disorder_evaluation(Newborn,Visit,Diagnosis,Plausi,Soundness)
```

The various diagnoses or groups of diagnoses are evaluated individually depending on their plausibility and sound basis. A plausible and sound diagnosis results either from

- the fact that the sufficient conditions have or the necessary conditions have not been satisfied or
- the combination of all valid probability factors that point to a particular diagnosis, with the soundness depending on the number of the valid parameters.

The following rules illustrate these relationships:

```
not(satisfies_necessary_condition(Newborn,Visit,Diagnosis)
   → overall_plausibility(Newborn,Visit,Diagnosis,none)

unknown(not(satisfies_necessary_condition(Newborn,Visit,Diagnosis))&
satisfies_sufficient_condition(Newborn,Visit,Diagnosis)
   → overall_plausibility(Newborn,Visit,Diagnosis,max)

unknown(not(satisfies_necessary_condition(Newborn,Visit,Diagnosis)))&
unknown(satisfies_sufficient_condition(Newborn,Visit,Diagnosis))&
overall_plausibility_value(Newborn,Visit,Diagnosis,Overall_plausi)&
evaluation_overall_plausibility(Overall_plausi,Evalu)
   → overall_plausibility(Newborn,Visit,Diagnosis,Evalu)
```

The soundness of a diagnosis is similarly formulated. Again, the control of the diagnosing process is encoded using the autoepistemic operator **unknown**. The constant **none** is assigned to a particular diagnosis and visit, if necessary conditions do not hold. The constant **max** is assigned, if sufficient conditions are fulfilled, but the necessary conditions are not yet known. If both types of conditions are unknown, then no constant is assigned. A variable (**Evalu**) gets its value by evaluating the overall plausibility of the diagnosis.

Determining Plausibility. The computation of plausibility factors differentiates the three plausibility models (overall, based on laboratory, based on clinical parameters). The overall plausibility model, for example, is based on the following rule:

```
overall_plausibility_model(Diagnosis) &
sum_of_clinical_probability_factors(Newborn,Visit,
                                    Diagnosis,Clinical_points) &
sum_of_lab_probability_factors(Newborn,Visit,Diagnosis,Lab_points)&
sum_of_anamnesis_probability_factors(Newborn,Visit,
                                    Diagnosis,Anamnesis_points)&
add(Clinical_points,Lab_points,C_plus_L_points) &
add(C_plus_L_points,Anamnesis_points,Total_points)&
normalized_overall_plausibility(Diagnosis,Total_points,Norm_plausibility)
   → overall_plausibility_value(Newborn,Visit,
                                    Diagnosis,Norm_plausibility)
```

The sum of probability factors is determined using the autoepistemic operator **sum_of** (see section 3.2.3). For example, the following rule sums up all clinical probability points for all parameters for a particular diagnosis:

```
sum_of(points,
      valid_clinical_probability(Newborn,Visit,
                                    Diagnosis,Parameters,Points),
      sum)
   → sum_of_clinical_probability_factors(Newborn,Visit,Diagnosis,Sum)
```

The plausibility model for diagnoses more based on laboratory parameters than on clinical ones uses a rule which backwards chains to computing the soundness of parameter evaluation:

```
lab_stronger_than_clinical(Diagnosis) &
lab_soundness(Newborn,Visit,Diagnosis,Soundness)
   → soundness_value(Newborn,Visit,Diagnosis,Soundness)
```

```
number_labParameters(Diagnosis,Number_overall) &
number_valid_lab_parameters(Newborn,Visit,Diagnosis,Number) &
evaluation_soundness(Number_overall,Number,Soundness)
   → lab_soundness(Newborn,Visit,Diagnosis,Soundness)
```

The number of valid parameters is calculated by the count operator:

```
count(valid_lab_parameter(Newborn,Visit,Diagnosis,Value),Number)
   → number_valid_lab_parameters(Newborn,Visit,Diagnosis,Number)
```

Presenting a diagnosis A rule step leads from the disorder evaluation to the diagnosis. It is made when the disorder has been plausibly and soundly stated. The central rule is:

```
disorder_evaluation(Newborn,Visit,Diagnosis,Plausibility,Soundness)&
diagnosis_sound(Plausibiliy,Soundness)
   → diagnosis(Newborn,Visit,Diagnosis,Plausibility,Soundness)
```

What is important, when it comes to making a correct diagnosis or multiple diagnoses, is not to overlook the symptoms that have not been covered by an established diagnosis. Another forward inferencing step uses the diagnosis to produce the parameters not accounted for by the diagnosis and registers them as facts:

```
diagnosis(Newborn,Visit,Diagnosis,Plausibility,Soundness) &
high(Newborn,Visit,Parameter) &
valid_evaluation(Newborn,Visit,Parameter,Value) &
unknown(probability(Parameter,Value,Diagnosis,Points))
   → parameter_unexplained(Newborn,Visit,
                        Diagnosis,Parameter,Value)
```

This rule mainly unifies the parameters for which the probability is unknown with the third argument of the predicate parameter_unexplained.

The Planning Planning is one of the most crucial tasks of the system. Planning determines the laboratory tests that are to be arranged and the queries that are to be asked at the beginning of the next visit. The system computes the interest of each disorder: the more interesting a diagnosis, the more important the queries. The importance of a query depends on the efforts involved (costs incurred) and their usefulness in verifying or falsifying the diagnosis. This information is stored as facts.

The Clinical Assessment. Each new visit brings up queries in order to be able to assess the patient's clinical condition. As in the case of the plausbilility determination, this assessment results from the accumulation of the probability factors these parameters have.

The Interest. The interest is based on the plausibility, the soundness and the risk of the various disorders with a particular emphasis on the clinical condition of the patient. Altogether, there are 21 interest-computing rules such as:

```
not(clinical_extreme(Newborn,Visit) &
overall_plausibility(Newborn,Visit,Diagnosis,little) &
soundness(Newborn,Visit,Diagnosis,Soundness) &
ne(Soundness,optimum) &
risk(Diagnosis,yes)
    → interest(Newborn,Visit,Diagnosis,moderate)
```

Queries The laboratory queries, the diagnosis and the unexplained parameters are the results of the consultation. In the first visit the laboratory queries originate in the model of temporal development. In the other visits they arise from the interest in the various diagnoses. The interest determines both the cost level of the laboratory parameters and also the queries to be asked in the next visit and those to be used to assess a diagnosis. The system will request only those data that are likely to be invalid in the next visit:

```
time_until_next_visit(Newborn,Visit,Hours) &
visit(Newborn,Visit) & disorder(Diagnosis) &
interest(Newborn,Visit,Diagnosis,Interest) &
interest_of_parameter_compilation(Diagnosis,Parameter,Costs) &
interest_justifies_costs(Interest,Costs) &
is_lab_parameter(Parameter) &
presumably_invalid_or_no_evaluation(Newborn,Visit,
                                    Parameter,Hours)
    → lab_query(Newborn,Visit,Diagnosis,Parameter)
```

9.2.3 Icterus Consultations in MOBAL

The functionality of the ICTERUS system consists of compiling patient data in the course of several visits, searching for a diagnosis, and finally coming to a justified diagnosis. This functionality is also provided by MOBAL, although the MOBAL inference engine as such has not been built to control consultations.

The consultation is triggered by the forward-chaining inference mechanism (see section 3.3.1): the inference engine uses each fact that has been entered to prove the rules that contain the predicate as the premise. Then, the system attempts to prove the remaining premises using backward-chaining inference (see 3.3.2). The search depth is adjusted by a control parameter which specifies the number of rules that can be used in the backtracking process (see section 3.2.5). As the inference engine stores the result of each derivation step as a fact, these facts can also trigger new forward-chaining inferences.

The consultation is modeled using particular predicates in rule premises for control purposes. These predicates trigger forward-chaining inferences. Queries are triggered by the input of a fact with the predicate visit/2. The search for diagnoses is triggered by the input of a fact with the predicate input_terminated/2. The third and last control predicate time_until_next_visit/3 activates the planning process, i.e. determining which disorders or disorder groups are interesting. Backward inferencing supplies the system with all the information about parameter evaluation and sufficient and necessary conditions for diagnoses. The control predicates are represented in the very same way as other predicates. Hence, only the knowledge engineer interprets them as control predicates - MOBAL does not notice the difference between control predicates, which represent knowledge about the consultation process, and predicates that represent medical knowledge about disorders.

9.2.4 An Assessment

The ICTERUS domain modeled by Stollmann Ltd has posed challenges that the MOBAL system had not been developed to meet. In fact, MOBAL was not only used as a knowledge acquisition system but also as a kind of expert system shell. This section assesses the experience in working with MOBAL to represent the ICTERUS world from the point of view of the involved expert and the knowledge engineer.

- How adequate was the representation formalism?

- What kinds of problems were posed by the modeling process?
- How did the system support the modeling of the domain and the use of the represented knowledge?

The Adequacy of the Representation Formalism

The MOBAL representation formalism enables a simple and semantically well-defined modeling of the domain. The structure of the system consisting of facts and rules was relatively comprehensible. There were hardly any difficulties in representing knowledge in MOBAL. The autoepistemic operators such as unknown, sum-of and count (see section 3.2.3) play an important role in ICTERUS.

Unknown The use of unknown allows the system to make default conclusions, if a fact is unknown. In the modeling process this was necessary to obtain the following functionality:

- Determining the queries at the beginning of a visit: queries are to be requested if a parmeter is needed and there is no valid evaluation for it. When in one of the last few visits the system had registered a valid evaluation for the parameter, then it is possible to compute its invalidity, if not; the lack of an evaluation can safely be used to conclude that there is none at all. Unknown could only be avoided if in each visit the system states for any parameter which is to be compiled, but which was not requested, that it was not entered.
- The plausibility and soundness of a diagnosis can be determined by the accumulation of probability factors and by counting the valid evaluations of parameters. This is not necessary if it is already known that the the sufficient conditions are satisfied or the necessary conditions are not satisfied. If the sufficient conditions are satisfied or the necessary conditions are not satisfied, the plausibility must not be computed from the sum of probability points. Otherwise, this could lead to two different results. In order to avoid the use of unknown, the negation of the sufficient and necessary conditions ought to be formulated.
- The data compiled from the first visit are used to compute a model of temporal development. This information determines the data compilation process for the second visit. If the data do not provide any information, a standard course of the dialog session will be assumed.

sum_of and count Knowledge assessment in this model primarily results from the accumulation of probability factors and the counting of the valid parameter evaluations describing various disorders. This leads to the justification of the diagnosis being plausible and sound. It would also be possible to use rules instead, where each item is listed as a premise whose arguments would then be added up individually.

The non-monotonic operators unknown, count and sum-of provide a very powerful and useful extension to the MOBAL knowledge representation system. Not only the ICTERUS domain can make use of them.

Thanks to the thorough support provided by the inference engine, these functions can easily be used to retract nonmonotonic inferences. Only in connection with the search depth limitations they sometimes produce unintentional (even though correct) results, since these functions refer to the inferences that are possible within the resource limits (search depth) and not to the overall-possible inferential closure of the knowledge base. Consequently, it can happen that a proposition is evaluated to be unknown, although it would be proven given an increased depth of the search tree. Also, when it comes to adding up the factors, only those facts that can be proven within the predefined depth of the search tree will be summed up.

General Problems in Domain Modeling

One of the major problems posed by domain modeling is the choice of the appropriate objects, properties and relations. This is reflected in the choice of predicates and argument positions. As all the knowledge - the facts and the rules - is made up of predicate relations, the choice of a predicate definition is one of the most important decisions in building a system. MOBAL supports the user in that it allows a predicate to be defined or provides predicate definitions itself by learning. MOBAL compares the facts and rules with the definitions to find out whether they are correct. Moreover, the general problem of representation needs not be solved once and for all, due to MOBAL's approach of sloppy modeling.

In principle, the choice of predicate definitions poses three problems. The first problem lies in deciding what to represent as a predicate and what as an argument. The proposition "Anne has a high fever" can be represented as

temperature(anne,high)

or as

high(temperature,anne)

The second problem consists of determining the necessary argument positions. In the ICTERUS system, for example, the consultation related data not only depend on the newborn but also on the number of the visit, as some of them are only valid in one visit.

The third problem refers to the question as to how much information is to be contained in the predicate and how much in the arguments. The proposition "Anne has a high fever" can be represented as

temperature(anne,high)

or with a more general predicate as

evaluation(anne,temperature,high)

The first case provides a simplified interpretation of the proposition, while the second representation enables the formulation of relationships between all these general propositions.

The description of such relationships in complex domains often requires the use of very general predicates consisting of an unmanageably large number of argument positions. These predicates will have to be specified in advance. It would certainly be desirable if MOBAL could provide support for the modification of predicate definitions. This would fit into the framework of MOBAL but has not yet been implemented.

System Support in the Modeling Process

Modeling the ICTERUS domain the inductive learning tools were not used because neither case data of patients nor real-world data from visits were available (cf. section 9.2.5).

The structure of the ICTERUS domain only incorporates sorts entered by the user. This model does not have an automatic definition and verification of sorts because the knowledge engineer primarily needed the predicate declarations for keeping track of many predicates with higher arity.

The inference engine actively supports the modeling process: the input of facts and rules causes the engine to check the data's logical consistency with the prerequisite knowledge and adds newly derived facts or contradictions to the database, i.e. it is possible to check the modeling result incrementally.

The topology was used to examine the (inferred and entered) facts at each level (or of each group) and at any time. The system's processes are transparent: the various (mediating) results - in this case propositions about plausibility, soundness, valid evaluations, etc. - enable the user to keep track of the processes. The topology supported the inspection of the knowledge base.

The knowledge revision with its derivation trees allowed erroneously entered facts to be immediately detected and rectified. The revisability was supported in this way. Unfortunately, modifications, especially in a complex system, take time. It is true that the rules and facts to be updated can be called with the help of the focus mechanism, but the system will at first have to retract all the derivations upon deletion and then compute them again when they are re-entered (depending on the predefined forward-inferencing depth). Regardless of the time needed, it is very helpful for the knowledge engineer to have the opportunity to discover and rectify errors and then to have the improved version displayed during a dialog session so that the consultation can proceed.

The aim of the MOBAL system development was to use it in accordance with the philosophy of second-generation expert systems, which advocates a clear-cut separation of different knowledge types [Clancey, 1986]. In contrast to that, the expertise to be used in the ICTERUS model and to be implemented in MOBAL had a rather "compiled" structure, i.e. some parts of the actual expertise were mixed with control knowledge. Though we first had some reservations about the adequacy of MOBAL to build such a compiled model, the ICTERUS experiment has finally proven that MOBAL is sufficiently powerful to be used as an expert system and that it is as operational as expected. However, the intended use is more of the kind described in the next section.

9.2.5 The Interaction of MOBAL and TWAICE

The cooperation of the three partners who intended to create a model of the ICTERUS domain was very intensive. Stollmann Ltd elicited the medical knowledge to create the domain model. To be able to process this, Nixdorf Computers AG extended their system TWAICE, and MOBAL was used to reconstruct the domain model. Without any consultations, which lead to many new facts being created, the ICTERUS model implemented in MOBAL contains 800 facts and 267 rules. Note, that translating facts and rules of MOBAL into the formalism of TWAICE gives about ten times as many rules. One fact in MOBAL corresponds to up to six rules in TWAICE.

Coupling the expert system shell TWAICE with MOBAL showed a new perspective on how to achieve the separation of domain and consultation knowledge and use the knowledge acquisition system also during consultations. TWAICE was used as the consultation system responsible for the control knowledge. Using the pipe concept of UNIX, TWAICE put queries to MOBAL whenever domain knowledge was needed. MOBAL answered the queries. The input data about a new patient were also passed from TWAICE to MOBAL. From these new data, MOBAL learns new rules and invents new concepts so that the knowledge base is maintained because of consultations. The knowledge base was enhanced by a new concept which was defined by the system in the following way:

compiled_earlier(X,Y) & constant_parameter(X)
→ concept1(X,Y)
recompiled(X,Y) → concept1(X,Y)

This new concept could be used by the following (learned) rule:

indication(X,Y) & pathological(X,Z) & concept1(X,Z)
→ interesting(Y,Z)

The rule states that a parameter which is linked to a diagnosis and whose value is pathological is interesting for further evaluation only if it is either a constant parameter or a parameter compiled in this visit. This is not a particularly "exciting" rule. However, knowledge engineers tend to forget the simple rules. Therefore, it is good to have the system add those necessary rules in the course of using the knowledge base for consultations.

9.3 The Telecommunications Security Domain

In this section, we briefly describe a prototypical application of MOBAL to a telecommunications security problem developed in cooperation with Alcatel Alsthom Recherche, Paris, in the *Machine Learning Toolbox* (MLT) ESPRIT project[6]. This application is of particular interest for demonstrating the learning and knowledge revision capabilities of MOBAL in an interactive setting, and for illustrating a usage scenario of the system. We begin with a short introduction to the problem, and then describe some of the modeling efforts that were done by Alcatel Alsthom Recherche and GMD.

[6] MOBAL has been applied to several other problems within MLT which we do not have the space to describe here (see [Work Package 8 Partners, 1991]).

9.3.1 Problem description

The MOBAL application being described in this section has been developed in the context of a research project on telecommunications security being conducted at Alcatel Alsthom Recherche, Paris. The problem addressed by this project is the following [Fargier, 1991]. A telecommunications network generally consists of a number of regionally distributed switching systems that are responsible for allocating network resources and implementing the connections requested by end users. These switching computers may be installed on the premises of the network provider, or on the premises of customers needing local equipment. They may be owned and operated by the network provider, or owned, rented, and operated in whole or part by customer companies.

In such a complex environment, it is a serious problem to ensure that only personnel authorized to perform a particular class of operations can actually access the switching systems and perform the operations. Currently, this access control task is often addressed by manually established access control lists. These lists, however, are error-prone, and it is impossible to guarantee that a consistent *security policy* is being followed throughout. The goal of the project at Alcatel Alsthom Recherche is to develop an approach for formally specifying, validating, and using an explicit security policy that could replace the above-mentioned manual methods. By using formal methods, a security policy could be proved consistent, and it could be guaranteed that the policy is being followed in all cases. As a language for the expression of security policies, a Horn-clause-like representation was chosen.

9.3.2 Use of MOBAL in SPEED

There are several aspects in which MOBAL offers support for the construction of a system that addresses the above access control problem. First of all, since the language for security policies is essentially of a Horn-clause form, the representation of access control rules in MOBAL is directly possible (with the exception of constraints, which are not currently supported by MOBAL). Similarly, the required background information about the available switching systems, their locations, owners, and employees can be represented. Table 9.6 shows some of the predicates used for representing this kind of information in an initial MOBAL prototype developed by Hélène Fargier at Alcatel Alsthom Recherche [Fargier, 1991], and then extended by Edgar Sommer at GMD [Sommer, 1992].

may-operate/3: <user>, <component>, <operation>.
optype/2: <operation>, <operation-type>.
rented-by/2: <switch>, <company>.
dept/1: <department>.
manages/2: <department>, <switch>.
manager/1: <user>.
operator/1: <user>.
works-in/2: <user>, <department>.
threshold/2: <error-counter>, <value>.
subsystem/2: <switch>, <subswitch>.
location/2: <switch>, <region>.
covers/2: <company>, <region>.
owner/2: <switch>, <company>.
applicable/2: <operation>, <component>.

Table 9.6: Subset of Predicates used in Telecom Security Domain

The meaning of most of these predicate declarations should be clear from their names alone. The most important "target" predicate in this domain is may_operate, which specifies that a certain user may perform a specific operation on a particular network component.

Although a comparison of RDT and other learning algorithms is not a central topic here, different algorithms can be and have been integrated into MOBAL. A brief review of testing FOIL [Quinlan, 1990] on the SPEED data may be of interest [Sommer *et al.*, 1993a]. The comparison shows the effect of the closed world assumption. When entering 587 positive examples of `may-operate` into FOIL[7], it applied the closed world assumption and found two good rules and an incorrect one in 252.5 seconds. The rules covered 21 percent of the examples. For the same data, RDT found 14 rules (including one learned by FOIL) in 443.0 seconds. The rules covered 89 percent of the examples. When adding one negative example to the data set, FOIL no longer applies the closed world assumption and so finds four strange rules with a coverage of zero percent[8]. RDT delivered the same rules as before.

[7]This large number is a concession to FOIL - RDT learned rules with far fewer examples.

[8]In these rules, not all variables were bound in the premise, effectively inferring access rights for arbitrary users (or arbitrary operations and components). MOBAL's inference

This illustrates the importance of the assumption about knowledge. If we have a domain with a big and completeable set of examples, FOIL is very fast and efficient. If we do not know in advance how many examples we will have and how representative they are, RDT is a good choice for learning. In this experiment, we had 587 examples from 8775 possible instances of `may-operate`. The examples represent only 6.7 percent of this theoretical total, and we cannot guarantee that we do in fact know all intended legal access privileges at any given point in time. This is no problem though, as MOBAL supports an incremental modeling style and can handle incomplete knowledge.

The usage scenario for MOBAL in the application domain is that MOBAL forms part of an interactive system for security managers with which they can specify, evaluate, and use security policies. To illustrate this scenario, a special-purpose user interface for MOBAL was constructed at GMD. in This user interface differs from the generic MOBAL knowledge acquisition environment mainly in its use of special-purpose buttons and displays that are labeled with domain terminology instead of the generic MOBAL terms. MOBAL supports the construction of such special-purpose interfaces through its documented program interface (PI), and a set of special-purpose routines to access the PI and MOBAL's display routines directly from the display server via message passing.

Within the above usage scenario, there are several possible services that MOBAL can provide in this domain. First of all, the manual knowledge acquisition and inspection environment can be used by the security manager to input manually security policy rules and the necessary background knowledge. This can be done with MOBAL's generic interface, or with a specialized version as mentioned above. Once input, the inference engine can be used to apply the rules to derive individual users' access rights. More importantly, MOBAL can help to acquire and revise security policies automatically. If an access or importing facility from the existing, manually constructed access right databases were available, the learning module RDT could be used to analyze the manual data, and extract the implicit policies according to which they may have been constructed. For example, in the prototype model, RDT discovered the following rule (here shown with meaningful variable names):

manages(Dept,Switch) & works-in(Person,Dept) &
manager(Person) & optype(Op,log-create) →

engine does not apply such faulty rules (non-generative rules in the terminology of [Muggleton and Feng, 1990]).

may-operate(Person,Switch,Op)

which states that the managers of a department may all perform a certain type of operation on all equipment operated (managed) by their department.

For both manually input and inductively acquired policies, it is furthermore possible for the security manager to avoid having to inspect and evaluate the set of rules in the abstract by relying on MOBAL's knowledge revision capabilities. The access rights derived using the general rules can simply be checked on the level of individual users, and whenever a user is granted incorrect access rights, KRT can be employed to trace back to the responsible rule and to modify it as necessary. The system will even automatically detect and point out the conflict if some rules are contradictory. In one of the prototype models, KRT was used to modify rules which finally led to the creation of a new "senior operator" concept by CLT, which had previously been missing from the model.

9.3.3 Summary

The application described in this section differs from the rest of the applications described in this chapter in both its emphasis on an interactive use of MOBAL as part of an application system, and in its advanced state of development in an industrial context. Since the task of developing and maintaining formal security policies is of an ongoing nature due to changes in stated policy or network structure, this application is also a prime example of the *balanced cooperative modeling* paradigm that underlies the design and implementation of MOBAL (see chapter 1).

Bibliography

[Abrett and Burstein, 1987] G. Abrett and M. H. Burstein. The KREME knowledge editing environment. *International Journal of Man-Machine Studies*, 27:103–126, 1987.

[Amarel, 1968] S. Amarel. On representations of problems of reasoning about actions. In B. Meltzer and D. Michie, editors, *Machine Intelligence*, volume 3, pages 131–171. Edinburgh University Press, Edinburgh, 1968. Reprinted in *Readings in Artificial Intelligence*, B. L. Webber and N. J. Nilsson, editors, Morgan Kaufmann, 1981.

[Angluin and Smith, 1983] D. Angluin and C. Smith. Inductive inference - theory and methods. *Computing Surveys*, 15(3), 1983.

[Anjewierden *et al.*, 1990] A. Anjewierden, J. Wielmaker, and C. Toussaint. Shelley - computer aided knowledge engineering. In B. Wielinga, editor, *Current Trends in Knowledge Acquisition*, pages 41–59. IOS Press, Amsterdam, 1990.

[Attardi and Simi, 1984] G. Attardi and M. Simi. Metalanguage and reasoning about viewpoints. In *European Conference on Artificial Intelligence*, 1984.

[Bachant and McDermott, 1984] J. Bachant and J. McDermott. R1 revisited: Four years in the trenches. *The AI Magazine*, 5(3):21–32, 1984.

[Badre, 1984] A. Badre. Designing transitionality into the user-computer interface. In G. Salvendy, editor, *Human-Computer Interaction*. Elsevier, Amsterdam, 1984.

[Bareiss and Porter, 1987] E. Bareiss and B. Porter. Protos: An exemplar-based learning apprentice. In P. Langley, editor, *Proc. 4th Int. Workshop on Machine Learning*, pages 12–23. Morgan Kaufman, 1987.

[Barsalou, 1983] L. W. Barsalou. Ad hoc categories. *Memory & Cognition*, 11(3):211–227, 1983.

[Belnap, 1976] N. Belnap. How a computer should think. In G. Reyle, editor, *Contemporary Aspects of Philosophy*. Oriente Press, 1976.

[Benjamin, 1990] D. P. Benjamin, editor. *Change of Representation and Inductive Bias*. Kluwer Academic Publishers, Dordrecht, Netherlands, 1990.

[Biedermann, 1988] A. Biedermann. Wissenserwerb und Lernen zum Einsatz von Dienstleistungs-Expertensystemen. Interner BMFT-Bericht, Nr.9, 1988.

[Biedermann and Müller-Wickop, 1988] A. Biedermann and J. Müller-Wickop. Wissenserwerb und Prototyp-Konzeption des Expertensystems Ikterus. Interner BMFT-Bericht, Nr.5, 1988.

[Blair and Subrahmanian, 1989] H. A. Blair and V. S. Subrahmanian. Paraconsistent logic programming. *Theoretical Computer Science*, 68:135–154, 1989.

[Boose, 1985] J. H. Boose. A knowledge acquisition program for expert systems based on personal construct psychology. *Int. Journal of Man-Machine Studies*, 23:495–525, 1985.

[Boose and Bradshaw, 1987] J. H. Boose and J. M. Bradshaw. Expertise transfer and complex problems using aquinas as a knowledge acquisition workbench for expert systems. *Int. Journal of Man-Machine Studies*, 26:3–28, 1987.

[Bowen, 1985] K. Bowen. Meta-level programming and knowledge representation. *New Generation Computing*, 3:359–383, 1985.

[Brachman and Levesque, 1985] R. J. Brachman and H. J. Levesque, editors. *Readings in Knowledge Representation.* Morgan Kaufmann, 1985.

[Brachman and Schmolze, 1985] R. J. Brachman and J. Schmolze. An overview of the KL-ONE knowledge representation system. *Cognitive Science*, 9(2):171–216, 1985.

[Brazdil, 1986] P. Brazdil. Transfer of knowledge between systems: A common approach to teaching and learning. In *ECAI-86*, volume II, pages 73–78. Brighton, 1986.

[Brazdil, 1987] P. Brazdil. Knowledge states and meta-knowledge maintenance. In I. Bratko and N. Lavrac, editors, *EWSL-87, Bled, Yugoslavia*, pages 138–146. Sigma Press, Wilmslow, 1987. Progress in Machine Learning.

[Buchanan and Mitchell, 1978] B. Buchanan and T. M. Mitchell. Model-directed learning of production rules. In D. Waterman and F. Hayes-Roth, editors, *Pattern-Directed Inference Systems.* Academic Press, New York, San Francisco, London, 1978.

[Buntine, 1988] W. Buntine. Generalized subsumption and its applications to induction and redundancy. *Artificial Intelligence*, 36:149–176, 1988.

[Ceri *et al.*, 1990] S. Ceri, G. Gottlob, and L. Tanca. *Logic Programming and Databases.* Springer, Berlin, New York, 1990.

[Cestnik *et al.*, 1987] B. Cestnik, I. Kononenko, and I. Bratko. Assistant 86: A knowledge-elicitation tool for sophisticated users. In I. Bratko and N. Lavrac, editors, *Progress in Machine Learning*, pages 31–45. Sigma Press, Wilmslow, 1987.

[Chandrasekaran, 1989] B. Chandrasekaran. Task-structures, knowledge acquisition, and learning. *Machine Learning*, 4:339–345, 1989.

[Charniak and McDermott, 1984] E. Charniak and D. McDermott. *Introduction to Artificial Intelligence.* Addison-Wesley, Reading, 1984.

[Chomsky, 1965] N. Chomsky. *Aspects of the Theory of Syntax.* MIT Press, Cambridge, Mass., 1965.

[Christaller *et al.*, 1989] T. Christaller, F. di Primio, and A. Voß, editors. *Die KI-Werkbank Babylon, eine offene und portable Entwicklungsumgebung für Expertensysteme.* Addison-Wesley, Bonn, Reading, Menlo Park, New York, 1989.

[Clancey, 1986] W. J. Clancey. From GUIDON to NEOMYCIN and HERACLES in twenty short lessons: Our final report 1979-1985. *The AI Magazine*, pages 40–60, 1986.

[Cox and Blumenthal, 1987] L. Cox and R. Blumenthal. Krimb: An intelligent knowledge acquisition and representation program for interactive model building. In *First European Workshop on Knowledge Acquisition for Knowledge-Based Systems.* Reading University, UK, 1987.

[Davies and Russell, 1987] T. Davies and S. Russell. A logical approach to reasoning by analogy. In *Procs of IJCAI-87*. Morgan Kaufmann, San Mateo, 1987.

[Davis, 1979] R. Davis. Interactive transfer of expertise: Acquisition of new inference rules. *Artificial Intelligence*, 12:121–157, 1979.

[Davis, 1982] R. Davis. Applications of meta-level knowledge to the construction, maintenance, and use of large knowledge bases. In R. Davis and D. B. Lenat, editors, *Knowledge-Based Systems in Artificial Intelligence*. McGraw-Hill, New York, 1982.

[De Jong and Mooney, 1986] G. De Jong and R. Mooney. Explanation-based-learning: A alternative view. *Machine Learning*, 2(1):145–176, 1986.

[De Kleer, 1986] J. De Kleer. An assumption-based truth maintenance system. *Artificial Intelligence*, 28(2):127–162, 1986.

[De Raedt, 1991] L. De Raedt. *Interactive Concept-Learning*. PhD thesis, Catholic University of Leuven, Leuven, Belgium, February 1991.

[De Raedt and Bruynooghe, 1989a] L. De Raedt and M. Bruynooghe. Constructive induction by analogy: a method to learn how to learn? In *Proc. Fourth European Working Session on Learning (EWSL)*, pages 189–199. Pitman/Morgan Kaufman, London/Los Altos, CA, 1989.

[De Raedt and Bruynooghe, 1989b] L. De Raedt and M. Bruynooghe. Towards friendly concept-learners. In *Proc. of the 11th Int. Joint Conf. on Artif. Intelligence*, pages 849–854. Morgan Kaufman, Los Altos, CA, 1989.

[De Raedt and Bruynooghe, 1992] L. De Raedt and M. Bruynooghe. Interactive concept-learning and constructive induction by analogy. *Machine Learning*, 8(2):107–150, 1992.

[Diederich *et al.*, 1987] J. Diederich, M. Linster, I. Ruhmann, and T. Uthmann. A methodology for integrating knowledge acquisition techniques. Technical report, GMD, Sankt Augustin, 1987.

[Dietterich and Michalski, 1985] T. G. Dietterich and R. S. Michalski. Discovering patterns in sequences of events. *Artificial Intelligence*, 25:187–232,, 1985.

[Doyle, 1979] J. Doyle. A truth maintenance system. *Artificial Intelligence*, 12(3):231–272, 1979.

[Džeroski *et al.*, 1992] S. Džeroski, S. Muggleton, and S. Russell. Pac-learnability of determinate logic programs. In *Proc. of the 5th ACM Workshop on Computaional Learning Theory (COLT)*, 1992.

[Easterlin and Langley, 1985] J. D. Easterlin and P. Langley. A framework for concept formation. In *Seventh Annual Conference of the Cognitive Science Society*, pages 267–271. Irvine, CA, 1985.

[Emde, 1987] W. Emde. Non-cumulative learning in METAXA.3. In *IJCAI-87*, pages 208–210. Morgan Kaufman, Los Altos, CA, August 1987. An extended version appeared as KIT-Report 56, Technical University of Berlin.

[Emde, 1989] W. Emde. An inference engine for representing multiple theories. In K. Morik, editor, *Knowledge Representation and Organization in Machine Learning*, pages 148–176. Springer, New York, Berlin, Tokyo, 1989. Also: KIT-Report Nr. 64, TU Berlin, 1988.

[Emde, 1991] W. Emde. *Modellbildung, Wissensrevision und Wissensrepräsentation im Maschinellen Lernen.* Informatik-Fachberichte 281. Springer, Berlin, New York, 1991. PhD thesis.

[Emde and Morik, 1989] W. Emde and K. Morik. Consultation-independent learning in BLIP. In Y. Kodratoff and A. Hutchinson, editors, *Machine and Human Learning.* Michael Horwood Publ., East Wittering, England, 1989.

[Emde and Schmiedel, 1983] W. Emde and A. Schmiedel. Aspekte der Verarbeitung unsicheren Wissens. Technical Report KIT-Report 6, Technical University of Berlin, Berlin, 1983.

[Emde *et al.*, 1983] W. Emde, C. Habel, and C.-R. Rollinger. The discovery of the equator or concept driven learning. In *IJCAI-83*, pages 455 – 458. Morgan Kaufman, Los Altos, CA, 1983.

[Emde *et al.*, 1989] W. Emde, J.-U. Kietz, I. Keller, K. Morik, S. Thieme, and S. Wrobel. Wissenserwerb und Lernen zum Einsatz von Dienstleistungsexpertensystemen — Abschlußbericht des KIT-LERNER projektes. Technical Report KIT-REPORT 71, Technical University of Berlin, Berlin, 1989.

[Eshelman *et al.*, 1987] L. Eshelman, D. Ehret, J. McDermott, and M. Tan. Mole: A tenacious knowledge acquisition tool. *Int. Journal of Man-Machine Studies*, 26(1):41–54, 1987.

[Everitt, 1980] B. Everitt. *Cluster Analysis.* Heinemann Educational, London, 1980.

[Falkenhainer, 1987] B. Falkenhainer. Towards a general-purpose belief maintenance system. Report UIUCDCS-R-87-1329, Department of Computer Science, University of Illinois at Urbana Champaign, 1987.

[Fargier, 1991] H. Fargier. Using Mobal: overview and remarks. Technical note AAR/P2154/40/1, Alcatel Alsthom Recherche, August 1991. Personal Communication.

[Feng and Muggleton, 1992] C. Feng and S. Muggleton. Towards inductive generalization in higher order logic. In D. Sleeman, editor, *Procs. Of IML-92.* Morgan Kaufmann, San Mateo, CA, 1992.

[Fikes *et al.*, 1972] R. E. Fikes, P. E. Hart, and N. J. Nilsson. Learning and executing generalized robot plans. *Artificial Intelligence*, 3:251–288, 1972.

[Filman, 1988] R. E. Filman. Reasoning with worlds and truth maintenance in a knowledge-based programming environment. *Communications of the ACM*, 31(4):382–401, 1988.

[Fisher, 1987] D. H. Fisher. Knowledge acquisition via incremental conceptual clustering. *Machine Learning*, 2:139–172, 1987.

[Floyd *et al.*, 1988] C. Floyd, W. Langenheder, and D. Siefkes. Software development and reality construction. In Budde, Floyd, Keil-Slawik, and Züllighoven, editors, *Software and Reality Construction, an Invited Working Conference.* GMD Bonn, Bonn, 1988.

[Freksa *et al.*, 1984] C. Freksa, U. Furbach, and G. Dirlich. Cognition and representation - an overview of knowledge representation issues in cognitive science. In Laubsch, editor, *GWAI-84*, pages 119–144, 1984.

[Fu and Buchanan, 1985] L.-M. Fu and B. Buchanan. Learning intermediate concepts in constructing a hierarchical knowledge base. In *Proc. 9th International Joint Conference on Artificial Intelligence*, pages 659–666. Morgan Kaufman, Los Altos, CA, 1985.

[Gärdenfors, 1988] P. Gärdenfors. *Knowledge in Flux — Modeling the Dynamics of Epistemic States.* MIT Press, Cambridge, MA, 1988.

[Garey and Johnson, 1979] M. R. Garey and D. S. Johnson. *Computers and Intractability - A Guide to the Theory of NP-Completeness.* Freeman, San Francisco, Cal., 1979.

[Garfinkel, 1967] H. Garfinkel. *Studies in Ethnomethodology.* Prentice-Hall, Englewood Cliffs, N.J., 1967.

[Garfinkel, 1973] H. Garfinkel. Das Alltagswissen über soziale und innerhalb sozialer Strukturen. In *Alltagswissen, Interaktion und gesellschaftliche Wirklichkeit*, pages 189–262. rororo studium, Reinbeck bei Hamburg, 1973.

[Gennari *et al.*, 1989] J. H. Gennari, P. Langley, and D. H. Fisher. Models of incremental concept formation. *Artificial Intelligence*, 40:11–61, 1989.

[Gold, 1967] E. M. Gold. Language identification in the limit. *Information and Control*, 10:447–474, 1967.

[Gruber and Cohen, 1987] T. R. Gruber and P. R. Cohen. Design for acquisition: Principles of knowledge-system design to facilitate knowledge acquisition. *Int. Journal of Man-Machine Studies*, 26:143–159, 1987.

[Habel, 1986] C. Habel. Prinzipien der Referentialität — Untersuchungen zur propositionalen Struktur von Wissen. *Informatik-Fachbericht 122*, 1986.

[Habel and Rollinger, 1981] C. Habel and C.-R. Rollinger. A sketch on acquisition of higher cognitive concepts. Technical Report Bericht 81-11, Technical University of Berlin, 1981.

[Habel and Rollinger, 1982] C. Habel and C.-R. Rollinger. The machine as concept learner. In *ECAI-82*, pages 158–159. Orsay, France, 1982.

[Hanson and Bauer, 1989] S. Hanson and M. Bauer. Conceptual clustering, categorization, and polymorphy. *Machine Learning*, 3(4):343–372, 1989.

[Haussler, 1989] D. Haussler. Learning conjunctive concepts in structural domains. *Machine Learning*, 4(1):7–40, 1989.

[Hayes-Roth, 1983] F. Hayes-Roth. Using proof and refutations to learn from experience. In R. Michalski, J. Carbonell, and T. Mitchell, editors, *Machine Learning — An Artificial Intelligence Approach*, pages 221–240. Tioga, Palo Alto, CA, 1983.

[Hecht and Leufke, 1992] A. Hecht and A. Leufke. Case Study: MLT Algorithms Applied to Message Burst Analysis. Technical Note Siemens/P2154/3/1, Machine Learning Toolbox ESPRIT Project P2154, September 1992.

[Helft, 1989] N. Helft. Induction as nonmonotonic inference. In *Proceedings of the 1st International Conference on Knowledge Representation and Reasoning*, 1989.

[Herkner, 1980] W. Herkner. *Attribution - Psychologie der Kausalität.* Hans Huber Publishers, Bern, Stuttgart, Wien, 1980.

[Hermes, 1967] H. Hermes. *Einführung in die Verbandstheorie.* Springer, Berlin, Heidelberg, 1967. 2. Auflage.

[Hinton, 1986] G. E. Hinton. Learning distributed representations of concepts. In *Proc. Eigth Annual Conf. of the Cognitive Science Society*. Lawrence Erlbaum Associates, Hillsdale, NJ, 1986.

[Johnson, 1987] N. Johnson. Mediating representations in knowledge elicitation. In *First European Workshop on Knowledge Acquisition for Knowledge-Based Systems*. Reading University, Reading, UK, 1987.

[Jung, 1993] B. Jung. On inverting generality relations. In *Proc. of 3th Inductive Logic Programming Workshop, ILP-93*, pages 87 – 101, 1993.

[Kalish and Montague, 1964] D. Kalish and R. Montague. *Logic - Techniques of Formal Reasoning*. Hartcourt, New York, 1964.

[Karbach and Voß, 1992] W. Karbach and A. Voß. Model-k for prototyping and strategic reasoning at the knowledge level. In J.-M. David, J.-P. Krivine, and R. Simmons, editors, *Second Generation Expert Systems*. 1992.

[Karbach *et al.*, 1991] W. Karbach, A. Voß, R. Schukey, and U. Drouven. MODEL-K: Prototyping at the knowledge level. In J. Rault, editor, *Proceedings of the 11th International Conference Expert systems and their applications*, volume 1 (Tools, Techniques & Methods), pages 501–511. EC2, Avignon, 1991.

[Kauffman and Grumbach, 1987] H. Kauffman and A. Grumbach. Multilog: Multiple worlds in logic programming. In B. Boulay, D. Hogg, and L. Steels, editors, *Advances in Artificial Intelligence II 7th ECAI-86, Brighton, England*, pages 233–247. Elsevier Pub. (North Holland), Amsterdam, 1987.

[Kearns, 1990] M. J. Kearns. *The Computational Complexity of Machine Learning*. Distinguished Dissertation. MIT Press, Cambridge, Mass., 1990.

[Kelly, 1955] G. Kelly. *The Psychology of Personal Constructs*. Horton, New York, 1955.

[Kietz, 1988] J.-U. Kietz. Incremental and reversible acquisition of taxonomies. *Proceedings of EKAW-88*, pages 24.1–24.11, 1988. Also as KIT-Report 66, Technical University of Berlin.

[Kietz, 1992] J.-U. Kietz. A comparative study of structural most specific generalizations used in machine learning. In *Proc. of 3th Inductive Logic Programming Workshop, ILP-93*, pages 149 – 164, 1992. Also as Arbeitspapiere der GMD No. 667.

[Kietz, 1993] J.-U. Kietz. Some lower bounds for the computational complexity of inductive logic programming. In *Proc. Sixth European Conference on Machine Learning (ECML-93)*, pages 115 – 123, 1993. Also as Arbeitspapiere der GMD No. 718.

[Kietz and Morik, 1991a] J.-U. Kietz and K. Morik. Constructive induction: Learning concepts for learning. Arbeitspapiere der GMD 543, GMD (German Natl. Research Center for Computer Science), 1991. Presented at the Workshop on Concept Formation in Man and Machine, May 1991.

[Kietz and Morik, 1991b] J.-U. Kietz and K. Morik. Constructive induction of background knowledge. In *Proc. of Workshop W8 at the 12th IJCAI-91: Evaluating and changing representations in machine learning.*, 1991.

[Kietz and Morik, 1993] J.-U. Kietz and K. Morik. A polynomial approach to the constructive induction of structural knowledge. *Machine Learning*, 1993. To appear.

[Kietz and Wrobel, 1991] J.-U. Kietz and S. Wrobel. Controlling the complexity of learning in logic through syntactic and task-oriented models. In S. Muggleton, editor, *Proc. of Int. Workshop on Inductive Logic Programming*, pages 107–126. Viana de Castelo, Portugal, 1991. Also available as Arbeitspapiere der GMD No. 503.

[Klingspor, 1991] V. Klingspor. MOBAL's Predicate Structuring Tool. Deliverable 4.3.2/G, Machine Learning Toolbox ESPRIT Project P2154, September 1991.

[Knoblock, 1990] C. A. Knoblock. Learning abstraction hierarchies for problem solving. In *Proc. 9th National Conference on Artificial Intelligence*, pages 923–928, 1990.

[Kodratoff, 1986] Y. Kodratoff. Learning expert knowledge by improving the explanations provided by the system. Technical report, Université Paris-Sud, Orsay, France, 1986.

[Kodratoff and Ganascia, 1986] Y. Kodratoff and J.-G. Ganascia. Improving the generalization step in learning. In R. S. Michalski, J. G. Carbonell, and T. M. Mitchell, editors, *Machine Learning - An Artificial Intelligence Approach*, volume II, chapter 9, pages 215–244. Morgan Kaufman, 1986.

[Korf, 1980] R. E. Korf. Toward a model of representation changes. *Artificial Intelligence*, 14(1):41–78, 1980.

[LaFrance, 1987] M. LaFrance. The knowledge acquisition grid: a method for training knowledge engineers. *Int. Journal of Man-Machine Studies*, 26:245–256, 1987.

[Laird *et al.*, 1986] J. E. Laird, P. S. Rosenbloom, and A. Newell. *Universal Subgoaling and Chunking.* Kluwer Academic Publishers, Boston, Dordrecht, Lancaster, 1986.

[Langley and Nordhausen, 1987] P. Langley and B. Nordhausen. Towards an integrated discovery system. In *10th IJCAI-87, Milano*, pages 198–200. Morgan Kaufman, Los Altos, CA, 1987.

[Langley *et al.*, 1986] P. Langley, J. M. Zytkow, H. A. Simon, and G. L. Bradshaw. The search for regularity: Four aspects of scientific discovery. In R. Michalski, J. Carbonell, and T. Mitchell, editors, *Machine Learning–An Artificial Intelligence Approach*, volume II, pages 425–469. Morgan Kaufman, Los Altos, CA, USA, 1986.

[Langley *et al.*, 1987] P. Langley, H. A. Simon, G. L. Bradshaw, and J. M. Zytkow. *Scientific Discovery - Computational Explorations of the Creative Processes.* MIT Press, Cambridge, Mass., 1987.

[Lawler, 1976] E. L. Lawler. *Combinatorial Optimization, Networks and Matroids.* Holt, Rinehard and Winston, New York, 1976.

[Lebowitz, 1987] M. Lebowitz. Experiments with incremental concept formation: UNIMEM. *Machine Learning*, 2:103–138, 1987.

[Lenat, 1982] D. B. Lenat. AM: Discovery in mathematics as heuristic search. In R. Davis and D. Lenat, editors, *Knowledge-Based Systems in Artificial Intelligence*, pages 1–225. McGraw-Hill, New York, 1982.

[Lenat and Guha, 1990] D. B. Lenat and R. Guha. *Building Large Knowledge-Based Systems - Representation and Inference in the CYC Project.* Addison-Wesley, Reading, Massachusetts, 1990.

[Levesque and Brachman, 1985] H. J. Levesque and R. J. Brachman. A fundamental tradeoff in knowledge representation and reasoning (revised version). In H. J. Levesque and R. J. Brachman, editors, *Readings in Knowledge Representation*, pages 41–70. Morgan Kaufman, Los Altos, CA, 1985.

[Ling, 1991] C. Ling. Non-monotonic specialization. In *Proc. Inductive Logic Programming Workshop, Portugal*, 1991.

[Linster, 1992] M. Linster. Linking modeling to make sense and modeling to implement systems in an operational modeling environment. In T. Wetter, editor, *Proc. of EKAW-92*. Springer, Berlin, New York, Tokyo, 1992.

[Lloyd, 1987] J. Lloyd. *Foundations of Logic Programming*. Springer, Berlin, New York, 2nd edition, 1987.

[Marcus, 1988] S. Marcus. SALT - a knowledge acquisition tool for propose-and-revise systems. In S. Marcus, editor, *Automating Knowledge Acquisition for Expert Systems*. Kluwer Academic, Boston, Dordrecht, London, 1988.

[McAllester, 1982] D. McAllester. Reasoning utility package user's manual. AI Memo 667, AI Laboratory, MIT, Cambridge, Mass., 1982.

[McDermott, 1983] D. McDermott. Contexts and data dependencies: A synthesis. *IEEE Transactions of Pattern Analysis and Machine Intelligence*, PAMI-5(3):237–246, May 1983.

[Mendelson, 1987] E. Mendelson. *Introduction to Mathematical Logic*. Wadsworth & Brooks, Belmont, CA, 3rd edition, 1987.

[Mettrey, 1987] W. Mettrey. An assessment of tools for building large knowledge-based systems. *AI-Magazine*, pages 81–89, 1987.

[Michalski, 1983] R. S. Michalski. A theory and methodology of inductive learning. In *Machine Learning — An Artificial Intelligence Approach*, volume I, pages 83–134. Morgan Kaufman, Los Altos, CA, 1983.

[Michalski, 1986] R. S. Michalski. Understanding the nature of learning. In Michalski, Carbonell, and Mitchell, editors, *Machine Learning - An Artificial Intelligence Approach*, volume II. Morgan Kaufmann, Los Altos, California, 1986.

[Michalski, 1990] R. S. Michalski. Learning flexible concepts: Fundamental ideas and a method based on two-tiered representation. In Y. Kodratoff and R. Michalski, editors, *Machine Learning - An Artificial Intelligence Approach*, volume III, pages 63–102. Morgan Kaufmann, San Mateo, 1990.

[Michalski and Stepp, 1983] R. S. Michalski and R. E. Stepp. Learning from observation: Conceptual clustering. In R. Michalski, J. Carbonell, and T. Mitchell, editors, *Machine Learning*, volume I, pages 331–363. Tioga, Palo Alto, CA, 1983.

[Michalski and Winston, 1986] R. S. Michalski and P. H. Winston. Variable precision logic. *Artificial Intelligence*, 29:121–146, 1986.

[Mitchell, 1982] T. M. Mitchell. Generalization as search. *Artificial Intelligence*, 18(2):203–226, 1982.

[Mitchell *et al.*, 1986] T. M. Mitchell, R. M. Keller, and S. T. Kedar-Cabelli. Explanation-based generalization: A unifying view. *Machine Learning*, 1:47–80, 1986.

[Morik, 1987] K. Morik. Acquiring domain models. *Int. Journal of Man-Machine Studies*, 26:93–104, 1987. Also appeared in *Knowledge Acquisition Tools for Expert Systems*, volume 2, J. Boose, B. Gaines, editors, Academic Press, New York and London, 1988.

[Morik, 1989] K. Morik. Sloppy modeling. In K. Morik, editor, *Knowledge Representation and Organization in Machine Learning*, volume 347 of *Lecture Notes in Artificial Intelligence*, pages 107–134. Springer, Berlin, New York, 1989.

[Morik, 1990] K. Morik. Integrating manual and automatic knowledge aquisition - BLIP. In K. L. McGraw and C. R. Westphal, editors, *Readings in Knowledge Acquisition – Current Practices and Trends*, chapter 14, pages 213–232. Ellis Horwood, New York, 1990.

[Morik, 1991] K. Morik. Underlying assumptions of knowledge acquisition and machine learning. *Knowledge Acquisition Journal*, 3, 1991.

[Morik and Rieger, 1993] K. Morik and A. Rieger. Learning action-oriented perceptual features for robot navigation. Technical Report LS 8 3, Univ. Dortmund, 1993.

[Morik and Rollinger, 1985] K. Morik and C.-R. Rollinger. The real estate agent - modeling users by uncertain reasoning. *The AI Magazine*, pages 44–52, 1985.

[Morik *et al.*, 1993] K. Morik, G. Potamias, V. Moustakis, and G. Charrissis. Knowledgable learning using MOBAL - a case study on a medical domain. In Y. Kodratoff and P. Langley, editors, *Real-World Applications of Machine Learning*, 1993.

[Muggleton, 1987] S. Muggleton. Structuring knowledge by asking questions. In I. Bratko and N. Lavrač, editors, *Proc. Second European Working Session on Learning (EWSL)*, pages 218–229. Sigma Press, Wilmslow, UK, 1987.

[Muggleton, 1990] S. Muggleton. Inductive logic programming. In *Proceedings of the 1st conference on Algorithmic Learning Theory*, 1990.

[Muggleton and Bain, 1992] S. Muggleton and M. Bain. Non-monotonic learning. In S. Muggleton, editor, *Inductive Logic Programming*. Academic Press, London, New York, 1992.

[Muggleton and Buntine, 1988] S. Muggleton and W. Buntine. Machine invention of first-order predicates by inverting resolution. In *Proc. Fifth Int.. Conf. on Machine Learning*. Morgan Kaufman, Los Altos, CA, 1988.

[Muggleton and Feng, 1990] S. Muggleton and C. Feng. Efficient induction of logic programs. In *Proceedings of the 1st Conference on Algorithmic Learning Theory*, 1990.

[Musen *et al.*, 1987] M. A. Musen, L. M. Fagan, D. M. Combs, and E. H. Shortliffe. Use of a domain model to drive an interactive knowledge-editing tool. *International Journal of Man-Machine Studies*, 26(1):105–121, January 1987.

[Nebel, 1989] B. Nebel. *Reasoning and Revision in Hybrid Representation Systems*. Springer, Berlin, New York, 1989. Doctoral Dissertation.

[Neches *et al.*, 1985] R. Neches, W. R. Swartout, and J. D. Moore. Enhanced maintenance and explanation of expert systems through explicit models of their development. *IEEE Transactions on Software Engineering*, SE-11(11):1337–1351, 1985.

[Nelson, 1983] K. Nelson. The derivation of concepts and categories from event representations. In E. K. Scholnick, editor, *New Trends in Conceptual Representation: Challenges to Piaget's Theory?*, chapter 6, pages 129–149. Lawrence Erlbaum Associates, Hillsdale, NJ, 1983.

[Newell, 1982] A. Newell. The knowledge level. *Artificial Intelligence*, 18:87–127, 1982.

[Nilsson, 1982] N. J. Nilsson. *Principles of Artificial Intelligence.* Springer-Verlag, Berlin, 1982.

[Oberschelp, 1962] A. Oberschelp. Untersuchungen zur mehrsortigen Quantorenlogik. *Mathematische Annalen,* 145, 1962.

[O'Keefe *et al.*, 1987] R. O'Keefe, O. Balci, and E. P. Smith. Validating expert system performance. *IEEE Expert,* 2(4):81–90, 1987.

[Pagallo, 1989] G. Pagallo. Learning dnf by decision trees. In *Proc. 11th International Joint Conference on Artificial Intelligence,* pages 639–644. Morgan Kaufman, Los Altos, CA, 1989.

[Paredis, 1988] J. Paredis. Qualified logic as a means of integrating conceptual formalisms. In Y. Kodratoff, editor, *8th European Joint Conference on Artificial Inteligence (ECAI-88).* Pitman, London, 1988.

[Parsons and Puzey, 1992] T. Parsons and N. Puzey. Case Study: MLT Algorithms applied to Design for Manufacture. Technical Note BAE/P2154/mlt226/1, Machine Learning Toolbox ESPRIT Project P2154, April 1992.

[Plotkin, 1970] G. D. Plotkin. A note on inductive generalization. In B. Meltzer and D. Michie, editors, *Machine Intelligence,* volume 5, chapter 8, pages 153–163. American Elsevier, 1970.

[Plotkin, 1971] G. D. Plotkin. A further note on inductive generalization. In B. Meltzer and D. Michie, editors, *Machine Intelligence,* volume 6, chapter 8, pages 101–124. American Elsevier, 1971.

[Potamias *et al.*, 1992] G. Potamias, V. Moustakis, M. Blazadonakis, P. Vassilakis, and L. Gaga. Case study: Theurapeutic treatment of maldescensus testis using machine learning. Technical Note FORTH/P2154/cs1/1, Machine Learning Toolbox ESPRIT Project P2154, September 1992.

[Puerta *et al.*, 1991] A. Puerta, J. Egar, S. Tu, and M. A. Musen. A multiple-method knowledge-acquisition shell for the automatic generation of knowledge acquisition tools. In *Procs. of AAAI-KAW,* 1991.

[Puppe, 1986] F. Puppe. *Assoziatives diagnostisches Problemlösen mit dem Expertensystem MED2.* PhD thesis, University of Kaiserslautern, June 1986. PhD thesis.

[Quinlan, 1983] J. R. Quinlan. Learning efficient classification procedures and their application to chess end games. In R. Michalski, J. Carbonell, and T. Mitchell, editors, *Machine Learning - An Artificial Intelligence Approach,* pages 463–482. Tioga, Palo Alto, CA, 1983.

[Quinlan, 1990] J. R. Quinlan. Learning logical definitions from relations. *Machine Learning,* 5(3):239–266, 1990.

[Reinfrank, 1985] M. Reinfrank. An introduction to non-monotonic reasoning. Technical Report Memo-Seki-85-02, University of Kaiserslautern, Kaiserslautern, 1985.

[Reiter and Criscuolo, 1981] R. Reiter and G. Criscuolo. On interacting defaults. In *7th International Joint Conference on Artificial Intelligence (IJCAI).* Vancouver, 1981.

[Rendell and Seshu, 1990] L. Rendell and R. Seshu. Learning hard concepts through constructive induction: framework and rationale. *Computational Intelligence,* 6:247–270, 1990.

[Rollinger, 1983] C.-R. Rollinger. How to represent evidence - aspects of uncertain reasoning. In *IJCAI-83, Karlsruhe, 1983.* Karlsruhe, 1983.

[Rollinger, 1984] C.-R. Rollinger. *Die Repräsentation natürlichsprachlich formulierten Wissens — Behandlung der Aspekte Unsicherheit und Satzverknüpfung.* PhD thesis, Technical University of Berlin, Berlin, 1984. PhD thesis.

[Rouveirol, 1991] C. Rouveirol. Semantic model for induction of first order theories. In *Proc. 12th International Joint Conference on Artificial Intelligence*, 1991.

[Rouveirol and Puget, 1989] C. Rouveirol and J. F. Puget. Beyond inversion of resolution. In *Proc. Sixth Int. Workshop on Machine Learning*, pages 122–130. Morgan Kaufman, Los Altos, CA, 1989.

[Rouveirol and Puget, 1990] C. Rouveirol and J. F. Puget. Beyond inversion of resolution. In B. Porter and R. Mooney, editors, *Proc. Seventh Int. Conf. on Machine Learning*, pages 122–130. Morgan Kaufmann, Palo Alto, CA, 1990.

[Russell, 1985] S. Russell. The complete guide to MRS. Technical Report KSL-85-12, Knowledge Systems Laboratory, Stanford, CA, 1985.

[Salzberg, 1985] S. Salzberg. Heuristics for inductive learning. In *IJCAI-85*, pages 603–609. Los Angeles, CA, 1985.

[Sammut and Banerji, 1986] C. Sammut and R. B. Banerji. Learning concepts by asking questions. In R. Michalski, J. Carbonell, and T. Mitchell, editors, *Machine Learning — An Artificial Intelligence Approach*, volume II, chapter 7, pages 167–191. Morgan Kaufman, Los Altos, CA, 1986.

[Schlimmer, 1987] J. C. Schlimmer. Incremental adjustment of representations for learning. In *Proc. Fourth Intern. Workshop on Machine Learning*, pages 79–90. Irvine, CA, 1987.

[Schütz, 1962] A. Schütz. *Collected Papers.* Nijhoff, The Hague, 1962.

[Scott, 1983] P. Scott. Learning: The construction of a posteriori knowledge structures. In *AAAI-83.* Washington, 1983.

[Sedgewick, 1988] Sedgewick. *Algorithms.* Addison-Wesley, 1988.

[Shapiro, 1981] E. Shapiro. An algorithm that infers theories from facts. In *Proc of the seventh IJCAI-81*, pages 446–451, 1981.

[Shapiro, 1983] E. Y. Shapiro. *Algorithmic Program Debugging.* ACM Distinguished Doctoral Dissertations. MIT Press, Cambridge, Mass., 1983.

[Shortliffe, 1976] E. H. Shortliffe. *Computer based medical consultations: MYCIN.* Elsevier, New York, Amsterdam, 1976.

[Shrager, 1987] J. Shrager. Theory change via view application in instructionless learning. *Machine Learning*, 2, 1987.

[Silverstein and Pazzani, 1991] G. Silverstein and M. Pazzani. Relational cliches: Constraining constructive induction during relational learning. In Birnbaum and Collins, editors, *Procs. of the Eighth International Workshop on Machine Learning*, pages 203–207. Morgan Kaufmann, San Mateo, CA, 1991.

[Simon, 1983] H. A. Simon. Why should machines learn? In R. Michalski, J. Carbonell, and T. Mitchell, editors, *Machine Learning: An Artificial Intelligence Approach*, pages 25–38. Tioga, Palo Alto, CA, 1983.

[Smith and Medin, 1981] E. E. Smith and D. L. Medin. *Categories and Concepts.* Harvard University Press, London, England, 1981.

[Sommer, 1992] E. Sommer. Using MOBAL: Incremental design of the SPEED domain. Technical Note GMD-P2154-26-1, GMD, St. Augustin, 1992. Personal Communication.

[Sommer, 1993] E. Sommer. Cooperation of data-driven and model-based methods for relational learning. In *Second International Workshop on Multistrategy Learning Workshop.* Harpers Ferry, West Virginia, USA, 1993. to appear.

[Sommer *et al.*, 1993a] E. Sommer, K. Morik, J. Andre, and M. Uszynski. What on-line learning can do for knowledge acquisition - a case study. Arbeitspapiere der GMD, GMD (German Natl. Research Center for Computer Science), P.O.Box 1316, 53731 Sankt Augustin, Germany, 1993.

[Sommer *et al.*, 1993b] E. Sommer, W. Emde, J.-U. Kietz, K. Morik, and S. Wrobel. Mobal 2.0 user guide. Arbeitspapiere der GMD, GMD (German Natl. Research Center for Computer Science), P.O.Box 1316, 53731 Sankt Augustin, Germany, 1993.

[Steels, 1990] L. Steels. Components of expertise. *AI Magazine*, pages 28–49, Summer 1990.

[Stepp and Michalski, 1986] R. E. Stepp and R. S. Michalski. Conceptual clustering of structured objects: A goal-oriented approach. *Artificial Intelligence*, 28:43–69, 1986.

[Subramanian, 1990] D. Subramanian. A theory of justified reformulations. In D. P. Benjamin, editor, *Change of Representation and Inductive Bias*, pages 147–167. Kluwer, Boston, 1990.

[Subramanian and Genesereth, 1987] D. Subramanian and M. Genesereth. The relevance of irrelevance. In *Proc. 10th International Joint Conference on Artificial Intelligence*, pages 416–422. Morgan Kaufman, Los Altos, CA, 1987.

[Swartout, 1983] W. R. Swartout. Xplain: a system for creating and explaining expert consulting programs. *Artificial Intelligence*, 21:285 –325, 1983.

[Swartout and Smoliar, 1989] W. R. Swartout and S. Smoliar. Explanation: A source of guidance for knowledge representation. In K. Morik, editor, *Knowledge Representation and Organization in Machine Learning.* Springer, Berlin, New York, Tokyo, January 1989.

[Thieme, 1989] S. Thieme. The acquisition of model knowledge for a model-driven machine learning approach. In K. Morik, editor, *Knowledge Representation and Organization in Machine Learning*, pages 177–191. Springer, Berlin, New York, 1989.

[Uszynski and Niquil, 1992] M. Uszynski and Y. Niquil. Case Study: The SPEED Application. Technical Note AAR/P2154/68/1, Machine Learning Toolbox ESPRIT Project P2154, April 1992.

[Utgoff, 1986] P. E. Utgoff. Shift of bias for inductive concept learning. In R. Michalski, J. Carbonell, and T. Mitchell, editors, *Machine Learning — An Artificial Intelligence Approach*, volume II, pages 107–148. Morgan Kaufman, Los Altos, CA, 1986.

[Valiant, 1984] L. G. Valiant. A theory of the learnable. *Communications of the ACM*, 27(11):1134–1142, 1984.

[van Melle, 1981] W. J. van Melle. *System Aids in Constructing Consultation Programs.* UMI Research Press, Ann Arbor, Michigan, 1981.

[Vere, 1977] S. A. Vere. Induction of relational productions in the presence of background information. In *Proc. of the 5th International Joint Conference on Artificial Intelligence*, pages 349–355, 1977.

[Wachsmuth and Gängler, 1991] I. Wachsmuth and B. Gängler. Knowledge packets and knowledge packet structures. In O. Herzog and C.-R. Rollinger, editors, *Text Understanding in LILOG - Integrating Computational Linguistics and Artificial Intelligence*, volume 546 of *Lecture Notes in Artificial Intelligence*, pages 380–393. Springer-Verlag, Berlin, 1991.

[Wahlster, 1981] W. Wahlster. *Natürlichsprachliche Argumentation in Dialogsystemen. KI-Verfahren zur Rekonstruktion approximativer Inferenzprozesse.* Springer, Berlin, Heidelberg, New York, 1981.

[Wielinga and Breuker, 1986] B. Wielinga and J. Breuker. Models of expertise. In *Proceedings of ECAI-86*, pages 306–318, 1986.

[Winston, 1975] P. H. Winston. Learning structural descriptions from examples. In P. Winston, editor, *The Psychology of Computer Vision.* McGraw-Hill, 1975.

[Wirth, 1989] R. Wirth. Completing logic programs by inverse resolution. In K. Morik, editor, *Proc. Fourth European Working Session on Learning (EWSL)*, pages 239–250. Pitman/Morgan Kaufmann, London/San Mateo, CA, 1989.

[Work Package 8 Partners, 1991] Work Package 8 Partners. Description of the Applications Chosen for the MLT, Phase 2. Deliverable 8.1.2, Machine Learning Toolbox ESPRIT Project P2154, April 1991.

[Wrobel, 1987] S. Wrobel. Higher-order concepts in a tractable knowledge representation. In K. Morik, editor, *GWAI-87 11th German Workshop on Artificial Intelligence*, Informatik-Fachberichte Nr. 152, pages 129–138. Springer, Berlin, New York, Tokyo, October 1987.

[Wrobel, 1988a] S. Wrobel. Automatic representation adjustment in an observational discovery system. In D. Sleeman, editor, *Proc. of the 3rd Europ. Working Session on Learning*, pages 253–262. Pitman, London, 1988.

[Wrobel, 1988b] S. Wrobel. Design goals for sloppy modeling systems. *Int. Journal of Man-Machine Studies*, 29:461–477, 1988. Also appeared in The Foundations of Knowledge Acquisition, vol. 4, J. Boose and B. Gaines, eds., Academic Press, 1990.

[Wrobel, 1989] S. Wrobel. Demand-driven concept formation. In K. Morik, editor, *Knowledge Representation and Organization in Machine Learning*, pages 289–319. Springer, Berlin, Tokyo, New York, 1989.

[Wrobel, 1991a] S. Wrobel. Concepts formation in man and machine: Fundamental issues. Arbeitspapiere der GMD 560, GMD (German Natl. Research Center for Computer Science), P.O.Box 1316, 53731 Sankt Augustin, Germany, 1991. Presented at the Workshop on Concept Formation in Man and Machine, May 1991.

[Wrobel, 1991b] S. Wrobel. Towards a model of grounded concept formation. In *Proc. 12th International Joint Conference on Artificial Intelligence.* Morgan Kaufman, Los Altos, CA, 1991. To appear.

[Wrobel, 1993a] S. Wrobel. Concept formation and knowledge revision — a demand-driven approach to representation change. Doctoral disseration, Universität Dortmund, June 1993.

[Wrobel, 1993b] S. Wrobel. On the proper definition of minimality in specialization and theory revision. In *Proc. Sixth European Conference on Machine Learning (ECML-93)*, pages 65 – 82, 1993. Also as Arbeitspapiere der GMD No. 730.

[Wrobel, 1994] S. Wrobel. Concept formation during interactive theory revision. *Machine Learning*, 1994. To appear.

[Wygotski, 1964] L. S. Wygotski. *Denken und Sprechen.* Conditio humana. S. Fischer, 1964. (First published in Russian 1934, English translation "Thought and language" 1962 by MIT Press).

Author Index

Boldface page numbers refer to the page where the complete reference is given. Italic page numbers refer to *et al.* citations where the name of the author is not explictly shown.

Name Index

This index contains all references to system names.

Subject Index

Boldface page numbers refer to definitions.